W9-BKS-913

SCALING GLOBAL CHANGE

SCALING GLOBAL CHANGE

A SOCIAL ENTREPRENEUR'S GUIDE TO **SURVIVING** THE **START-UP PHASE** AND **DRIVING IMPACT**

ERIN **GANJU**
CORY **HEYMAN**, PhD

WILEY

Room to Read®
World Change Starts with Educated Children.®

Published by John Wiley & Sons, Inc., Hoboken, New Jersey.
Published simultaneously in Canada.

For general information on our other products and services or for technical support, please contact our Customer Care Department within the United States at (800) 762-2974, outside the United States at (317) 572-3993 or fax (317) 572-4002.

Wiley publishes in a variety of print and electronic formats and by print-on-demand. Some material included with standard print versions of this book may not be included in e-books or in print-on-demand. If this book refers to media such as a CD or DVD that is not included in the version you purchased, you may download this material at http://booksupport.wiley.com. For more information about Wiley products, visit www.wiley.com.

Library of Congress Cataloging-in-Publication Data:

Names: Ganju, Erin, 1969– author. | Heyman, Cory, 1969– author.
Title: Scaling global change : a social entrepreneur's guide to surviving the start-up phase and driving impact / by Erin Ganju, Cory Heyman, Ph.D.
Description: Hoboken, New Jersey : Wiley, [2018] | Includes index. |
Identifiers: LCCN 2017058572 (print) | LCCN 2018008558 (ebook) | ISBN 9781119483885 (epub) | ISBN 9781119483939 (pdf) | ISBN 9781119483854 (cloth)
Subjects: LCSH: New business enterprises. | Social entrepreneurship.
Classification: LCC HD62.5 (ebook) | LCC HD62.5 .G364 2018 (print) | DDC 658.1/1—dc23
LC record available at https://lccn.loc.gov/2017058572

Cover Design: Wiley

Printed in the United States of America

10 9 8 7 6 5 4 3 2 1

To Heather and Jeetu, whose love and encouragement have made this book—and all we do—possible; and to Cassie, Josephine, Julia, and Scott, whose passion for life and opportunities to live their dreams is something we hope can extend to every child.

Also to all past, present, and future Room to Readers. This is our story.

Proceeds from this book will go to Room to Read.

Room to Read®

World Change Starts with Educated Children®

Contents

About the Authors

Photo credit: Sergio Villareal.

Erin Ganju is the cofounder and a member of Room to Read's Emeritus Board, an organization that believes World Change Starts with Educated Children.® She is a Managing Director at Echidna Giving, a fund that invests in girls' education in lower-income countries. She was CEO of Room to Read from 2009 to 2017 and, from the early start-up days of Room to Read, has been instrumental in the design and implementation of the organization's scalable, replicable model for improving the quality of education around the world. As CEO and prior to that as COO, she oversaw Room to Read's global operations across 14 countries; a technical assistance unit called Room to Read Accelerator; fundraising teams in North America, Europe, Australia, and the Asia Pacific region; and a worldwide staff of more than 1,500 employees.

Under her leadership, Room to Read was recognized with prestigious awards, including the U.S. Library of Congress Literacy Award (David M. Rubenstein Prize), the UNESCO 2011 Confucius Prize for Literacy, and the Skoll Award for Social Entrepreneurship. In addition, Erin has been selected as one of the World Economic Forum's Schwab Foundation Social Entrepreneurs (2014); recognized as a Global Impact Featured Member for 2017 by the Young Presidents' Organization; and honored with the Women's Bond Club Isabel Benham Award (2014). Erin was named one of Fast Company's Extraordinary Women (2012) and is a contributor to Fortune's Most Powerful Women Insider Network.

Before founding Room to Read, Erin worked at Unilever; Goldman, Sachs & Co.; as well as a couple of technology start-ups. She has spent extensive time working and living in Asia, where she saw firsthand the need to enhance countries' educational systems. Erin holds a bachelor's degree from Johns Hopkins University and a master's degree in international relations from the School of Advanced International Studies in Washington, D.C.

Dr. Cory Heyman is chief innovation officer and executive director, Room to Read Accelerator of Room to Read. Cory oversees Room to Read's external technical assistance projects, and visioning for the longer-term programmatic growth and strategic positioning of the organization as a whole. Previously Cory served as Room to Read's chief program officer as well as a member of Room to Read's global advisory board.

Cory is also a franchisee of CoreLife Eatery restaurants, an expanding restaurant concept that provides healthy, great-tasting food as part of a healthy life. His first restaurant is scheduled to open in May 2018.

Having worked at the nexus of public, private, and nonprofit sectors, Cory has managed large-scale educational projects in the United States, Latin America, Eastern Europe, the Middle East, South Asia, and southern Africa for more than

Photo credit: Sergio Villareal.

25 years. He has served as a professional staff member in the United States Senate; executive director of the Potomac Regional Education Partnership; principal research scientist at the American Institutes for Research; and vice president at the Academy for Educational Development.

A specialist in applied quantitative and qualitative research methods, Cory has worked to increase access to quality educational opportunities for underserved children in lower-income countries. Cory is the author of more than 20 academic and professional publications. He has presented at forums such as the Skoll Foundation for Entrepreneurship, World Bank, Brookings Institution, U.S. Peace Corps, U.S. Agency for International Development, the White House, and the British House of Commons. Cory received a BA in political economy and an MPP in public policy from the University of California, Berkeley, and has a PhD in sociology from Johns Hopkins University.

Framing the Issues

1

Introduction:
Go Big or Go Home

At Room to Read, our first major identity crisis came when we were eight years into our work. Over the years, we'd achieved rapid growth in revenue and staff. We'd also expanded the number of elementary schools with our literacy program and the scale of our girls' education program every year. Yet we had serious concerns about the quality of our programs. Were we really improving children's learning? Was our model sustainable? Were we doing our absolute best to ensure children had better educational outcomes—or were we just pursuing growth for growth's sake?

While we were asking ourselves these questions, we were getting more requests to extend our services. Our country teams were asking us to help teachers do a better job of teaching children to read. However, this would have pushed us deeply into the unknown, way past our comfort zone. We would be striking at the heart of schools' core responsibilities. Would schools even allow us to help? In our Girls' Education Program, country teams wanted to hire more full-time staff. They suggested creating "social mobilizers" to help girls to develop more consistent life skills.

These were huge new opportunities. They were exciting to consider, but did we have the talent and money to pull it off?

Investors were beginning to ask more specific questions about our impact. *What difference were we really making? Were children reading better? Were governments adopting our programs? How do we define success, and what is our end game?*

We excelled at establishing well-functioning libraries at government primary schools in lower-income countries and filling them with exciting local language books. But we didn't know whether these resulted in better reading skills for the children we were targeting. Was it time to be more ambitious?

Although some investors and board members cautioned against it, our senior management team argued persuasively that Room to Read needed to move fast to stay relevant. It was imperative that we deepen our impact. The benefits far outweighed the risks.

The result: We outlined an ambitious 2010–2014 global strategic plan that would transform our organization's mission and operations. Our bet was to invest heavily in Room to Read's operational support systems, thought leadership, and monitoring and evaluation processes. We would investigate our impact and adjust our programs accordingly. This approach would help us through our identity crisis—our "sophomore slump"—and position us for success in the next major phase of our development.

It was a bet that paid off.

The Rise (and Often Fall) of the Entrepreneurial Social Enterprise

The world faces no shortage of challenges. Climate change, infectious diseases, terrorist attacks, ethnic and gender discrimination, failing public healthcare and education systems, underemployed and alienated youth, food security, and water security—the list goes on. These large crises threaten the ability for all of us to enjoy peaceful, productive, and sustainable lives. The world requires daring, innovative solutions. And when we find those solutions, we need to scale them quickly and effectively to make a difference globally.

One way to do this is through entrepreneurial social enterprises (ESEs) such as Room to Read. ESEs take an entrepreneurial approach to addressing social issues. They combine for-profit and nonprofit business practices and approaches to find scalable, replicable, and sustainable solutions to social and environmental problems. Disruptive in solving problems, ESEs fall somewhere between traditional nonprofit and for-profit organizations in their management styles.

"ESE" is not a formal business term. There are no specific criteria, minimum financial thresholds, levels of proficiency, or annual ESE rankings in business magazines. The Bureau of Labor Statistics does not track the number of ESEs in the United States. The IRS does not grant special tax breaks. An ESE is more of a mindset, an approach to organizational leadership and development. Foundations such as Ashoka, Draper Richards Kaplan, and Skoll identify ESEs and build networks among social entrepreneurs. Business schools teach courses in social entrepreneurship and write case studies about ESEs. One can even earn a PhD in the subject. We think of ESEs as a smart way to structure socially oriented work for maximum impact.

We live in an inherently unfair and unjust world. If you have traveled widely like we have, you have experienced this yourselves. You have seen firsthand the difficult circumstances in which many people struggle to survive daily and how lucky you are in life that you do not live in that situation. That you have this book in your hands and can read it means that you are among an elite and privileged group. You are literate and can afford to buy a book, check out a book from the library, or have the means and skill to download it. Your life experience is far different from the people served by ESEs.

People approach this kind of inequity in one of two ways. Some people recognize that the world is unfair but shrug their shoulders. "What can I do about it?" they ask. They believe that their job is to look out for themselves and their families, make the best of their own situations, and work hard to end up on the better side of the household income statistics.

The other approach does not accept the status quo and is determined to change it. These people lie awake at night thinking of ways to create a better world—a more free, sustainable, and just world. They are passionate about their ideas for changing the system.

For those of you who fall into this second category, you may be a social entrepreneur—a person driven to establish an organization to solve big global problems or effect social change. Even if you don't have the entrepreneurial bug to start an organization, you may be a social change champion who wants to support and rally around innovative, disruptive ideas and help turn them into reality. In either case, we firmly believe that "To whom much is given, much is expected."

If we are to improve the circumstances of our planet, we must grow and harness the power of social enterprises. Like most business start-ups, nonprofits find it difficult to break through the initial rush of enthusiasm and early successes and develop a stable path toward longer-term growth, stability, and impact. The start-up years are invigorating, but building a strong organizational foundation to get to scale takes grit and perseverance.

Helping uncover why some entrepreneurial social enterprises make it—and how you can take steps to put your organization on the path to success—is the purpose of this book. This book is written *by* social entrepreneurs *for* current and aspiring social entrepreneurs and the social change champions who support them. We feel that you are our "tribe"—our peer group—and we hope our experiences can help you.

What's in a Name?

What is the difference between organizations described, alternatively, as nonprofit, charity, social impact, and entrepreneurial social enterprise? It is a valid question and one that has confused many of us. As practitioners, our answer to the question is "Not much." These are all terms that refer to an organization working to improve the lives of people who are underserved—often poor or otherwise disenfranchised. They all aspire to address social issues and create positive change in our communities. One can argue more specific definitions based on accounting and legal differences, but for the sake of this book we will generally use the layperson definition of "nonprofit" to refer to non-governmental or nonbusiness organizations whose purpose is to further a social cause. As a subset of the nonprofit sector, we will often employ the terms "entrepreneurial social enterprise" and "social entrepreneurs." ESEs tend to be more innovative, disruptive, and risk-taking in the approaches they employ to achieve social change and make an impact on a large scale.

Who We Are

Room to Read is frequently cited as an early example of a successful social enterprise. It is among the organizations that received the first *Fast Company/Monitor* Social Capitalist Award for innovation and social impact. It was also among the early grantees of foundations investing in social entrepreneurs such as the Skoll and Draper Richards Kaplan Foundations.

Room to Read is an international nonprofit organization that helps improve educational opportunities for children in lower-income countries. Our goal is twofold: to develop reading skills and the lifelong habit of reading among younger children, and to help adolescent girls complete high school and make smooth transitions to the next phases of their lives. We won't be going deeply into the details of our founding and early successes. These have been well documented in John Wood's award-winning memoir, *Leaving Microsoft to Change the World*. But we will be discussing our challenges, experiences, and lessons learned later in the journey.

As is typical of many social enterprises, many of our first staff members had business backgrounds. We chose to leave successful careers to establish and grow Room to Read. We were committed to developing innovative solutions. We sought change at a global scale and persevered against the odds. We were risk-takers and passionate advocates for our cause. We were on fire to change the world for the better. So many challenges in the world are fueled by terror, fear, and hate. We sought to counter this by focusing on a solution filled with hope, courage, and optimism.

Let us briefly introduce ourselves.

Erin did not necessarily consider herself a social entrepreneur when she cofounded Room to Read. In fact, the term was not yet commonly used when Room to Read was founded in 2000! But as time evolved, she recognized her own determination to "be the change you want to see in the world," as Mahatma Gandhi said so beautifully. She cashed in her business aspirations to become a social entrepreneur.

Erin's Story

"After a successful business career starting with Goldman Sachs, Unilever, and then two tech start-ups, and more stress than was worth the paycheck—especially when the stock options became worthless—I started to question what the heck I was doing with my life. So, I self-imposed a sabbatical and time out to reset my priorities. I thought back to the times I was happiest in life, and most of them related to times I was volunteering for causes that mattered to me, or traveling and interacting across cultures. I taught English in a government school in Vietnam and helped Unilever Vietnam build its corporate social responsibility initiatives, doing things like establishing a preschool in a community where one of our factories was under construction. My mother was a social worker and part of the first thousand volunteers for the Peace Corps in her youth. My father was a university professor and was the first person in his family of Irish Catholic immigrants to go to college (he ended up getting his PhD). Their expectations for my sister and me were that we would go to university and make use of the opportunities a good education can provide to follow our bliss. I realized I was passionate about combining my belief in the transformative power of education with my love for cross-cultural collaboration. I was determined to find a way to help children—especially girls—in low-income countries be empowered in their lives through education."

—Erin, Women of Influence event, 2009

At Room to Read's "10 millionth child" celebration in Cambodia in 2015, Erin gave a shout out to her two cofounders, Dinesh Shrestha and John Wood, in her speech, expressing her astonishment and gratitude that they were all still in the trenches together 15 years later: "Ten million children's lives changed. Brighter futures for kids who deserve it. Happy, joyful readers exploring the world of books. Empowered girls knocking down doors and breaking through glass ceilings. We invested in the future, working hard towards our bold goal and got there five years faster than we planned. I am profoundly grateful that I partnered with you."

Erin's passion for Room to Read's mission is still as great as when she started. She remembers sitting on a floor in a school in the Mekong Delta reading the first books Room to Read delivered in Vietnam to a group of eager kids. In the years since, some of her best work days have been in Room to Read partner schools across Asia and Africa, sharing her love of reading.

As one of the early adopters in the Room to Read movement, Cory has been deeply involved in its growth. In 2004, just a few years after Room to Read was founded, Erin was looking to build a more robust monitoring and evaluation system to chart the organization's impact. She asked around for recommendations of experts in the field to consult. She contacted several people, but most didn't return her calls. They probably felt Room to Read was too small to be worthy of their time. Cory, on the other hand, not only took Erin's call, but willingly offered to get involved on a volunteer basis and offer guidance and advice. At the time, Cory was working at an education research and consulting organization in Washington, D.C. He was not put off by this disruptive, crazy start-up in San Francisco that audaciously sought to influence the international education sector. In fact, he embraced its boldness and new ways of working and actively collaborated for many years before Erin was finally able to convince Cory to make Room to Read his full-time focus in 2010.

Cory and Erin believe this book is for all those social entrepreneurs and champions who are dedicating their time, talent, and lives to helping create a better world. It is filled with the advice and tips that we wish someone had shared with us as we were growing Room to Read from start-up through scale-up.

Cory's Story

"I was one of the people who knew what I wanted to do professionally as far back as my freshman year of college. I decided then to pursue a career in international education. There were no doubts in my mind. I did not know my exact path at the time, but I did know that I wanted to do something related to helping children in underserved communities around the world. There were two motivators for my early career choice. The first came from an experience during my last year in high school. I was an international exchange student in Denmark and became fascinated with the Holocaust. Being so close to Germany and Poland sparked a visceral desire to read books and visit concentration camps. The outcome of my experience was a deep belief that education could be a strategy for promoting world peace. The logic was that a good education can promote critical thinking, and a society of people who have strong critical thinking skills can make better decisions and stave off threats of totalitarianism and brutal dictatorships. The second motivator was reading Paulo Freire's *Pedagogy of the Oppressed* in a freshman development studies class. This book and others helped me to understand the transformative power of education. Education really could be the great equalizer."

—Cory, Symposium on the Contributions of Arab Women toward a Lasting Peace, 2016

At least once a month, Erin and Cory meet with would-be social entrepreneurs. These people, brimming with bold new ideas and big visions, seek advice on how to turn those ideas and visions into reality. Quite often these entrepreneurs are relatively early in their careers and have more ideas and passion than actual business experience. But their willingness to experiment and devote themselves to social justice as well as their unflappable belief that making a positive difference in the world is possible are things we admire tremendously. They are the future heroes of this planet.

However, we often struggle with what to say to these bright comrades in arms. How can we support and motivate them while simultaneously giving them a dose of reality about all the challenges they will inevitably face? There are the long hours, the doors closed, the many trips crisscrossing the globe on a limited budget, and the never-ending to-do list. And there isn't a big paycheck or stock to cash in at the end of the road. There is only a sense of accomplishment that you have left the planet a better place than when you arrived.

In one such conversation, Erin found herself saying, "If I knew now how hard it would be to grow Room to Read, I am not sure I would do it again." The crushed look on the young leaders' faces made Erin realize how important it was to be constructive when encouraging the next generation of social entrepreneurs. And, happily, at the heart of the Room to Read story are many incredibly positive lessons to share.

But where do we start, and what is most relevant and transferable to others? Most of the entrepreneurs we help write e-mails thanking us for our time. The comments we really appreciate are the ones that tell us what was particularly useful in our conversation—the specific nuggets of information that resulted in "aha" moments for them. This book is our attempt to bring those nuggets together. It's also an explanation of the blood, sweat, and tears, as well as tossing and turning in many sleepless nights wondering in the most desperate moments if the work it took to grow Room to Read was worth it. Spoiler alert: The answer is unquestionably *yes*.

We are sharing our story because we have faith that together we can create the world we all want to live in. Knowing that we are co-conspirators, doing the messy, hard work in support of each other, is inspiring to us. We strongly believe the world needs us to win—together—before it is too late. This is a playbook for winning as social entrepreneurs and champions.

Big Ambitions

Started as a small, country-specific charity called Books for Nepal, Room to Read is now one of a handful of international education nonprofits launched in this millennium that has broken the US$50 million annual operating budget barrier. Today we have programs in 14 countries, impacting the lives of more than 15 million children and their families. During our early days when Dinesh, Erin, and John were working hard to establish the organization, it was unclear whether Room to Read would be viable. We would tell each other, "Go big or go home," meaning we would shoot for the moon when trying to build a dynamic, high-growth organization. If we failed in our dreams of scale, we would go back to our day jobs. But as ultracompetitive business types, we had high expectations and a deep commitment to success.

The big need we were attempting to address was the fact that there are more than 750 million illiterate people on earth. Approximately two-thirds of them are women and girls. Yet we envisioned a world in which all children could pursue a quality education in their local communities that would enable them to reach their full potential and contribute to their local communities and countries. Our early plan, which continues to this day, was to work with families, schools, local communities, partner organizations, and governments to make this possible.

In our Girls' Education Program, we work with cohorts of middle and high school girls in their schools, providing life-skills education, mentoring, targeted money for fees and tuition, and activities to increase community support for girls to complete high school. In our Literacy Program, we help establish elementary school libraries, fill the shelves of those libraries with fun storybooks, train school staff to integrate library activities into the school day, and help first- and second-grade teachers learn to teach their students to read and write. What is most innovative about Room to Read is our ability to identify, package, and scale effective practices. We are good at choosing effective strategies from the range of options based on our knowledge of what works on the ground. Our programming is deeply rooted in scientifically validated practices that we test, refine, and retest with our community partners to deliver the highest-quality, replicable activities in these two crucial areas of education—literacy and girls' education. We go deep in the development of high-quality teachers' guides, student workbooks, storybooks, and coaching for teachers and librarians, but always with an eye to figuring out how to go broad and make these activities possible for the larger school systems to take on as part of their core work. We are what one educational official in northern Sri Lanka called, "the quiet organization that does not say much but gets things done."

For us, what is truly game-changing about our programs is the transformative impact we witness in children's lives. An example is a young girl in Sri Lanka named Ara, whose day-to-day life came with its own unique challenges. Like thousands of other Muslim Sri Lankans from the Mannar district, Ara's family moved to the small village of Puttalam after being evicted during the country's 30-year civil war. The eldest of five children, Ara and her family became internally displaced people forced to move empty-handed to a district where girls' education is a low priority. Then, in 2007, Room to Read's Girls' Education Program arrived at Ara's school.

Through the help of the local Room to Read social mobilizer, Fazeena, Ara and her parents became excited about Ara's education. "Room to Read stepped into my life, and everything changed. Fazeena encouraged me to attend school every day, and by doing so, I gained so much knowledge that made me realize that I could do more if I learned more," says Ara.

Ara had busy days. She would wake up at 4:00 a.m. to study, and some days after school there would be Room to Read life-skills sessions. Then, she'd come home and fly through chores like cooking and caring for her sisters before going to bed. Her persistence paid off. Ara was not only the first female in her family to complete high school, but she also earned straight A's in every subject on her Advanced Level exam. She was accepted to the University of Colombo, a prestigious and competitive university in Sri Lanka—a feat even advantaged girls from the capital city rarely achieve. "Education benefits more than just the person being educated. Knowledge is a wealth that increases when you share it. I'm excited for my future and for the future of those I will cross paths with," says Ara.

Room to Read's approach focuses on deep, systemic trans-formation within government schools in lower-income countries during two time periods that are critical in a child's schooling: early elementary school for literacy acquisition and middle and high school for girls' education. With a focus on the quality of education services that governments are supposed to provide for their children, Room to Read has created reading and girls' education programs that governments and other organizations can localize, operate on their own, and sustain over time. Room to Read is helping to transform educational experiences and impacting future generations with a belief in our motto "World Change Starts with Educated Children®." We set measurable goals, collect and analyze data, and incorporate feedback into programming to ensure our work has impact while making the best use of every dollar.

Because we track metrics rigorously, we can tell you how many libraries we've established, books we've published, teach-ers we've trained, and girls we've served. We can also tell you how individual girls are progressing in school, how many books children are checking out of libraries, and how much children are improving in their reading over time. Similarly, we can tell you how children whose teachers participate in our programs are faring compared to their peers whose teachers do not. We can introduce you to families who made the difficult decision to send their daughters to school instead of keeping them home to work and the long-term economic payoff they get from taking that kind of risk. We can also tell you about thousands of struggling readers who, in just a few months, are reading well enough—finally—to understand the words they are seeing on the page.

Part of Room to Read's growing reputation is based on the scale of our activities. We've worked in more than 20,000 government schools. We've distributed more than 18 million books, produced nearly 1,400 storybook titles in more than 20 languages, and are helping more than 50,000 girls finish high school (often referred to as *secondary school* in our partner countries) in our Girls' Education Program. We have more than 1,500 full-time employees and a vibrant volunteer chapter network engaging over 16,000 volunteers who help raise funds in 16 countries. Everything we do, whether program development, operations, or fundraising, we do at scale. "Go big or go home" is still our ethos. We are known for our strong planning processes, for our careful tracking of expenditures and outcomes, for reporting our results openly, and for using information obsessively to improve our work.

Only now, after more than 18 years of hard work, would we begin to consider Room to Read a relatively "mature" social organization. This categorization helps us reflect on our stage of organizational development. In some ways, we feel we are in an evolutionary sweet spot. We are beyond the struggle of the early years but not yet of the size and scope to wrestle with bureaucratic sluggishness. Within a tumultuous nonprofit sector, our organization is relatively sustainable year after year, and we continue to grow. We remain small enough to be nimble, and continue to learn, evolve, and innovate. If this were *Goldilocks and the Three Bears*, Room to Read would not be too small nor too big, but *just right* for our current stage of growth.

One of our founders, John Wood, shared some of the Room to Read story in his two bestselling books, *Leaving Microsoft to Change the World* and *Creating Room to Read*, about his personal journey, the motivation to establish Room to Read, and the grueling yet exciting early years of our work. These books brilliantly answer the "what" and "why" questions about the genesis of our work. It is the excitement of these stories that has led people to ask the next question: *"How* did Room to Read do it?"

We are not claiming that Room to Read's experience is a perfect model for others. It just so happens that our one case study extends over many years and includes many instances of trial and error. In the same way that Gandhi viewed his life as "experiments with truth," Room to Read has worked through scores of organizational decisions and has tried to draw lessons from each experience to inform the next decision. Our process is to collect data and perspectives, debate, decide, execute, reflect, and modify as necessary. So, while we can't assert that any single decision is directly applicable to other organizations, our *process* has helped to build a strong organizational foundation and deliver substantial impact that we hope is transferable to similar situations.

Smashing the Sophomore Slump

One underlying theme of this book is that it takes an organization to achieve social solutions at scale. This can't be done by individuals acting on their own. It therefore follows that entrepreneurial leaders must first focus on helping their organizations thrive to achieve their social goals. This is important at all stages of development. At some point, though, the question changes from one about surviving to being able to scale sufficiently to have a system-level impact.

Unfortunately, we often see social enterprises suffer from sophomore slumps such as the one that we faced at Room to Read and described at the beginning of this chapter. This term typically refers to the challenging second year of high school or college, when the initial enthusiasm of a new school wears off and a student realizes that there is a still a lot of work to be done to earn a degree. It is like what breakthrough musical artists often face in cutting their second albums, or new writers when publishing their second books—often accompanied by disappointment after a tremendously successful debut. In these cases, it takes tremendous work to persevere and make it successfully to the other side. In the world of entrepreneurial social enterprises, we've witnessed this pattern many times.

Room to Read has been fortunate to have smashed through at least some of the barriers that have plagued some organizations trapped in the sophomore slump. Take the challenge we outlined at the beginning of the chapter. We worked our way through that stagnation and risk to effectiveness by being honest about our vulnerabilities, attacking them directly in our next five-year plan, and working diligently and patiently to help Room to Read usher in its next phase of development. We are excited to share some of these stories. The lessons reinforce the truism that the journey is just as important as the destination.

One misunderstanding about nonprofits is that they are somehow vastly different from organizations in the public and private spheres. In fact, the daily routines and decisions about organizational growth and development can be quite similar. Both sets of organizations have staffing structures with supervisors and direct reports. They have policies and procedures, invoices and investments, finances, and fundraising. Like private businesses, nonprofits are accountable for their products and services. They are accountable to investors, overseen by boards of directors, and have public reporting requirements.

Many people have unrealistic expectations about starting or working for a nonprofit. They may believe you don't have to work as hard since there is no bottom-line requirement of profitability. Or they believe that nonprofit workers are on the front lines battling evil and protecting the disenfranchised. Some of that is true. Those of us in the nonprofit space do spend all our time working toward our organizational missions. However, much of that means doing the same kind of office work and organizational development as would be the case anywhere else.

This realization can be frustrating, perhaps especially so for some people who choose to start their organizations to achieve an important social goal. They are driven by their hearts and often have little time or patience for details. Unfortunately, passion and drive can only go so far. *It is therefore essential that nonprofit organizations be as strong and robust as any other organization to achieve their missions.* The excitement and enthusiasm for a start-up—even in the nonprofit sector—can only go so far. It is just as important to grow a strong organization as it is to advocate for a worthwhile cause.

In the book *Beyond the Idea*,[1] Dartmouth business professors Govindarajan and Trimble contend that successful innovation is 5% idea and 95% execution. This rule of thumb is equally as important for the nonprofit sector as it is for profit-seeking businesses. As the nonprofit sector has grown, competition for charitable donations has become fierce. Investors have many choices. Although many people fund nonprofits that pull at their heartstrings, many others want proof that organizations are strong structurally and able to accomplish what they promise. Goodwill for new ideas and new leaders can go far, but it does not last forever. When we meet with a potential investor, we always bring a variety of background documents, from country and program overviews to success story summaries, to engaging photos of children and teachers hard at work, to our latest annual report and statistic summaries that show changes in key Room to Read indicators over time. When we can, we like to illustrate the stark comparisons between schools where Room to Read is involved versus those where we are not.

We find a huge chasm between nonprofits in start-up mode and those that are more mature. Like new organizations in any sector, many new nonprofits can enjoy an extended honeymoon period. They can identify a new social need or highlight a social cause that has not yet been met. They can have charismatic leaders or receive substantial publicity for a time-sensitive issue and build momentum and recognition for good deeds or other successes. Working in such an organization can be an intense and exhilarating ride. It can throw staff and volunteers into the spotlight or into new places with new resources—the exciting, new start-up with the breakthrough innovation that will change the world.

But maintaining momentum requires substantial effort, often on a shoestring budget. An organizational structure must constantly evolve to respond to the latest needs. It can be exhausting. Public interest can wane. The organizational mission can be achieved, or, more likely, some other cause can take its place in the spotlight. The founding team can burn out, or worse, attempt to run the organization by themselves longer than is productive, without bringing on the new skill sets and experience they may need to continue to grow and evolve.

So how can you transition from a start-up to a more mature organization? What does it take to break through the awkward teenage years of growth and development, when the excitement begins to dissipate but systems are still being developed, programming is still being refined, and staff are working hard to build evidence of the success of your approach?

These questions haunt any ambitious organization but may be particularly difficult for nonprofits. This is because the charitable sector is inherently more unstable than the for-profit or government sectors. After all, nonprofits exist because they focus on issues that do not have a private sector or profit motive and have not been identified as enough of a public challenge to receive government funding (or perhaps the government-funded approach is not sufficient to deliver quality results). As a result, nonprofits hold an unenviable ground between for-profits and government organizations.

We believe that the Third Sector, another name for the nonprofit, nongovernmental sector, has a critical role to play in society—much like a third leg of a stool alongside the public and private sectors that keeps us balanced. Nonprofits often offer new ways of thinking; create innovative business models; take catalytic, disruptive approaches; and drive accountability. These approaches can challenge the public and private sectors in a constructive way, forcing them to consider their impact on the people and resources on our planet and strive for greater efficiency and effectiveness when delivering their services. We need a thriving civil society with vibrant nonprofit organizations and social enterprises providing solutions to society's critical problems that would otherwise fall through the cracks.

We Do It Because We Love It!

Since you're reading this book, you probably agree that cultivating healthy, vibrant entrepreneurial social enterprises is important. You might have a cause you are passionate about. This work gives our lives meaning, and we love it. Passion to achieve some greater social goal must be the starting point and the fuel that brings joy to our work and helps us persevere during the tough times.

Inevitably, driving large-scale social impact makes all of us feel as though we are leaving the world in better shape. We choose to work for a nonprofit organization because it is one of the most effective ways to make a difference in this world.

Nothing fills us with greater hope than meeting the children who are benefiting from Room to Read's programs—like "Mr. Poet," as he is called by his friends and teachers, who studied at an elementary school in South Africa that Erin was fortunate to visit. Room to Read had supported Mr. Poet's school to establish a library, and he quickly became one of its most avid patrons. A well-stocked and well-run library was an exciting change to his school's environment, and it quickly became an oasis from the challenges in the students' lives. Mr. Poet, the title given to him by the other students and emblazoned proudly on this school uniform sweater, was so inspired by all the books he read that he started to write his own poems. He wrote one for Room to Read:

Miss Library

Miss Library, you are the quiet lady full of respect and dignity

You attend to people who take time to seek information

Your shelves are full of books filled with knowledge and inspiration

Through you, I shared in the ideas of important people like William Shakespeare and Desmond Tutu

The dinosaurs became extinct before our time, but you kept record and make them come alive for us

Anytime I visit you seeking knowledge, I depart more powerful

Knowledge is power

When I seek a good story, you leave me inspired

Oh, Miss Library you are one of a kind

You are the mother of all nations

You feed the nations with knowledge and wisdom

Feed us

In the following chapters, we have tried to capture some of the most inspirational and difficult lessons from our Room to Read journey that has impacted the education of millions of children such as Mr. Poet.

NOTE

1. Vijay Govindarajan and Chris Trimble, *Beyond the Idea: How to Execute Innovation in Any Organization* (New York: St. Martin's Press, 2013).

2

Vision and Execution:
Framing the Issues

The day begins at 4:30 a.m. You get out of bed, escaping the confines of a huge bed net and take a lukewarm shower. You grab a handful of peanuts and dried fruit that you brought with you because the lodge is not yet serving breakfast. You strategically consider the amount of coffee to make in your room's hot pot because you know that it will be hours on the road without a rest stop. You meet the driver and your two colleagues from the local Room to Read office who will be joining you for the day, all of whom you met only two days ago but have long since felt like long-lost friends and your lifeline to the world.

The van is comfortable enough, and the sunrise glorious as you watch it unfurl behind the high clouds. As you drive the three hours to the first school site, you get an important window into rural life. On some drives, the scenery is breathtaking: lush forests, ocean views, vast open spaces. Other drives are jam-packed with one industrial center after another, streets heaped with trash and air filled with car exhaust, with very little natural life evident. Irrespective of the views, it is always fun to observe the rituals of life: people getting up; preparing for the day; opening their shops, or walking or riding their bikes to morning destinations; stopping to talk with friends and neighbors along the way. In some countries, you see women carrying water or large packages on their heads. In other countries, you see very few women at all.

Afternoon drives are like morning drives but in reverse, as people return home to end the day. In both directions, you often see groups of schoolchildren dressed in their uniforms on the way to or from school. The long journeys are filled with conversation. This is a great opportunity to learn about your colleagues, their work, their families, and their interests. You ask about the local political and economic challenges facing the country as well as the nonprofit landscape impacting their work. You learn why they love to work for Room to Read and what they would recommend to achieve even more impact.

Stops along the way include school visits of every kind. Sometimes you are greeted with flower garlands, incense, long rows of singing children and smiling adults, and well-rehearsed classroom activities. Sometimes you can enter a school with little notice, with a brief courtesy discussion with the head teacher, and then an opportunity to sneak to the back of a classroom or library to observe normal day-to-day interactions. Other stops on these days include meetings with local government officials, partner organizations, or small field offices with other field-based Room to Read staff.

These days in the field are some of the most fun and satisfying in our jobs. But they are also exhausting. Long car rides that go off the main road into increasingly bumpy dirt roads for hours at a time are surprisingly hard on the body and mind. Often the last couple of miles require transferring to a motorcycle or going on foot because of the rough terrain. Meetings and conversations all day long require you to be "on" and remain communicative, upbeat, and reflective. It is also important amidst the bustle to record, at least in your mind, what is working well and what needs to be adjusted in the collective work of local staff, partners, and schools.

The regular day often ends with a meal and drinks with staff before you retreat to your hotel room for hours of e-mail.

You need to check in with your staff worldwide, approve work plans and invoices, review draft agreements, answer investor questions, complete slides for the board of directors, write a proposal or a report, and, of course, find time to say hello to your spouse and kids.

Workdays at home are just as busy. Although they may not start as early as 4:30 a.m., they can often last 12–15 hours. There are early-morning calls to Africa, late-night calls to Asia, and many more virtual and in-person meetings between the two. Sometimes, in the evenings, when your spouse asks about the day, it is hard to remember what you did (and not just because you are getting old!).

It can seem like a blur, an exciting but nonstop fire drill. Because the work of nonprofit leaders has many different facets, it is easy to go days, weeks, or even months and do nothing but simply respond to immediate needs. And because nonprofit leaders find it incredibly difficult to carve out the time to be forward-thinking, it's that much more important to be strategic in vision and planning. Reminding yourself of this larger vision and taking advantage of tools to track your progress toward it can help leaders be more focused and impactful when managing their time.

This chapter is meant to help social entrepreneurs to shape that vision. We explain why it is important to set a vision, what to prioritize in the major domains of work, and how we have done this at Room to Read. We then discuss how vision setting and execution likely change at different times of an organization's development.

Negotiating Urgent and Important Issues in Social Endeavors

Stephen Covey offers one strategy for digging out of this hole of endless overwhelming work (see Table 2.1). He suggests that we think about our daily tasks as falling into a simple

TABLE 2.1   Covey Time-Management Matrix.

	Urgent	Not urgent
Important	I	II
Not important	III	IV

time-management matrix.[1] One axis is labeled "urgency," the other "importance."

This small but powerful table encapsulates many important lessons. For our purpose, we highlight Covey's recommendation that people should organize their work so they focus over time on fewer activities that are urgent and not important (quadrant III) and more of time on activities that are important but do not always have to be urgent (quadrant II). Having the time and space to address important issues in a thoughtful way is better than being rushed. This is not easy to do. It requires hard work and thoughtful planning, and reorienting oneself to be a strategic, proactive planner instead of a task-oriented manager. It also takes discipline and the willingness to delay gratification in merely checking tasks off a list. In the private and public sectors, the process of organizing priorities should be relatively straightforward.

In business, for example, financial profit is an extremely strong motivator and unifying force. All actions are ultimately organized around how to make the most money in the most effective and efficient way. The organizing principle in the public sector is similarly strong. Most government offices that are responsible for public services should have a very clear mission that drives its work. In most instances, a government employee in a line agency who arrives at the office on a Tuesday *should* also have a very clear sense about how to organize his or her day. We would argue, perhaps not surprisingly, that the process of organizing work in a nonprofit organization is more fungible. (Everyone thinks their own situations are more complicated, right?) Those of us running nonprofits have a lot more discretion when thinking about how to organize our time.

Yes, in the long run, we are accountable both to our investors and the people whom we serve. However, in daily activities, we have substantial flexibility. This reality makes the challenge of time management more acute. We must be especially mindful of how we organize our work to move from activities that are urgent but not necessarily important to a situation in which we are operating strategically and with reasonable pacing. Otherwise, we overstretch ourselves and our staff. We burn out quickly and our otherwise fantastic social movements disappear quickly into the heap of nonprofit graveyards lined with good intentions and unfulfilled potential.

The Nonprofit Two-Step (Cha-cha-cha?)

Most nonprofit leaders are driven by powerful social goals. We have never met a sincere leader who has been motivated by a boring or inconsequential goal. What we often find, though, is that leaders assume that identifying important social goals is enough in and of itself to start an organization. The actual plan for achieving the goal is often an afterthought or conceived only at a high level at the beginning. This is not a criticism. Having the audacity to dream big and start something new is hugely laudable. However, having a passion is very different from the ability to assess local needs and gaps that are not being met, develop meaningful social products and services, and then grow them for large-scale success.

Leaders need to be clear about (1) *how*, at a high level, the organization is trying to tackle the large, underlying social goal; and (2) *what* specific approaches the organization will pursue to achieve success—hence, the "nonprofit two-step." Leaders must also then develop the discipline and grit to build organizational capacity and persevere through various stages of development to scale their impact.

Stephen Covey's recommendation that people move from tasks that are urgent but unimportant to those that are important but not urgent assumes that we have a good understanding about what is important. This is something that we think about all the time at Room to Read. It is imperative that leaders take the time to ask whether they themselves and their staff are focusing on the important issues of organizational development and execution. Our management team at Room to Read does this every quarter. We hold a one- or two-day offsite meeting to reflect on our progress over the past quarter and how we need to adjust for the next quarter. We track our metrics for success in a succinct organizational dashboard and regularly question whether individual metrics need to be added, deleted, or updated.

This reflection process becomes even more comprehensive during our annual planning process, which is rooted in five-year organizational strategic plans. In all instances, data are collected by our country teams and our global office, fed into the dashboard, analyzed, and shared with our directors across the organization for necessary action. This quarterly planning and reflection is grounded in a higher-level set of assumptions about how we strive to achieve our goals. The fancy term for this that has become fashionable in recent years is "theory of change." The idea is to have defensible assumptions about how the activities and processes that an organization puts in place help to achieve the expected outputs, and how those outputs are meant to contribute to longer-term outcomes and impact.

For example, Room to Read's theory of change is that by collaborating with local communities, partner organizations, and governments in literacy and girls' education, there will be more educated children in the world, which will result in more empowered, active, and responsible citizens.

Once again, the idea that we need to understand how organizational activities lead to desired outcomes might seem so obvious that it's not worth mentioning. However, as we speak to nonprofit leaders, it is often a missing piece in their thinking. We therefore argue that it's important for leaders of entrepreneurial social enterprises to think about their theory of change, be willing to poke holes (and have others poke holes) and question their assumptions about their approaches to achieving change, and be ready to adjust if they find their approaches falter or circumstances change over time.

The Three-Legged Stool Supporting a Theory of Change

Our thesis for scaling impact in entrepreneurial social organizations is that successful leaders must be clear about their theories of change and cognizant about how to evolve their related approaches in the different stages of organizational development.

In fact, leaders should think about three different approaches that, in unison, promote their audacious goals: (1) programmatic, (2) operational, and (3) strategic. Although each of these approaches is important by itself, they are all mutually reinforcing. An organization is in a much better position to succeed and scale if these approaches are clear and well understood by staff members, participants, investors, and other stakeholders.

A **programmatic approach** outlines your organization's activities, the expected outputs, and the intended impact you hope to achieve. It answers the question "What do you do and what impact are you hoping to create?" An **operational approach** then explains the "how." How will you implement those programmatic activities in terms of staffing, financing, legal, administrative, technology, marketing, and communications and fundraising structures and systems, as well as track success over time? Finally, a **strategic approach** defines your plans to scale up and leverage your organizational efforts for greatest impact and system-wide adoption.

Being clear about the programmatic, operational, and strategic approaches that reinforce your organization's theory of change builds confidence. You can then make the right day-to-day decisions to drive your organization forward. This clarity can also help guide action at any given stage of your organizational development so you know when to say "no" or "not yet" and focus on the most important activities. It can also help leaders understand when an approach has outlived its usefulness, and thus can be the impetus for change. Programmatic, operational, and strategic approaches need to be highly functional and mutually reinforcing to keep an organization balanced and increasingly impactful over time. The importance of this balance is shown in Figure 2.1.

Programmatic Approach

The first important approach, programmatic, explains how the activities your organization engages in work, and how activities affect desired outputs and outcomes. We define a program as a

FIGURE 2.1   The Three-Legged Stool.

set of linked activities that are meant to achieve specific goals. An easy way to organize one's thoughts about this is to develop a table that includes five columns: (1) activity, (2) input(s), (3) output(s), (4) intended outcome(s), and (5) explanation. We give two examples in Tables 2.2a and 2.2b for just one activity from each of the Room to Read's Girls' Education Program and Literacy Program, respectively.

Mapping these expectations in a simple way forces a leader to become clear about how the program is supposed to work and be in a better position to explain it to staff and supporters.

After completing this table for all activities in a program, it can be helpful to represent the logic of the overall program graphically, with arrows that specify the directional relationships among the inputs, outputs, and outcomes. We also include any important assumptions as part of the model.

Figure 2.2 summarizes the most recent logic model of Room to Read's overall Girls' Education Program.

Operational Approach

Having a strong programmatic approach is not in and of itself sufficient for long-term organizational success. Program activities can be implemented in an infinite number of ways. Some may be clearly superior to others. However, our experience is that making decisions about operational approaches is not simple. There are always trade-offs in deciding between two or more possible operational designs.

One common trade-off is between quality and cost. For example, at a relatively early stage in Room to Read's development, we made the decision to introduce local, school-based staff into our activities. Even though we were building some great momentum in establishing new projects in new communities and countries, we were becoming concerned that our school partners were not receiving sufficient support. So, we decided to expand our local staff in a big way. We would hire full-time

TABLE 2.2a   Illustrative Row in a Logic Model for a Programmatic Approach to a Room to Read Girls' Education Program Activity.

Activity	Input(s)	Output(s)	Intended outcome(s)	Explanation
Facilitating monthly life-skills sessions with adolescent girls	Tested and results-driven program design, instructional materials and training activities for social mobilizers, and regular check-in visits with program participants	Specific number of girls trained in life-skills education	Girls become competent in their decision making and skills to negotiate their life goals with family and community members	Many girls in underserved communities do not appreciate that they have the skills and rights to think about what they want to achieve in life. Life-skills sessions create this understanding and help girls communicate about this in a positive and respectful way.

TABLE 2.2b   Illustrative Row in a Logic Model for a Programmatic Approach to a Room to Read Literacy Program Activity.

Activity	Input(s)	Output(s)	Intended outcome(s)	Explanation
Developing grade 1 and 2 children's storybooks and nonfiction books	Tested and results-driven program design, instructional materials, and training activities for authors and illustrators	Trained authors and illustrators who create high-quality children's books, and books themselves	Children's access to more book content enhances their interest and increases opportunities to encourage reading habits	Many low-income countries do not have much experience with children's books—much less books of high quality—and therefore need model books to spark demand in schools and in the commercial book-publishing sector.

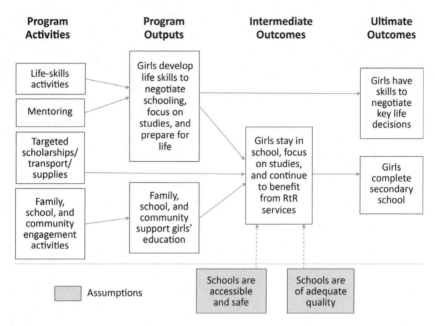

FIGURE 2.2   Logic Model of the Programmatic Approach to the Girls' Education Program.

employees from the communities in which we work to engage more frequently with the girls and schools.

Instead of simply hosting periodic workshops for teachers and administrators, or holding periodic meetings with families and communities, we invested in what we now call "social mobilizers" to work directly with girls; "library management facilitators" to help schools establish libraries and use library books in educational activities; and "literacy coaches" to help teachers improve the quality of the reading instruction.

This decision increased program costs substantially and sparked enormous changes in how our country offices organized, recruited staff, and interacted with the global office. We also had to come up with strategies for explaining the changes to our existing investors and making the case for higher program costs to new investors. This operational change was challenging to implement, but it was absolutely the right call. It does not make sense to create libraries, books, instructional programs, or girls' education programs if the work stops with the physical infrastructure and does not address the desired changes in behavior—the ultimate program outcomes. We had learned that the material inputs alone couldn't change behaviors.

The return on this investment was huge. Teachers noted substantial changes in the children's behavior. They were becoming quite proud of how they were improving children's reading skills and habits. The stories that motivated us the most were from veteran teachers—often teaching for decades—who were seeing many more students in their classrooms reading. Khieavanh Khanouthai, who taught first grade at Nongdern Complete Primary School in Laos for more than 22 years, shared with us, "No matter how much I tried, at the end of the semester my students could barely read and I had no idea why." After incorporating Room to Read's new instruction methods into her classroom techniques, and after her school was provided with our high-quality reading and instructional materials, Khieavanh saw substantial improvement in her students. "Children catch up fast. Now my students can sense how to blend new consonants with simple vowels, even before they open their textbooks!" said Khieavanh.

Namex Pen, a teacher at Kampong Thom Primary School in Cambodia for more than 28 years, had never had a library until her school partnered with Room to Read. What she found most helpful was the teacher training and ongoing coaching. Namex discovered that she could learn how to teach young students to read for fun. Even though Namex had read stories to her students for years, she had merely read from a government-issued textbook, which was limited in colorful illustrations, and asked students to summarize the story. Reading seemed like a chore. Her students were easily distracted. "The different read-aloud techniques that Room to Read taught me are so helpful," Namex said. She saw a huge improvement in the children's reading habits. "They borrow lots of books, especially after the library period," said Namex, "so many that I barely manage to write them all down in the logbook!"

Our experience is that defining a clear operational approach is not easy. This is even more important for organizations that work in the international space. Every part of the work becomes more challenging, from communications to oversight, to cultural ways of working, to roles and responsibilities.

Strategic Approach

Last, all organizations have implicit or explicit expectations about how their strategies affect their ultimate goals. When your organization is ambitious and wants to make changes on a very large scale, your strategic approach becomes that much more important. You need to figure out how one organization can make a difference across large groups of people, perhaps over numerous geographies, to achieve some big change. When defining your strategic approach, you should consider issues of breadth, depth, sustainability, and the methods you will use to achieve system-level change.

People who study how organizations scale have different models to describe the scaling process. Most believe—as we do—that scaling must be an explicit part of one's plan from early in an organization's development. This is one of the core theses of the *Millions Learning*[2] study, conducted by Jenny Perlman and others at the Brookings Institution. Perlman and her colleagues asked the question, "What do organizations that have been successful in the international educational sector do to scale their programmatic impact?" Her team conducted more than a dozen detailed organizational case studies, including Room to Read, and identified four main elements of scaling success: (1) design, (2) delivery, (3) finance, and (4) enabling environment. The key finding from the study is that organizations need to plan for scale to be able to execute strategically at scale.

From its earliest days, Room to Read had an ambition to scale. The early team had the audacity to believe that it could help improve children's reading and girls' success in school for 10 million children in 20 years. Incredibly, Room to Read reached its 10 millionth child after only 15 years—five years earlier than expected. Between 2000 and 2011, Room to Read established long-term offices in 10 countries. We hired the best country teams and raised funds to implement more and more literacy and girls' education projects, honed our programmatic models to be more effective, and streamlined operations to stretch our resources as far as possible. The dominant strategic approach during that time was expanding direct programming ourselves in more communities and in more countries in Africa and Asia, as financial and human resources allowed.

As successful as Room to Read was during this vigorous and dynamic period, we also knew that our contribution was limited on a worldwide basis. What about the other 250 million children left behind? Could we wait another 150 years under our current growth trajectory to reach this mark? How many more children would be deprived of their right to education if Room to Read and other organizations did not help to end worldwide illiteracy or achieve gender equality in education in our lifetimes? This perspective was not ambition for ambition's sake. We simply knew that every day and year that children do not learn to read or have the chance to finish school, another generation will be lost to poverty and forces that will crush their opportunities.

This has been a growing part of our organizational mindset over the past five years and paramount in our deliberations as we worked on our 2015–2019 strategic plan. We considered views about scaling from organizations such as Management Systems International (MSI), the Brookings Institution, and others, which argued that scaling could be achieved through means other than through direct implementation. The MSI framework describes three ways that an organization can grow its work after demonstrating effective and efficient innovations: (1) expansion, (2) collaboration, and (3) replication.[3] *Expansion* is a strategic approach that Room to Read adopted initially, whereby we expanded the number of projects that we implemented directly over time with increased quality and productivity.

We've then used collaboration and replication to grow the impact of our work even more. *Collaboration* is the process of partnering with other organizations to achieve overall program goals, while *replication* is the process of releasing one's process, technology, or model of service for others to use. We have built both processes into our strategic plan under the auspices of "doing more with less."

Our strategic approach was to develop a new business practice area, launched in January 2015, called Room to Read Accelerator, which codevelops and adapts materials and trains other organizations in Room to Read approaches. By combining our direct implementation with external technical assistance, we have continued to innovate and expand our historical work while also helping others to learn to implement programs like ours—and in turn, setting up these organizations to train even more organizations or governments directly. We discuss the ways in which Room to Read evolved its approach to strategic influence in Chapter 9.

From Start-Up to Maturity, and Everything Between

What should be clear from the discussion thus far is that well-articulated programmatic, operational, and strategic approaches, embedded in a clear theory of change, are important tools for focusing organizations' planning and execution.

This is key even from the earliest days of an organization's life. However, it is often the case that these approaches change over time, too. Leaders of ESEs need to be sensitive to environmental and organizational shifts as well as their own learning and adjust their approaches as necessary. In reflecting on Room to Read's own history, we believe that we have achieved a good balance between continuity and change. We have held fast to our highest-level organizational priorities instead of succumbing to the temptations of enticing new opportunities. We have even reduced the scope of our work at times to focus it more on what was strategically important to us. From our inception, we have also maintained a core set of values that have driven our organizational culture since its inception.

We have also made major adjustments over time, too. Could we have evolved differently? Could we have leapfrogged over some phases of our development and gotten to the result sooner? Perhaps. Clearly, organizations can always be more thoughtful in daily decision making. However, we also believe that it took a certain amount of grit, experience, and organizational learning to move from one phase of growth to another. All in all, we believe that the 18 years it has taken for us to make it this far were well spent. Our organizational foundation is solid for future scale *because* we have grappled deeply with the different phases of our work over time. We needed to build the organizational culture, infrastructure and support systems, program designs, proofs of concept, and recognition to achieve the kind of impact now that we sought from the beginning of our work. We also needed time to make mistakes and correct them along the way.

Can other organizations evolve to maturity faster than we have done? Yes! In fact, that is the intent of this book. We hope that other organizations can learn from not only our successes but also our mistakes and avoid some common pitfalls. At the same time, we also recommend strongly that organizations not try to push too far too fast and take shortcuts that could limit their long-term impact. For example, don't go after that mega-grant before you have the capacity to implement it well. Don't make people think that your organization has achieved its aspirational goals before it really has done so. Premature pronouncements about success can lead to unproductive decision making.

Social entrepreneurs are impatient. We want to achieve world change as quickly as possible. This is not necessarily for our egos or personal ambitions (though we need to check these regularly, too!) but because we want the world to benefit from what our organizations offer. In many cases, our work can make the difference between life and death. So we feel a sense of urgency to scale our work as soon as possible. However, it is important that leaders resist the urge to do too much too quickly. It is only through this discipline that leaders can move into the coveted Covey quadrant of important but not urgent work. One of the ways to do this is to have a good sense of how mature your organization is at any time.

For this book, we would like to focus our discussion about the importance of time and organizational development phases to three: (1) start-up, (2) transition, and (3) maturity. *Start-up* extends between the time that a new organization is a flicker in the eye of its founders to the initial stages of development. It is the time when initial organizational missions, structures, and approaches are conceived, seed funding is raised, a core team is built, and initial program activities get off the ground. At the other end of the spectrum, *maturity* is the phase of organizational development when major systems are in place, programmatic approaches and operational systems have been tested thoroughly and validated, at least some leadership has been in place long enough for there to be institutional memory, and there is deep, enduring support for the organization's work among investors, partners, and other stakeholders in the organization's success.

The *transition* phase is everything in between start-up and maturity. It is the tough phase of adolescence in which participants can see the possibilities of scaling and success but do not yet have all the experience or pieces in place to realize the organization's full potential.

What is important to note about the three stages of organizational development is that there are no hard and fast beginning and ending points. In many ways, they blend into each other. We liken the stages to William Bridges's "transition theory" as explained in his book, *Managing Transitions*,[4] that we have used in times of change management at Room to Read. Bridges describes the process of transitioning from an old way of working to a new way of working and the "neutral zone" that sits between the two. This construct also works well for our concept of the phases of organizational development. We adapt Bridges's graphic, in Figure 2.3, as follows.

This diagram is powerful for several reasons. First, it illustrates that while the phases of organizational development are somewhat fluid and overlapping, organizations are largely in start-up, transition, or maturity at any one time. An organization's theory of change and related approaches need to

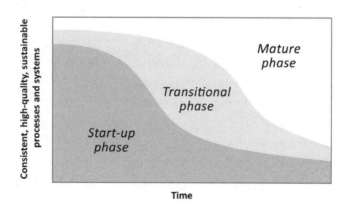

FIGURE 2.3 Overlapping Phases of Organizational Development.

consider its phasing so as not to overstretch its resources but also to take full advantage of its situation. Knowing when your organization is deep in the transition stage is particularly important, as this is the time when the sophomore slump discussed in Chapter 1 can weigh you down, overwhelm your efforts, and stifle development. You must be patient but also deliberate in your efforts to break through and enjoy the benefits of maturity on the other side. The need for organizational determination is at its peak at this transition stage as you no longer have the same start-up enthusiasm as in early days but also do not yet have mature systems in place to take up the slack. Knowing that you are in the transition stage can push you to develop your human resource systems further to retain talent, or begin to codify your standard operating procedures to reduce duplication, complexity, and workloads and therefore the need for additional staff.

Table 2.3 describes the relationship between organizational approaches and phases of organizational development. It summarizes how Room to Read has conceptualized these relationships over time.

Although the specific content of each cell may be different for every organization, the descriptors can also be used as a reasonable guide for newer organizations seeking to scale.

The following chapters delve deeper into these relationships between organizational change and implementation strategies. We share some of the stories of success and failure that have shaped Room to Read's path, as well as our current thinking about the next step in our own organizational journey. We also describe how we have tried to balance our unending quest for improvement and greater impact with the need for pacing, stability, and the understanding and enthusiasm of the tens of thousands of people who make this work possible.

TABLE 2.3 Organizational Approaches and Phases of Organizational Development.

Organizational approach	Phase of development		
	Start-up	**Transition**	**Maturity**
Programmatic	Implement projects with best-in-class program elements based on research literature and adapted from other organizations	Draw on local innovation to develop and test missing program elements for longer-term project success, with an emphasis on enhancing program quality	Implement strong organizational programming at scale and with evidence that is impactful, scalable, sustainable, and cost effective
Operational	Emphasize implementation via local experimentation	Consolidate lessons from local implementation, with emphasis on program quality	Target support to enhance program outcomes efficiently and with more globally consistent practices
Strategic	Implement many projects and with an extensive geographical footprint to pilot activities and increase visibility	Deepen programmatic approach with strong monitoring and evaluation to prove program concept and increase stakeholder and partner support	Continue to implement individual projects but with a growing emphasis on support for system-level change and adoption by others

NOTES

1. Stephen R. Covey, *The 7 Habits of Highly Effective People: Powerful Lessons in Personal Change* (New York: Simon & Schuster, a Fireside Book, 1989), 149–156.
2. Jenny Perlman Robinson and Rebecca Winthrop with Eileen McGivney, *Millions Learning: Scaling Up Quality Education in Developing Countries* (Washington, DC: Center for Universal Education, Brookings Institution, 2016).
3. Larry Cooley and Richard Kohl, *Scaling Up—From Vision to Large-Scale Change: A Management Framework for Practitioners* (Washington, DC: Management Systems International, 2012), 10–12.
4. William Bridges with Susan Bridges, *Managing Transitions: Making the Most of Change*, 3rd ed. (Boston, MA: Da Capo, 2009), 99–102.

3

Communications:
Telling the Story

Authenticity shines through when one is speaking from the heart about deep passions. We have all experienced connecting to a story that is delivered with honesty. One of the things that has impressed us the most about social entrepreneurs is that most can tell personal and passionate stories about the work that they are doing. This powerful ability to link a story to the mission of your organization is one of the best ways for social entrepreneurs to engage people in your work.

As we have shared, much of the motivation behind Room to Read comes from the children and their families with whom we are fortunate enough to interact with on a regular basis. The direct and honest way in which they communicate their circumstances, hopes, and desires for their futures moves us to share their stories, garner support, and advocate for our cause. They tell the impact of Room to Read's work better than anyone.

Suma Tharu, from Nepal, provides a great example of the power of sharing personal stories. Suma comes from the Tharu community, which is an indigenous ethnic group that lives in the Terai in the southern foothills of the Himalayas. When she was six years old, she was given by her parents to a wealthy family to serve as an indentured servant in their home. This is a traditional practice called the Kamlari system. Both of Suma's parents had been indentured servants, too. They had six other children besides Suma and could not take care of all of them, so they felt they had no choice. The Kamlari system is outlawed by the government of Nepal now, but it is still practiced in desperately poor families. Suma served three different families from age six to 12 and described her experience as "being treated like a dog. … You're basically captive in the house. … To be a Kamlari is to lead the life of slavery."

Several nonprofits have been working to free children like Suma still serving as Kamlari girls and to prevent the practice from continuing.

Room to Read started our Girls' Education Program in 2008 in this region of Nepal to partner with organizations rescuing the girls and to help mainstream the girls back to school. The goal was to help families see there are other options and to understand the value of educating their daughters so that in the long term the girls would have more choices in life and have brighter futures.

Room to Read has worked with 1,500 Kamlari girls in this region to date. But Suma's story is unique. After being selected to participate in Room to Read's Girls' Education Program, she was chosen by a partner documentary film group called *Girl Rising* to be featured in a film of the same name. The film told the stories of nine girls from nine different countries and showed how investing in the education of adolescent girls was game changing for them, their families, and their communities. Suma writes her own folk songs in the Tharu language about the difficult life she has led. Writing and singing songs has helped her cope. "My songs have always centered me," she says. "They tell me where I have been, where I have come from, and how far I have to go." As part of the promotion of *Girl Rising*, Suma was invited to New York City to sing on center stage at Lincoln Center at the Women in the World Conference, which aims to bring to life firsthand stories from around the globe of what it is like to be a woman. An excerpt from Suma's song she sang that day:

Thoughtless were my mother and father, they gave birth to a daughter …
Did you want to see me suffer, Mother?
Did you want to see me suffer, Father?
Then why did you give birth to a daughter?
My brothers go to school to study
While I, unfortunate, slave at a master's house …
Abused every day by the landlord's wife
It's a hard life, being beaten every day …
Thoughtless were my mother and father …
They gave birth to a daughter …

After she sang at the conference, Suma was interviewed on stage and shared, "I'm singing for me and thousands of other girls still caught in a house, struggling for their life … I want to fight for the rights of women." She was an incredible representative for the voice of young women around the world who want to be valued and given the opportunity to reach their full potential in life. Once Suma was freed and going to school, she said, "Education is like the light in our eyes. We don't know anything until we get an education, we don't ever know where to go. … It's not just in order to have a job, it's also something you have to do for yourself, and others can never steal it. It always stays with you."

Erin had the pleasure of spending a few precious days in New York with Suma and her chaperone and translator, a Nepal Girls' Education Program senior staff member. Suma, having never even been to her country's major city of Kathmandu, was having a once-in-a-lifetime adventure in New York City. She stayed calm and measured throughout it all. She was not that impressed with the glitz and glamour of the city, which was somewhat disappointing to New Yorkers who love their city! She instead missed the open landscape, food, and simple pleasures of home. Suma, having spent most of her life walking or riding her bicycle everywhere, would get sick in every form of transportation we tried, from subway, bus, or taxi. We instead walked wherever we could.

On one of these walks, Erin asked Suma what was different and what was similar between New York and her home. Suma said that in her country, people would not show affection in public, noting that New Yorkers were always kissing, hugging, and holding hands. Suma then went on to poignantly point out what was similar to Nepal: Darker-skinned people seemed to do most of the hard work. Suma, who is dark-skinned herself, had hoped this would have been different in America. But when she looked around, the darker-skinned people were driving the taxis, opening the doors at the hotels, and clearing the dishes at restaurants. Everything Suma said was honest, straight to the point, and made you think deeply. These were phenomenal observations for a young woman who was just 16 years old at the time of her visit.

Stories like this help us build awareness of the need to improve the quality of education for all children. The hard part is that so many stories exist about so many important issues. As a social entrepreneur, you must excel at telling your organization's story to cut through the noise and win people over.

Planning Your Communications

From the start of our work, Room to Read has always tried to be thoughtful about how we communicate our story, even if the process was ad hoc and opportunistic in our early days. As we have grown, we have learned a lot and now annually update comprehensive marketing and communications plans for key areas. We have a communications department that oversees our global efforts in marketing, investor communication, media relations, crisis management, and internal communications. Given our limited financial and human resources, the key is to be well organized, strategic, and efficient in communications. Our annual communications calendar maps out all external communications, target audiences, frequency and timelines, channels (online or offline), persons responsible, budgets, and methods to track and evaluate results.

This plan also helps us to segment our communications to be relevant to different audiences and not bombard people with too many points of contact. For each communication piece, we have a primary goal of what we are hoping to achieve (for example, inspire donations or engage and update our supporters), and we craft our message to underscore the unique value proposition that highlights what differentiates Room to Read's work from other entrepreneurial ventures. Whether it's our website, blog, *Annual Report, Global Results and Impact Report*, or social feeds, we regularly hear from our wide network of supporters that our communications are informative and uplifting, and encourage people to join the cause and act. Mission accomplished!

We, of course, didn't start out with this level of planning. As we discussed in Chapter 2, the methods and tools we have used to create momentum around telling our story have evolved with our organization. We use the framework of start-up, transitional, and mature stages of organizational development to explain how you can best promote, advocate, and build public awareness and action for your mission.

Start-Up Stage: Building the Personality of Your Brand

Right from the beginning, Room to Read's founders agreed quickly on what the "personality" or brand of Room to Read would be. We wanted to stand for hope, optimism, the belief that large-scale, positive change in the world can be achieved, and that education is a cornerstone solution to helping solve every other problem today. Since we were solely focused on serving children, we wanted our brand to be playful, youthful, and fun. As a social enterprise headquartered in San Francisco, near Silicon Valley, we also wanted to be known for being results oriented, disruptive, innovative, and entrepreneurial. We wanted people to think of us as managed as well as any highly profitable business but with the heart of a leading social-mission-driven organization. It was a tall order.

We landed on the name Room to Read, with our logo representing a schoolhouse filled with colorful books, the tagline of "World Change Starts with Educated Children," and all our reports and external communication being upbeat, results and data driven, transparent, and ambitious. To illustrate our attention to detail, our tagline was "World Change Starts with Educated Youth" for 48 hours until we decided that "children" was a warmer, more approachable word that better represented our brand.

Every organization has a brand personality. It is crucial to figure out early on what you want yours to be so you can shape it and communicate it consistently. In building our brand, we focused on our organizational name, logo, tagline, visual identity, and the experience we wanted people to have when interacting with us. Although it is important to focus on internal issues like program delivery and operations, the founding team also needs to focus on communicating externally and building a movement around the mission and organization.

As social entrepreneurs, we all ultimately seek to launch a movement of change. We realize we cannot do it alone and must create a cadre of champions around us to be partners, volunteers, and investors. Some of the greatest movements in history, such as the civil rights movement in the United States or the nationalist movement in India for independence from the British, were successful because of the collective action they inspired. At Room to Read, we realized early on that we were in the movement-building business and identified different categories of key stakeholders to tailor our message to motivate, engage, and inspire action.

Receptive audiences come in all shapes. The following list exemplifies the various types and venues for initial target audiences:

- Room to Read–organized events, which ranged from small dinner salons in investors' homes to larger events in public spaces
- Media outlets of all kinds, from newspapers, magazines, and radio to television, as well as online media
- Corporate speaking opportunities, from "lunch and learns" that engaged employees, to executive or client conferences where we were keynote inspirational speakers
- Already assembled audiences, or "Triple As" as we nick-named them, which could range from a Rotary Club to a professional association to a conference
- Schools and universities, which often lead to making connections to parents and young professionals starting out their careers

We were constantly pitching anyone who would listen and said yes to almost every opportunity in those early days to talk about our work. Many people heard our story. Some chose to donate to us, and the truly converted became part of our volunteer chapter network and have been active partners in building our global movement.

Much of the brand building and external communications at this early stage involves envisioning the change you desire and painting a picture for the audience. It is aspirational in nature as the organization is still in the proof-of-concept stage. The ESE is still building its body of evidence to prove its impact. Often, you have to describe the intended impact you believe you are having rather than providing detailed evidence for the simple reason that as a start-up, you are still collecting the evidence. It takes a leap of faith.

We found the public, key partners, stakeholders, and investors to be understanding about this. At Room to Read, we described what it was like to be a student in a dilapidated school before and after Room to Read support. We painted a vivid picture of a run-down, crumbling, overcrowded school building transformed into a newly constructed, larger school, complete with a child-friendly library filled with local language books and staffed by a trained librarian. We would then share that we had replicated this transformation 50 times in one country, and scores of times across all our countries of operation in that year alone. This story of the change we were creating in hundreds of schools a year felt tangible because we rooted it in the story of the transformation of just one school community.

The challenge at this early stage of development is that sometimes the vision and story you are telling can get ahead of reality. We had to be careful because our stories of the changes we had effected in one community might or might not be replicable or scalable across all the school communities in which we were working. In a quick, inspiring snapshot of one successful school, the complexities and nuances of the hard work we were engaged in could be lost. It could appear that the solutions to real-world, complex problems are too easy or simple. Social entrepreneurs run the risk of their messaging getting ahead of the content and evidence—the aspirational desire to highlight stories of change to engage others in your cause can precede the reality of proving the model.

Being aware of this risk means we must be cautious about oversimplifying our messaging as well. At Room to Read, we realized many of our supporters didn't fully understand our model. They didn't realize we were working exclusively in government school systems, not building and running our own private schools. They didn't realize our literacy work was at primary schools for both boys and girls and that our

Girls' Education Program operated at secondary schools. They thought we were exclusively working with girls. Many of details of the "what" and "how" of our work were lost as we successfully engaged and inspired people to care and invest.

At this early stage of development, some of this disconnect is to be expected as the experiment of trying something new means all the details are not necessarily known at the beginning. Some larger and more traditional nonprofits in the international education space, however, criticized us for getting a lot of media attention and private investor funding without having the depth or scale of programming to warrant it. To some extent, they were right.

We took that misalignment in our messaging to heart, and it motivated us to bridge those gaps. We wanted to build a reputation based on evidence for the depth and quality of our work, not just for the story of the growth and scale of it. Room to Read's experiences demonstrate that it's possible to create an aspirational vision of where you want to go. Although success stories can get ahead of your evidence, it is both a risk and an opportunity that ESEs can adroitly manage to their benefit to drive their scale without misleading anyone. Disrupting the status quo has risks to it, but those risks should be managed ethically and transparently.

Transition Phase: Widening the Circle

As Room to Read grew, we focused not just on defining and sharing our message ourselves but also on empowering others to be storytellers for us. In today's world, people crave involvement in activities that are aligned with their values and that have real meaning. ESEs are in the unique position of being able to engage people in constructive ways to change the world—which is the kind of meaning people are seeking.

We invited people to do this through our volunteer chapter network, where we encouraged people to devote their time and talent to helping Room to Read raise public awareness and much-needed funding. We started our volunteer chapter network in the first few years of Room to Read as a way to encourage people in different cities around the world to be the local face of the organization in their communities. Chapters largely organized fundraising events, thereby reaching out to their networks to support our mission and having a huge multiplier effect on the amount of funds and brand awareness we could build as a small nonprofit. Our chapter network rapidly grew in our first 15 years to more than 40 cities in 16 countries with more than 16,000 volunteers.

The unifying force of our chapter network is that everyone in it believes that education is a powerful tool for changing the world. Often, people join our chapter network because education defined their experiences in their own lives, which opened doors and created opportunities that didn't exist for previous generations in their families. These individuals have been incredible brand ambassadors for Room to Read. We'll talk more about how we manage our chapter network in Chapter 8.

We hold chapter leadership conferences (CLCs) regularly in which the leaders from different cities gather for four days in San Francisco to share upcoming plans and best practices, be inspired, and celebrate each other's successes. CLCs are a highlight of our year at Room to Read, both positive and uplifting, knowing that these inspirational volunteers dedicate extensive time to help us.

We hear many stories at the CLCs. People share narratives of being the first generation in a family of immigrants that gave up everything to raise their children in a country where they could obtain a quality education. Or they share how they were the first women in their families to earn higher degrees, have successful careers, and choose their own spouses because their mothers and fathers broke from tradition. We at Room to Read have been lucky to tap into a powerful group of individuals who are willing to move mountains to make change happen.

Our job at Room to Read is to create the space and provide the tools to unleash the energy of these volunteers to represent us in their local communities. In the transitional stage of rapid growth, it sometimes felt like we couldn't keep up with the boundless energy of our chapter network. We provided Power-Point slide decks for them to use when speaking to audiences, event-planning toolkits for organizing fundraising events, and ways to connect across chapters to share and learn from each other. Because of this, our local chapters have played a huge role in the growth of our brand as well as revenues.

Many of our volunteers first learned about Room to Read through John Wood's first book, *Leaving Microsoft to Change the World.* Having a charismatic, visible leader like John writing a compelling book helped us recruit motivated people who wanted to get involved. And the book was a natural calling card to many media opportunities, like John being a guest on *Oprah* and getting stage time at various conferences. As our communication messaging began to evolve beyond our start-up story, we regularly found ways to use media opportunities to attract new champions to our movement.

Events were another key way to widen the circle. We hold a wide variety of events, often driven by our volunteer chapter network, that range from large galas with a key theme like "Destination Literacy" to more intimate salon dinners, to casual gatherings like beers for books or Bollywood girls' night out parties. Events succeed because key leaders and spokespersons can share their personal narratives as well as build a collective commitment of the group to act in supporting an organization's mission. A challenge for all spokespersons at Room to Read was how to tell the story in the most powerful and engaging way for each type of audience. We learned some best practices over time:

- Share your personal journey and what drives you to do this work. This will connect with your audience.
- Shock people into understanding the need by using statistics and data.
- Use stories of direct beneficiaries of your work to connect people at a human level as well to the cause.
- Use more images and fewer words when presenting with visual aids.
- Back up your claims of success with impact and output data.
- Share examples not just about your programs but also about your operations to build confidence that you are a solid and transparent organization.
- Always close with an ask—to donate, volunteer, or take some sort of action.
- Take questions, if appropriate, from the audience so you can have a two-way conversation.

Tailoring the messaging to fit the audience involves customizing the style and tone of communicating as much as the actual content—perhaps even more so. After being on the BBC *Women's Hour* radio show, Erin received compliments from Room to Read's London-based supporters that they almost forgot she was an American because she altered her pace and tone so effectively to match the interviewer. This was a different style than what she would use for an audience of bankers at a corporate speaking engagement in New York, or for a group of parents and children at a school in Singapore.

Another challenging aspect of this transition phase was developing the skills of staff members—and of people in our chapter network—so that they could represent Room to Read in compelling ways. That way, we would not always be dependent on Room to Read leadership.

This proved to be a much harder challenge than we at first realized. We struggled for years to find the best way to build the capacity of others to tell the Room to Read story and engage a wider audience. Fortunately, a great opportunity presented itself when Ketchum, a global communications firm, selected us to be their long-term pro bono corporate social responsibility partner. They used their tested and proven model of creating compelling messaging and tools to help us empower anyone to represent Room to Read.

The central part of their process is creating a message map for your organization and then training your key spokespeople how to use it effectively. The goal of the Ketchum communications training process is to ensure all people in your organization can easily tell your story clearly, consistently, and with passion in every opportunity. As Ketchum says, it is a rigorous approach that combines style with substance. The goal is to identify the "radiant core" of your story, distill it down to key points, and highlight proof points to back up and support each element and to overcome any objections that arise.

In Figure 3.1, we share a recent version of Room to Read's message map. Accompanying the map is a more detailed training document that has the supporting proof points for each box in the message map. In Figure 3.2, we give a few examples of these proof points.

The message map is not static. We overhaul it for each of our five-year global strategic plans. We also update and refine the map and proof points annually with the latest evidence. We then roll out the map and train any new staff members. We also use the map with volunteers, board members, and advisors—anyone representing Room to Read.

The message map is a great tool because it reminds us there is no single way to tell the Room to Read story. You can

Room to Read: Changing 15 Million Children's Lives through Education

WHY WE EXIST

Quality of life, health and economic opportunity all depend on education, and right now there remains an education crisis in low-income countries. Literacy is the foundation for all future learning yet nearly 750 million people are illiterate and 2/3 are women and girls. Even with increased access to school, many children aren't learning the basics while in primary school due to underprepared teachers, inadequate funds, lack of books and school infrastructure challenges and it gets worse for girls in secondary school when female student enrollment sharply drops due to societal and economic challenges.

WHAT DIFFERENTIATES US

- Room to Read targets two critical milestones during a child's school years that can dramatically impact a child's life and their future generations. We concentrate on literacy learning during 1st and 2nd grades because we know that once a child reaches 3rd grade without basic literacy skills, it is extremely difficult for the child to catch up. To us this means a child develops both the skills and the habit of reading which we believe together contribute to lifelong learning. We also concentrate efforts during a girl's transition into secondary school in 6th and 7th grades when she has a high risk of dropping out of school because we know that wages for girls increase by 15–25% for each additional year a girl remains in secondary school.

- We use data to evolve and improve our programs each year. Over the years, our hard work and commitment to our mission have resulted in our ability to measuring our results and reporting these results to our stakeholders as we consider transparency central to our success. This includes developing rigorous methods for determining results through regular data collection against key indicators at more than 3,500 sites annually.

- As an organization recognized for its transparency and financial excellence and listed in Charity Navigator's top 1% of organizations that are fiscally sound and responsible, we work to ensure that each dollar invested is maximizing the impact on each child and school we benefit.

WHO WE ARE

Founded in 2000, Room to Read believes that World Change Starts with Educated Children.®

We envision a world in which all children can pursue a quality education that enables them to reach their full potential and contribute to their communities and the world.

We create long-term systemic change in the 14 countries where we work.

We are a learning organization that finds innovative solutions to challenges and acts quickly to achieve results. We hold ourselves accountable to both the children and communities we serve and our investors.

INTEGRATED MESSAGE

Many world problems can be solved through one tool: education. Room to Read's innovative model focuses on deep, systemic transformation within schools in low-income countries during the two most critical periods in a child's schooling: early primary school for literacy acquisition and secondary school for girls' education. With a focus on the quality of education provided in the communities and ensuring this outcome is measured, Room to Read created a model that can be replicated, localized and sustained by governments. Room to Read is transforming educational experiences and impacting future generations with the belief that World Change Starts with Educated Children.®

OUR FUTURE

Room to Read focused its start-up years on achieving tremendous programmatic growth. Over the years, our hard work and commitment to our mission have resulted in our ability to systematize and institutionalize best practices. It has also paved the way for governments to start adopting our work to benefit more children. We are now focused on scaling our impact even further in the countries where we work and beyond for long-term systemic change in literacy and gender equality in education. We will do this through our core programmatic work, which aims to impact the lives of nearly one million children each year. We will also do this through Room to Read Accelerator, our technical assistance unit that shares and trains other organizations and government partners to implement similar models, thus amplifying Room to Read's reach into additional regions and countries.

WHAT WE DO

We collaborate with local communities, partner organizations and governments to ensure that we achieve the outcomes we desire: primary school children can become independent readers and girls can complete secondary school with the skills necessary to negotiate key life decisions. We set measurable goals and are committed to collecting action-oriented data to ensure our programs are run with quality and impact, while maximizing cost efficiencies.

LITERACY PROGRAM

Room to Read provides much more than a space for storing books.

Room to Read's **Literacy Program** transforms primary schools into child-friendly learning environments that enable children to develop the **skills and habit of reading** throughout primary school and become life-long, **independent readers.** Our intervention includes ensuring the school has a library with books in the children's local language, as well as teachers and librarians who are trained in the best practices of reading and writing instruction. Key to our program is ensuring that families, communities and governments are all engaged in the transformation of the school and committed to its success. This includes working closely with governments to integrate library services and books into national government curriculum and instruction.

GIRLS' EDUCATION PROGRAM

Room to Read provides much more than material support to girls.

Room to Read's **Girls' Education Program** ensures that **girls complete secondary school and have the skills to negotiate key life decisions.** Our program reinforces girls' commitment to their own education, works with girls to develop essential life skills and increases support for girls' education among their parents, school staff, and communities. Key to our program are our social mobilizers, local women who are hired as mentors and work with girls and their families to ensure that girls stay in school, participate in activities, and navigate the challenges of adolescence with the ability to make their own life choices, both personally and professionally.

GLOBAL IMPACT

Room to Read has benefited more than 15 million children by developing literacy skills and a habit of reading among primary school children and by supporting girls to complete secondary school with strong life skills. We have grown from supporting fewer than 100,000 children per year during the early stages of our organization, to reach approximately one million new children each year.

Our Literacy Program has made a difference in over 20,000 government schools. We have data showing children check out approximately 11 million books annually and learn how to read with fluency and comprehension at a greater rate than they would without the presence of our program. Our Girls' Education Program has supported more than 50,000 girls, and 95% either remained in school or graduated from secondary school in 2016.

FIGURE 3.1   Room to Read Message Map.

WHO WE ARE

Founded in 2000, Room to Read believes that World Change Starts with Educated Children.®

We envision a world in which all children can pursue a quality education that enables them to reach their full potential and contribute to their communities and the world.

We create long-term systemic change in the 14 countries where we work around the world.

We are a learning organization that finds innovative solutions to challenges and acts quickly to achieve results. We hold ourselves accountable to both the children and communities we serve and our investors.

1. We are a global organization with headquarters in San Francisco, USA that employs over 1,500 staff across 17 countries. Of those staff, 90% are employed in our program countries.

2. We have full-country program operations in Asia and Africa in the following countries: Bangladesh, Cambodia, India, Laos, Nepal, Sri Lanka, South Africa, Tanzania and Vietnam.

3. Long-term systemic change to us means that governments will adopt our work at scale, or the elements of our work that are most scalable and impactful. Through country-wide government support to scale our programs, we can impact and benefit more children.

   • We have seen examples of our influence on education systems through our Literacy Program. For example, in India we were invited to scale our literacy instruction activities at 360 state government schools across the two states of Uttarakhand and Chhattisgarh for five academic years, starting in 2015. We are working to build the states' systemic capabilities so they can implement effective literacy interventions independently in the future.

   • We have also seen examples of systemic change through our Girls' Education Program. For example, our life skills curriculum is being integrated into standard school curriculum in Prey Veng and Kampong Cham Provinces in Cambodia. We are now using this success to advocate for additional integration of life skills education into the national secondary school curriculum across the country.

4. We have an annual budget of approximately US$50 million, a financial scale that few nonprofits ever reach.

   • We are one of a handful of international and education-focused non-profits founded since 2000 to have broken the US$50 million annual operating budget barrier.

   • We have fundraising operations across North America, Europe, Asia and Australia in the following locations: Delhi, Hong Kong, London, Mumbai, New York, San Francisco, Singapore, Sydney, Tokyo and Zurich.

   • We have an active network of nearly 16,000 volunteers across approximately 40 cities around the world that significantly contributes toward our fundraising goals.

5. In our first 15 years, Room to Read benefited 10 million children, which was a goal we set for ourselves when the organization was founded and one we reached five years earlier than expected.

WHAT DIFFERENTIATES US

We use data to evolve and improve our programs each year. Room to Read is committed to measuring our results and reporting these results to our stakeholders as we consider transparency central to our success. This includes developing rigorous methods for determining results through regular data collection against key indicators at more than 3,500 sites annually.

1. Every year we collect a range of key data points at more than 3,500 schools and nearly 50,000 girls. We maintain accountability by committing to publish these figures in our publicly available Global Results and Impact Report each year.

2. Beyond the Global Results and Impact Report each year, Room to Read's research, monitoring and evaluation unit releases several additional reports about our research and evaluation activities, and each country team completes research projects on topics of critical interest to programs teams.

FIGURE 3.2 Proof Points.

WHAT DIFFERENTIATES US

As an organization recognized for its transparency and financial excellence and listed in Charity Navigator's top 1% of organizations that are fiscally sound and responsible, we work to ensure that each dollar invested is maximizing the impact on each child and school we benefit.

1. Room to Read leadership has been awarded for their innovation and entrepreneurism. Recognition includes:
   - World Children's Prize, Honorary Award Laureate, 2014, Awarded to John Wood on behalf of Room to Read
   - Schwab Foundation for Social Entrepreneurship, World Economic Forum/Social Entrepreneur of the Year, 2014, Awarded to Erin Ganju on behalf of Room to Read

2. We have won awards that demonstrate our impact and program quality including:
   - Library of Congress Literacy Award, Rubenstein Prize, 2014
   - UNESCO, Confucius Prize for Literacy, 2011

3. We have won more than 20 book awards that demonstrate the quality of our local language children's books, including an award from UNICEF for best early childhood development publication of the year (2012).

4. We have won awards for our fiscal excellence including earning eleven Charity Navigator 4-star ratings since 2007.
   - This award has been given to Room to Read each year since 2007 and recognizes us among the elite organizations that "outperform most other charities in America."

5. We are committed to ensuring that at least 80% of our funding goes directly to our work, while investing in high-quality infrastructure that supports our long-term health and effectiveness.

FIGURE 3.2 *(Continued)*

start at any point in the map and jump to any box as fits the situation. For any interaction to be compelling, though, it must be authentic to the person telling it and fit into the flow of the conversation. Because it simplifies message training, people can easily get comfortable with it, allowing us to widen the circle of those capable of telling the Room to Read story in compelling and consistent ways. The message map and accompanying proof points are not shared externally, but only used internally as training materials to build staff's capacity to tell the Room to Read story in a meaningful way.

Since one of the best ways to make Room to Read's work come alive is through the stories of the people whose lives have been transformed, we have hired communications officers in most of our country offices to collect and share these stories of success. We use stories in our blog on our website, investor reports, media stories, and public presentations. Everyone who travels for Room to Read is also always on the lookout for great stories that dramatize our message: the power of education to create a brighter future for the world's children. We weave these into conversations and presentations, because although audiences appreciate statistics, they frequently connect best to the personal stories of transformation.

Often just weaving in a quick story makes a point come alive. When Erin talks about our Girls' Education Program, she usually shares a recent interaction from a country she visited that year. She collects jewels such as what one of the girl graduates in Cambodia told her: "Education is like oxygen—it is what gives me hope for a brighter future for myself and my family." Or she'll relate experiences such as what happened when she attended a life-skills workshop for the girls in Tanzania. The topic was delaying marriage until after secondary school graduation. When the group asked Erin when she had gotten married, she told them she had waited until she was 34 years old—after she had established her career and met the right man for her. This news was greeted with spontaneous applause and a dance by the girls to congratulate Erin on being "smart" enough to wait. Or Cory brings alive how we work with governments, by discussing a recent visit with Ministry of Education officials in Nepal, the types of issues they raised, and the feedback they provided on our program.

Using stories to highlight the importance of issues is probably done best by Nicholas Kristof, an op-ed columnist for the *New York Times* and winner of two Pulitzer Prizes. In his columns, Kristof regularly talks about causes he's passionate about through the personal experiences of people. As Kristof says, "Individual storytelling is incredibly powerful. We as journalists know intuitively what scientists of the brain are discovering through brain scans, which is that emotional stories tend to open the portals, and that once there's a connection made, people are more open to rational arguments." Room to Read was fortunate to have Kristof visit our work in Vietnam in 2011 and again in 2014 and write about one of Girls' Education Program participants, Dao Ngoc Phung. After losing her mother to cancer, 14-year-old Phung had to assume many of her family's household responsibilities. During the week, Phung's father had to work extra jobs in the city to pay down the family debt, so Phung had full responsibility for her younger siblings in addition to keeping up with her schoolwork and other chores. Yet despite this heroic multitasking—which would be overwhelming in and of itself—Phung was determined to stay in school so that she could become an accountant one day. Kristof's inclusion of Room to Read in his column was one of the most powerful media exposures we have received.

Mature Phase: Amplifying the Message

When we reflect on Room to Read's evolution over the past 18 years, we are quite proud that we have built such a trusted brand in global education. As we discuss in following chapters, we made several key pivots in how we evolved our programs and operations as we have scaled Room to Read. Through these changes, we retained and grew our support base because of the strength of our brand. Corporate brands that thrive often represent lifestyles instead of products and indeed transcend traditional product lines—think Nike or Apple. Successful ESEs must do the same.

As we are all aware, the Internet has significantly changed the ways in which you can share your message and reach a wider audience. It allows you to amplify your message at lower costs than ever before. Technology is a great equalizer. Although most of today's current technology platforms didn't exist when we started Room to Read, we now actively manage our online presence to reach audiences through blogging; posting on Twitter, Facebook, YouTube, and Instagram; and through our own custom-built peer-to-peer fundraising platform.

We collaborated with the online and mobile fundraising platform for social impact organizations, Classy, to develop and be first to market with a cross-currency platform that allows our individual and corporate supporters to run a campaign that accepts donations and offers tax receipting in all our major fundraising currencies. These tools help our messages go viral, encourage others to tell our story, and spread news of the work we are doing. We also view our website as one of our most central external communication tools and devote a lot of time and attention to ensuring it is compelling, delivers a positive user experience, and drives visitors to action—either by investing in us or advocating on our behalf.

One the best examples of generating interest in and awareness for our work was our "Do Not Read This" video. The video was a challenge to viewers not to read anything for 24 hours and experience what your life would be like if you were illiterate. As you watch the video you experience what it feels like to go through life unable to read a street sign, medicine bottle, map, book, or website—something that more than 750 million people do every day. It was created by our communications department for less than $400 and went viral, being viewed more than a half million times. It was ranked in the top 10 social impact videos on YouTube in 2014 and won a 2015 SABRE Award, the biggest public relations award in the industry. Campaigns don't have to be expensive or complex. Instead they can be disruptive, thought provoking, and, most importantly, easy to share to encourage people to spread the word about your cause.

Building brand awareness is more successful when social media campaigns are combined with our supporters' individual networks and the networks of corporate partners. One of our media partners, Bloomberg, ran the "Do Not Read This" video in Asia as a free public service ad when it had space. This helped raise awareness for Room to Read as well as for eradicating illiteracy. We earned greater name recognition in prominent business circles from outreach like this. And we have received substantial exposure more broadly, as demonstrated by an experience our board chairperson had while traveling on a personal trip to Myanmar (a country in which Room to Read had at the time not yet worked). His tour guide asked him what he did. After mentioning his work with Room to Read, the young man replied, "Oh, Room to Read is very famous. We see it on TV, and we are all waiting for Room to Read to come to Myanmar."

In recent years, the Internet has raised awareness and much-needed financial support through crowdfunding, where you fund a project by raising monetary contributions from many people, and peer-to-peer fundraising, a method of fundraising that leverages your supporters to fundraise on your behalf. Room to Read has recently invested heavily in building our technology platform to support peer-to-peer fundraising in multiple countries and currencies. This is a natural extension of our successful volunteer chapter network, building off the same principle that most people give to a nonprofit organization if they are asked by a trusted friend or colleague.

Erin remembers sitting in an Internet café in Ho Chi Minh City in Room to Read's early days, overhearing backpackers searching the Internet for a nonprofit they could support after being moved by the poverty they had seen throughout Vietnam. At the time, Google was giving us free ad space, so a link to Room to Read appeared. The backpackers said, "Room to Read—never heard of them. Let's keep searching." At that point, Erin introduced herself to the two women and showed them her business card. They were mildly interested but not convinced. But today, many more people have heard of Room to Read from their trusted networks. Happily, now when we meet people on an airplane, at a friend's party, or a networking event, they often say, "Oh, of course I have heard of Room to Read. My friend told me about you." It is extremely gratifying to hear these responses, particularly when faces light up upon hearing our name.

We also have engaged in several "cause marketing" partnerships. Cause marketing is a collaboration between a corporation and a nonprofit designed to promote the former's sales and the latter's cause. It has become increasingly popular.

A great example of a successful cause marketing partnership for Room to Read has been with Atlassian, a technology company that builds collaboration software to help teams organize, discuss, and complete shared work. In 2009, Atlassian's two founders came to Room to Read early in the company's history offering to donate all revenue from every starter license subscription. The goal was to sell starter license subscriptions for five users, for $5 each, for five days to raise $25,000 for Room to Read.

As Atlassian was a relatively new technology company based in Australia, we had no idea of the value this was likely to generate, but willing to embrace innovative new ideas, we readily agreed. The $25,000 goal was reached in less than 24 hours. At the end of the five-day period, $100,000 had been raised. The starter license program soon became $10 for ten users, all donated to Room to Read, resulting in literally millions of dollars for girls' education. Eight years later, Atlassian is one of our largest corporate supporters and has provided approximately US$7 million to date through our multiyear partnership agreement. As it has grown, so does its contribution to Room to Read.

Atlassian went on to become one of the founding companies of "Pledge 1%," which is a corporate philanthropic movement dedicated to making the community a key stakeholder in every business. Pledge 1% encourages and challenges individuals and companies to pledge 1% of equity, profit, product, and employee time to their communities. Atlassian's co-CEOs often speak publicly to incentivize other companies to join the Pledge 1% movement and highlight the success of their partnership with Room to Read. This kind of exposure from well-regarded, successful business executives could never be bought by money.

Atlassian and Room to Read continue to find ways to support each other's cultures and growth. Atlassian in recent years has focused on getting its workers involved through an employee giving campaign called Dollars-a-Day, in which employees can donate out of their paycheck to support Room to Read's Girls' Education Program. We also host an annual trip for select Atlassian employees to Cambodia to see the work they are supporting firsthand. This is a great way to recognize and motivate top supporters of our cause.

One of our other successful cause marketing partnerships is with Tatcha. Tatcha is a high-quality line of beauty and skin care products. A highly accomplished female executive, Tatcha's founder and CEO is a source of inspiration and role model for young women. When she started her business, she decided she didn't want to just build a profitable business. More importantly, she and her cofounder wanted to improve the world for girls everywhere. The company launched the "Beautiful Faces, Beautiful Futures" campaign, in which Tatcha would donate the equivalent to one day of girls' education to Room to Read for every full-sized skincare item sold. We developed a "trust" logo with Tatcha that states it is a proud partner of Room to Read. This logo appears on all its full-sized skincare product packaging. Tatcha's initial goal was to support 35,000 days of school. Since 2014, however, Tatcha has grown so rapidly that it has already surpassed a million girl-days of school!

Again, Tatcha's investment in Room to Read grows along with the success of the business. And we gain exposure to customers who shop for Tatcha products in high-end stores like Barneys and Sephora. Tatcha builds us into every aspect of its corporate culture. It trains its staff to talk about Room to Read to customers and make the connection between buying Tatcha products and doing good for girls around the world. The brand exposure is something we could never achieve on our own.

Taking every opportunity to tell our story has been central from day one in being able to build a global movement around Room to Read and our cause. We encourage all social entrepreneurs to build a strong communication plan into their strategy early on so that it becomes a part of your approach to growth and development through every organizational stage. Whether you are on a stage in front of an audience, giving an interview to the media, creating a social media campaign, or empowering spokespeople to tell your story, the most important point is to maximize every chance you can to build awareness and advocates for your organization and cause—a crucial key first step in scaling up.

Key Takeaways

- **Create a complete brand personality or identity early** on which to build your external communication, focusing on your organizational name, logo, tagline, visual identity, and the experience you want people to have when interacting with your organization.

- **Take every opportunity to tell your story with simple, clear messages and powerful images** to a wide variety of audiences, from individuals at events to corporate gatherings, conferences and already-assembled audiences as an invited speaker, and in traditional and social media. Building **a wide and varied support base takes a commitment** to external communication.

- **Be careful that your message highlighting successes in your early stage doesn't get too far ahead of the reality of your work.** In the proof-of-concept stage, you need to rely on representative examples of your work to demonstrate impact, but be careful that the myth of your success doesn't grow faster than reality. Eventually, you will need to bring in "hard" evidence.

- As ESEs, we are in the **movement-building** business to drive social change. Use a **message map** communication tool and training process to **empower spokespeople** to be able to communicate your organizational story clearly, easily, and with passion.

- A **wide circle of storytellers** for your organization is essential for creating collective action around your cause. We invested in **user-friendly materials** and **training** to ensure our staff, volunteer chapter members, and board and advisors could effectively be our storytellers. We all own spreading our story as widely as possible together.

- One of the **most powerful ways to engage people in your cause is to tell stories of the personal experiences of the people impacted by your work**. These stories draw people in who then want to learn more about the facts, statistics, and details around your issue.

- Many **innovations are emerging that allow you to amplify your message** to engage audiences in low-cost, high-impact ways such as social media, peer-to-peer fundraising, crowdfunding, and cause marketing. Lean into these opportunities to widen the circle of advocates working to support your organization.

What We Do

4

Programs: A Theory (of Change) Is Just a Theory Until It Is Turned into Action

Starting Off Right

As recounted in John Wood's first two books, Room to Read's founding was somewhat unusual in the nonprofit world. John, a business executive on holiday in the magical mountains of Nepal, stumbles into a village school and realizes that children do not have books to read. He partners with a local Lion's Club member, Dinesh Shrestha—who understands Nepal's culture and mores—to deliver books to rural schools. Inspired by the community's reaction to the donations, John and Dinesh decide to devote their lives to this cause. Along the way, they meet another business leader, Erin, who had worked with schools in Vietnam. The three of them decide to build a nonprofit organization focused on scaling quality education programs in low-income countries. The rest, as they say, is history.

Every social enterprise begins with a story of inspiration. The question is, what happens after that inspirational start?

Why do some organizations grow while others simply maintain and still others fizzle out?

We know, looking back, that decisions made in Room to Read's early days increased the likelihood it would succeed. First, Room to Read focused on big, challenging, and consequential issues from its start. Helping girls to stay in school and helping girls and boys become lifelong readers are foundational for everything else that happens in their lives. Second, Room to Read hired the right people. These included subject matter experts and organizational leaders in the countries in which we work. Third, Room to Read was committed from early on to develop a strong organizational foundation—one with the resources to turn big ideas into action. We discuss the second and third issues later in the book. This chapter focuses on how we have designed our program activities.

The Right Issues

The scene is similar whenever we visit graduates of our Girls' Education Program, irrespective of whether we are in the shrimp farms of Vietnam, tea plantations of Sri Lanka, mangrove forests of Cambodia, or villages of Tanzania. Young women in their early twenties talk about their experiences in school and the role Room to Read played helping them in small but life-changing ways. Some were abused. Others were from poor families that did not have the money for tuition and fees. Still others were orphans and did not have practical guidance or support.

Common to all of them was the will to stay in school, work hard, and defy the odds for better lives. And when they reflect on their experiences, it was typically little things that made a difference. Whether a small stipend for textbooks or a home visit by a woman from the community who noticed that a girl had been absent from school the previous week, these gestures meant a lot. In all cases, the young women took full advantage of their high school diplomas and either continued into university or started jobs in business, education, medicine, or other skilled fields. Some of them tell us their stories with tears in their eyes. Others relate their narratives stoically with calm, matter-of-fact explanations. All of them speak passionately about ambitions to change the world and have clear plans for doing so.

We also visit primary schools where Room to Read has worked on reading. Our work is immediately visible. Rich libraries serve as magnets, drawing children and teachers for weekly library periods or separate visits in free time. Classrooms are colorful with student work, and posters with alphabets, vocabulary lists, sentences, and labeled body parts dominate the walls. Teachers work through their reading activities methodically, and children raise their hands exuberantly to answer teachers' questions. There is a strong culture of reading and learning. The entire school is alive.

It is good to intersperse these visits with stops in schools where Room to Read hasn't worked. Although heartbreaking to see the differences, it is affirming to know that teachers are trying to do the right thing. Unfortunately, most haven't had proper training and simply work through the curricula they've been given—if that. Often, they simply imitate what they remember learning from their school days. They sing songs, read passages authoritatively that children repeat on cue, and ask children to copy letters and words on chalkboards—always with vibrant smiles.

Middle and high school teachers run their classrooms similarly but often with more focus on boys. This is not always to praise the boys. Often, it is to discipline boys for goofing off. Girls and boys are treated quite differently. These dynamics repeat throughout tens of thousands of schools in scores of countries, losing generations of children who would have otherwise had opportunities to change their worlds if they'd only had a bit of guidance and support.

From Room to Read's earliest days, we have focused on two issues: reading and girls' success in school. Even now, we believe these early decisions were the right ones. We say "right" because these programs target children at important points in their schooling: at the very beginning stages of their reading development, when learning to read and a love of reading can make the difference in whether children learn anything more in school; and at the point when girls transition into middle and high school, when positive experiences can determine whether they stay in school and stay excited about education. Otherwise, girls drift back into their parents' homes, are married young into their husbands' homes, or sent into factories, people's homes as servants, or other low-wage jobs. These are not the *only* educational challenges in low-income countries—not by a long shot—but they are critical ones, and ones that the international community has paid increasing attention to in recent years.

For example, reading and girls' education are prioritized in the U.S. Agency for International Development's 2011–2015 strategy,[1] the *2016 U.S. Global Strategy to Empower Adolescent Girls*,[2] and the international community's Sustainable Development Goals for 2030.[3] This is because even now, more than a decade and a half after Room to Read's founding, more than 250 million children in the world still don't have foundational skills in reading, writing, math, and problem-solving to succeed in school and in life afterward. Similarly, there are still more than 60 million girls in the world who are not completing primary or secondary school. Addressing these challenges substantially impacts people's lives. What we and other educational organizations do ripples out from helping schoolchildren to advancing their communities, their countries, and the world.

The issues of reading and girls' education are similar in many ways. At Room to Read, we talk about transformational times in children's education. Perhaps the most important one is the first few years of a child's schooling. That is when students are set up for success or failure. If children in early grades do not develop at least some interest in reading, they cannot progress in school. Everything that follows depends on a child's ability to process information through the written word. At the same time, a secondary school degree—whether through an academic high school or career training—is quickly becoming the minimum credential necessary to acquire a job that offers reasonable pay and the potential for future advancement. Keeping girls in school and providing them with the skills to persevere and succeed and then to make good decisions about the next phases of their lives are essential to improving their lives and obliterating cycles of poverty.

When we started Room to Read, no one had identified good, practical solutions to either of these two challenges. As a result, no one was willing to do anything about them. Although many local and international organizations were working in this space, we felt Room to Read could offer an innovative solution—one that would work when others failed, and one that would increase people's confidence that something could indeed be done.

In short, by selecting the issues we did, and keeping our focus clear and constant, we established a foundation for success right from the beginning.

Evolving Our Program Approach

As we discuss throughout the book, an ESE's work can be much more successful if it is rooted in a clear "theory of change"; that is, if you are very clear about your assumptions regarding how the work drives the change that you are trying to achieve. Room to Read's theory of change is illustrated in Figure 4.1 below. The logic is that by collaborating in literacy and girls' education with local communities, partner organizations, and governments,

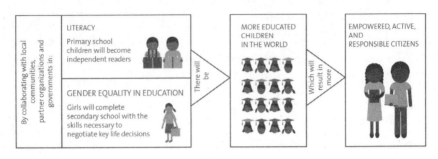

FIGURE 4.1   Room to Read's Theory of Change.

more educated children will be active in the world, which will result in more empowered and responsible citizens.

Having the right theory of change is essential to your long-term viability and the impact you can achieve. It is necessary for long-term success. Ideally, your approach should be based on previous evidence of success. Have other organizations used similar methods to achieve similar goals? Has the research literature shown that similar approaches have positive consequences? If not, at the very least, your proposed approach must pass the laugh test where your explanation is at least credible and sound enough not to garner any eye rolls or guffaws. Does it make sense to you? Does it add up to the people you're going to ask to perform the activities or fund the work? Do you have a clear sense of what you would observe if you took the actions you are considering?

Room to Read's work has always been grounded in our theory of change, even as our approach to our work has changed over time. We would even argue that being flexible enough to evolve our program activities and the ways in which we implement our programs has been one of the fundamental keys to Room to Read's success. An organization must focus on its existing approach but must also be nimble and open enough to change strategies midcourse based on new information.

For example, in 2000, Room to Read gave small scholarships for a small number of girls to stay in school and collected and donated children's books from the United States to send to a few skeletal libraries in Nepal. Many years later, we are implementing a comprehensive Girls' Education Program that emphasizes life-skills education, mentoring, and community engagement, with only a small amount of money spent on school tuition and fees. At the same time, our Literacy Program includes integrated support for school libraries, engaging storybooks in local languages, and support for teachers' reading instruction.

"New information" can be derived in a variety of ways. It may be from findings in an evaluation that shows your program results are underwhelming. It may be from a breakthrough innovation tested by local staff or something you learn from another organization. One way to think about it is that it is like how airline pilots or boat captains use "waypoints." Waypoints are the geographical markers that guide each step of a journey to help an airplane or boat to reach its destination. Similarly, organizations need to keep shorter-term goals in mind as part of their change theories as steps along the paths to longer-term social change.

Room to Read's monitoring and feedback system helps us learn about the need for course corrections. Take Hasana, for example, a girls' education associate in Bangladesh, who sees that girls in a school are dropping out of school at a higher rate than other schools. She can travel to the school and see whether there is something that Fatima, our local social mobilizer who worked with those girls, is missing. Perhaps Fatima needs to hold a meeting with school leaders and the community to solve the problem collaboratively. However, Hasana finds something completely different, and that requires a different solution. She sees a growing rate of dropouts in *all* the schools that we serve in the area; she therefore realizes that there may be some larger challenge with our programming. In fact, when we learned that many girls had failed their end-of-year exams a few years ago in Bangladesh, we changed the Girls' Education Program approach in that country to provide more intensive support for exam preparation. The result was that nearly all the girls passed their exams the following year.

It is through this kind of reflection and feedback that we regularly test whether our approach is working. When we realize that we are veering from our model, or that our model is not achieving the expected results, we update our approach.

For example, in 2014, we realized that our Girls' Education Program had become too complex for our social mobilizers to implement. We had been expanding our program activities in nine different content areas, from academic tutoring to gender-sensitivity training to large-scale community events. The women whom we had hired from local communities did not have the experience or time to manage everything that we were asking them to do. No one could have. It was just too much. This increasing realization created an opportunity for worldwide program designers in the global office to take a step back and streamline the approach. We changed the program to have fewer components and fewer activities per component.

Another way your approach might need to adapt is if you have a clear sense of the best way to implement an activity but do not yet have the funding, systems, guidance, or person power to take full advantage of that knowledge. Changes thus need to be incremental. This happened to us in 2015, as we began to think about how to make our support more consistent and of a higher quality. In all our countries, the global office trained country team members to take short videos of model teachers doing the routines that we trained them to do. ("Okay, children. We are now going to break up words into their sounds. Repeat after me: CAT. C-A-T, CAT.") Our idea was to make similar videos of all the reading activities in each country.

Unfortunately, we didn't have the extra staff time or money to complete this project right away. We had to stick with the first set of sample videos that we created until we had the funding and time to incorporate videos fully into our overall portfolio of school support resources. Implementation strategies must thus consider issues that apply for your stage of development at any given time in addition to the context in which you work.

One of Room to Read's core organizational strengths is that we have built in a healthy appetite for continuous learning and evolution into our organizational culture.

The Right Content

Promoting early-grade literacy and girls' success in school have been at the core of all Room to Read programming over the past decade and a half. Apart from a "Computer Room" program, which was also established early in our organizational history but was halted in 2009, we have focused exclusively on these two program areas. It has not been easy. There is always pressure to expand the scope of an organization's work, particularly given the vast needs exhibited by the world and the altruistic orientations of staff and supporters. But we have been clear from the beginning that we would rather be the best possible organization in a few content areas than have less impact with a broader scope of work.

We stopped the Computer Room program after analyzing our limited impact and finding our approach was not meeting its objectives. As painful as that was, our decision led to greater credibility with investors and enabled us to focus more strategically on our strengths. We have also started to deprioritize our school construction work. This has been an important strategy for creating extra library space in overcrowded schools. We still believe in the importance of this activity, but the work itself is too distant from our core expertise to remain an efficient part of our operations.

In our early days, we were lucky to receive advice from more established organizations. We begged and borrowed program content from others (but always with acknowledgment and never by stealing) that were identified as "best in class." By *program content* we mean the teaching and learning materials that we create and distribute and the related activities that we train teachers, librarians, authors, illustrators, and community members to implement. This could be a teacher manual, a student workbook, a short video clip of an ideal lesson, or a big storybook with funny pictures that a teacher can read out loud and show to children.

Over time, as we began to see gaps in the international education field, we have developed and honed our own program content. We have learned a lot about the elements of effective programming and have done our best to craft impactful, scalable, sustainable, and cost-effective programs. And at each stage of programming, we have always tried to be clear about *why* we attack the problems of reading and girls' education the way we do. It is just that the actual approach has changed over time.

Evolving Girls' Education Programming

Our Girls' Education Program,[4] for example, has gone through multiple changes in the last 18 years. The changes have not been linear. They have included various ups and downs, extensions, and, yes, contractions linked loosely to Room to Read's phases of growth. Each milestone in Figure 4.2 represents a change to our programmatic approach. The line represents the relative effort that we have put into our work with individual girls over time. This line grows substantially in earlier years and, in fact, tapers and decreases a bit as we have become more mature, more efficient in our service delivery, and more focused on system-level reform.

We've learned from many experiences over the years and have adjusted the Girls' Education Program accordingly. First, we decided to take a whole-school approach. This meant providing life-skills education and mentoring to all girls in a school and giving more targeted material and academic support to girls who had specific needs. That way we could promote a critical

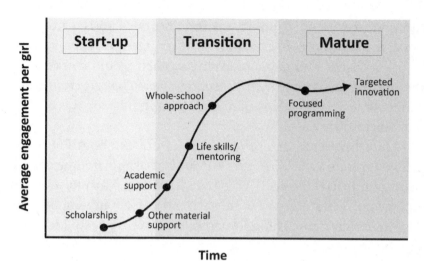

FIGURE 4.2 Evolving Program Approach to Girls' Education.

cluster of girls to work together and increase buy-in and collaboration from a larger school community. Our financial and time investments were necessarily larger, but they were also more targeted. This also meant that social mobilizers could concentrate their work on the same number of girls—the same 50 or so—but in a single school instead of multiple schools. In many cases, this meant deploying more than one social mobilizer in the same school if there was a large population of girls to support.

Second, we decided to focus on lower secondary school as the entry point for the program. This meant supporting individual girls for approximately six to seven years rather than 12 to 13 years from the beginning of primary school, as we had done previously. While this approach provides less overall support for individual girls, it targets the time in a girl's educational career when she is most vulnerable for dropping out and enables us logistically to work with an entire cohort of girls together in one school rather than primary school girls who might otherwise scatter to multiple schools when entering lower secondary school. And in identifying lower secondary schools in poor communities that had gender disparities, we had the opportunity to support entire cohorts of girls who could break through the proverbial grass, corrugated tin, or terra-cotta ceilings. These vanguards of young women would demonstrate the collective power of girls' success and change community views about the possibilities of girls completing schools and the benefits of their doing so.

The answer to the question "Why not the boys?" was that girls continue to be underserved and discriminated against in many places in the world. This is an issue that Murphy-Graham and Lloyd document well in their article about empowering adolescent girls in developing countries.[5] Girls need additional support to navigate what continues to be a biased world until such time that girls' completion of school and transition to the next phases of their lives is just as smooth as that of boys.

We also began to do a better job targeting schools and communities with clear gender disparities so that it would be obvious to all why girls deserved extra support. These responses have not allayed communities' concerns completely. In many poor places, where boys have almost as many challenges as girls, it can be difficult to provide services to some children but not others. On a personal level, it draws on one's heartstrings to see boys peeking in classroom windows to see what the girls are doing and not be able to join the activity. And in some cases, we do involve boys and men, particularly in the spirit of supporting their sisters and daughters. But we still believe that there are enough important challenges faced by half the world's population that a targeted and effective Girls' Education Program is essential for promoting an equitable world.

In our own neighborhoods as well as most of the communities in which we work around the world, we see that girls and boys still experience life in very different ways. Girls and boys arrive at school with different early childhood experiences in their homes, they have different experiences in classrooms and the larger school community, and they often need different skills when they finish school to be successful in the next phases of their lives.

This is the case irrespective of whether girls choose to attend university, join the workforce, or focus on family and public life.

By 2010, a decade after we first started the program, Room to Read had identified nine major components of an effective girls' education program: material support, academic support, life skills, mentoring, gender-responsive instruction, family and community engagement, effective partnerships with local organizations, government engagement, and monitoring and feedback. The plan was for country teams to complete content development for each program area over a four- to five-year period. Each did so with gusto. In fact, there was so much enthusiasm for ensuring that girls had all the supports necessary to be successful in school and life that the sheer amount of work that we expected became overwhelming.

Remarkably, and despite these challenges, we have experienced tremendous success in keeping girls in school and supporting their life-skills development. According to Room to Read's *2016 Global Results and Impact Report*,[6] for example, we are still seeing much lower dropout rates (6 percent) compared to the general population of girls. And among Girls' Education scholars who stay in school, 95% advance to the next grade, and 55% of Girls' Education graduates continue to tertiary education the year after they graduate even though they receive no additional support from Room to Read.

Yet by 2013 it was clear that we were asking the Girls' Education Program to do too much. We needed to streamline our program activities. Perhaps it was not urgent for teachers to become experts in the history of women's suffrage in their countries—which had become part of the program in some countries—but instead simply to recognize how classroom interactions are different for boys and girls. Perhaps it was not practical to ask that girls participate in weeklong residential life-skills camps if they only have a few weeks of vacation time per year. In attempting to streamline our programs, we did a lot of soul-searching and made uncomfortable—and unpopular—decisions about trade-offs.

The most difficult decision was about academic support. This was originally meant to help girls who were struggling to stay in school to receive targeted tutoring to pass their classes and exams. However, in many countries, it had become the most expensive program element (eating up more than a third of program costs) and was increasingly being used to provide regular tutoring for most girls in a school rather than targeting girls who had the greatest needs. This program element was attempting to compensate for the poor instruction in schools themselves. In some schools, we were hearing allegations that teachers were deliberately teaching at a low level during the regular school day so that they could then be paid to provide supplemental tutoring activities after hours (a claim that is often made against tutoring as an approach in general). To the extent this is true, this extra tutoring assistance for just a few girls was harming the broader population of students. Regardless of how pervasive this was throughout targeted schools, it would never be possible for limited Room to Read funding to counteract poor teaching.

For this reason, we made the difficult decision to limit academic support to life-skills activities that promote good study habits and peer tutoring. This decision was most difficult for social mobilizers and other staff who work closely with schools. It meant that certain girls would no longer be receiving a valuable service. However, most staff have accepted this change and have done a great job of reinvesting previous tutoring costs in more strategic and sustainable program activities, such as providing study sessions prior to big exams and helping girls organize study clubs among themselves.

The most important reason for streamlining was to make the Girls' Education Program more manageable for social mobilizers and other staff. This has meant reducing some of the other activities that may in fact have been benefiting the children whom we serve. Although home visits to talk with parents, for example, have a huge effect in shaping parents' views about school, we just do not have the person-power to visit every girl's home. We have had to limit visits to those situations in which girls are at risk of dropping out.

These close connections among content development, strategic implementation, and monitoring allow us to be more systematic when developing future programs without over-loading the system. For example, we have developed a "risk-and-response" protocol that identifies girls who are at risk of dropping out of school and uses that information to target services to them. The four risks that we monitor are (1) girls being out of school for three days or more, (2) girls missing life-skills education activities, (3) girls struggling academically, and (4) parents' or guardian's absences from parent meetings.

We prioritize these girls for one-on-one mentoring activities. For example, when Evelyne does not show up to school for a few days, her social mobilizer, Sonia, starts to talk to Evelyne's friends. If friends have not heard from Evelyne, Sonia makes a call to Evelyne's contacts, including Evelyne's parents. Sonia then stops by the parents' home to talk with them about Evelyne's whereabouts and brainstorm solutions with Evelyne and her parents about any bigger problems that jeopardize Evelyne's education.

Evolving Literacy Programming

Like the Girls' Education Program, Room to Read's Literacy Program has also undergone a substantial evolution over the last 18 years. Figure 4.3 identifies the new elements of our program-matic approach over time. The shape of the trajectory is also like that of the Girls' Education Program, as has been the progression from start-up, through transition, to more maturity.

Room to Read has added new program elements as we learned about the complexity of helping children to read. However, at a certain point, the work became so complicated and we had so many different staff members going to individual

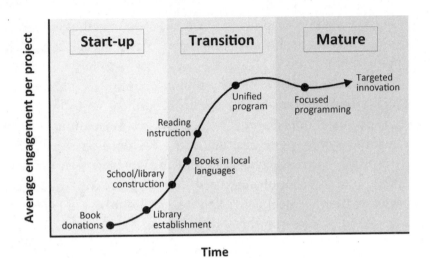

FIGURE 4.3 Evolving Programmatic Approach to Literacy.

schools that we began to stumble over one another. The schools themselves were becoming overwhelmed. We therefore needed to streamline and coordinate the work to make it easier to implement for ourselves and our partner schools.

The same open, data-driven, and reflective approach that shaped the Girls' Education Program also inspired better literacy programming over time. Room to Read's early staff recognized that school libraries were an important setting to promote reading. Libraries are places where children can see, touch, and experience the power of reading. They can go from one book on a shelf to the other and unlock powerful worlds to inspire their imaginations and understanding of the universe. We often say that Room to Read libraries are a window to the world as well as a mirror to one's own community and culture. An inviting library can be a sanctuary from the challenges of poverty. It can be a world that overwhelms children's senses in a positive way. Room to Read's first program, and perhaps the program for which it is still best known, establishes school libraries. This means converting an existing schoolroom into a library or making an existing library more enticing and accessible for children in primary schools. It also means ensuring that shelves are filled with hundreds of titles that children crave to read.

Nevertheless, even from Room to Read's earliest days, staff realized the challenges of these early aspirations. The two most urgent challenges were space and book content. Many schools in low-income countries are severely oversubscribed. They have too many children for the available teachers and schoolrooms. Although a school might allow Room to Read to use one of its existing classrooms to establish a new school library, the chances were very good that the library would be reconverted to a classroom or another function over time because space was at such a premium. Room to Read therefore began to work with communities to build additional structures. In some instances, it was a separate building that would be used for a school library. In others, it was a school block that would reduce crowding and make it more likely that the community would sustain a library in a new or existing room.

The second obvious early realization was that young children in a country such as Nepal—and many other places in the world—would have a hard time reading donated English books. While they could enjoy the illustrations, very few could read in English. Room to Read therefore decided to begin purchasing storybooks in local languages to fill libraries. The problem was that very few children's books existed in local languages, and the ones that did exist were often low in quality. This included the physical aspects of the book (for example, poor paper quality, fading inks, and weak binding) as well as content and illustrations. Many local storybooks were just not fun or enchanting enough to inspire a lifelong passion for reading. The books did not entice children into fantastical worlds that they could explore just as they were beginning to make sense of letters and sounds as Dr. Seuss and other authors did for us as children.

This lack of quality children's literature compelled us to act. Dinesh, who in 2003 was our country director in Nepal, went to all the bookshops and markets in Kathmandu looking for any title appropriate for children. He e-mailed Erin and John and told them all he could find were ten children's books, and they were not even great quality stories. Immediately, the three decided they had to find a way to help develop better books locally so they could support the nascent children's book industries in low-income countries. Since Room to Read was creating the demand for children's books by establishing school libraries, we needed to ensure capacity was built as well on the supply side of the equation by supporting the creation of the content.

For these reasons, Room to Read initiated the third component of our literacy program: to inspire and teach authors and illustrators to create storybooks for young children. We created training activities, developed competitions, and contracted with known authors and illustrators to develop new book titles, including fiction and nonfiction. We then used any books available or newly created that met minimum quality standards to fill new libraries.

Nothing is more inspiring than to work with a group of young, creative writers and illustrators; to help them apply their skills to develop a new genre of storybooks in a country; to see their photos on books that appear in schools throughout the country; and to see their careers take off in this new sector. In 2015, for example, two young Vietnamese artists, Phung Nguyen Quang and Huynh Kim Lien, who started their careers by attending one of Room to Read's writers' and illustrators' workshops three years earlier, won the Asia-wide Scholastic Picture Book Award competition. And in 2016, because of training a new group of young authors and illustrators in Indonesia, three of their resulting storybooks even won an international competition, the Samsung KidsTime Authors' Award in Singapore. The grand prize winner, *Lautkah Ini* by Yayasan Literasi Anak, translates to "Is This the Sea?" It is a beautifully illustrated book, using Indonesian batik designs, that depicts a conversation between two talking raindrops.

The Magic of Books

Almost all of us have had the experience of losing ourselves in a good book. We get sucked into the plot and cannot help but keep turning the next page to find out what happens next. Books give us the power to delve into other people's lives and unlock secret worlds. This diversion can be fun and entertaining and a nice distraction from our daily routines.

But for many children in the world, the magic of escape is even more important. It can protect from the most desperate situations. After the devastating Nepal earthquakes in 2015, the central government contacted Room to Read immediately to see how quickly we could get storybooks to children in the affected areas. Even though most schools were reduced to rubble, books were thought to be an important resource to provide some relief and happiness in children's lives. An infusion of books could also help maintain children's reading skills when it was not clear how quickly schools would open again. In a matter of weeks, we emptied our book warehouse and distributed approximately half a million books to as many communities as possible. This small gesture was widely touted by the government as a success and a small but bright light in an otherwise dark period.

We have also seen the power of books in war-affected countries such as Sri Lanka. We visited a school a few years ago that Room to Read had helped to construct in the northern part of the country that had seen the worst of the civil war. It was recently opened and primarily served families returning home after being displaced by the war. It was our job to give an award to the child in the school who had read the most books. The competition

(continued)

The Magic of Books (*Continued*)

was not even close. One boy had read all the books in the library—hundreds of them—many times over. He was a voracious reader and great student. Reading was his way of passing time in waiting for his dad to come home from the war. The school administrators had whispered to us before the ceremony that the boy had not been told that his father had been killed, but we had a sense that the boy knew anyway. In either case, books had become the boy's best friend and education his path to a better life.

Our other hope was to use supply to provoke demand. If children could borrow captivating books from school libraries and read to themselves or their families, perhaps parents would begin to appreciate children's books in a new way—tipping the scale toward promoting the culture of reading in communities that had never had books, newspapers, or street signs. Perhaps educational officials would also take notice and begin to incorporate children's books into their planning and budgeting. Perhaps, too, the authors and illustrators who created books for Room to Read could increase their visibility and be contracted by commercial publishers to write more titles, and so on.

These hopes have come to fruition in many countries in which Room to Read has worked. Several now have more robust children's book publishing industries. When Room to Read started to work in Nepal, for example, there were very few children's books available. Now, 18 years later, Nepal has a robust children's book publishing industry with hundreds of storybook titles available, some in multiple local languages. This is a fantastic example of a nonprofit organization playing a catalyzing role in creating a public or private good, and ensuring the long-term sustainability of a valuable product or service.

The next disruption in Room to Read's approach was a result of the first external evaluation of our programs (2006). We commissioned this study as an early attempt to learn about the benefits of our work and opportunities for program improvement. Paik and Walberg, the lead researchers, found that Room to Read had done a good job in constructing school blocks and separate library rooms, establishing child-friendly libraries, and filling the libraries with new children's books. However, the libraries themselves were underutilized. Children were not venturing into libraries on their own and checking out books at the rates that we had expected. The reason is that children had not developed the habit of reading or the reading skills necessary to take advantage of new library resources. One strategy was to hire a new cadre of school-level support staff to promote the habit of reading with families, school officials, and community leaders. This will be discussed shortly.

The other strategy was to launch an activity to help teachers teach children to read. This was the organization's most ambitious program decision to date. After all, teaching children to read is historically the purview of each country's ministry of education. What business did Room to Read have in delving into this work? Why did we believe that we could help improve children's reading in early grades in ways that each country's ministry had not been able to do? What expertise did we have? It turns out we were ahead of our time.

In recent years, helping teachers become better reading instructors has developed into one of the primary areas of financial investment among international development assistance agencies such as the U.S. Agency for International Development, the World Bank, the United Nations, and others for low-income countries. Hundreds of millions of dollars, euros, and pounds have gone into preservice and in-service teacher education to promote better reading instruction. However, Room to Read began to work on helping teachers teach reading more effectively long before the current influx of interest and cash.

What were we thinking? All we knew was that our other program activities would not be successful unless children in underserved communities learned to read. And if children could not learn to read, they could not become passionate, lifelong, independent readers. We therefore had to try to do something.

Fortunately, we had the benefit of outstanding staff and the goodwill of governments and communities to try some new approaches. We started in 2007 by creating "reading kits" that could be used in libraries. Later, and in line with our culture of research, monitoring, and evaluations, we conducted gap analyses of countries' early-grade reading textbooks and the support that teachers received as part of their ongoing professional development (or lack thereof) and created materials and strategies to fill the gaps. Still later, we began to develop entire early-grade reading programs that schools could use as alternatives to existing programs.

Our chief program officer at the time was an internationally renowned reading expert. We also sought extensive advice about reading instruction strategies from other experts. When we crafted our own philosophical approach to instructional support, it was rooted deeply in the scientific literature, particularly in the results of the National Reading Panel in the United States in 2000. In a nutshell, there are five major parts to children's reading: (1) the ability to understand sounds, (2) the ability to link sounds to letters and letters to words, (3) the speed and accuracy with which children can read words and string words together into sentences, (4) expanding vocabulary, and ultimately, (5) comprehension. We also add writing as an important part of children's literacy skills development. This is not just dictation, or the ability to pen letters and words, but also the ability to write ideas in complete sentences.

Determining the best way to teach children to read turns out to be an extraordinarily contentious issue, so much so that the controversies over time have been called the "reading wars." Although these debates continue to simmer around the world, Room to Read was neutral and agnostic initially but increasingly confident in our approach as we learned about the neuroscientific and linguistic underpinnings of effective instruction. With continuing focus, goodwill among partners and communities, and honest reflection and improvement, Room to Read has established one of the foremost reading skills programs in the international field.

Regular evaluation results indicate that children whose teachers participate in Room to Read professional development and coaching activities learn to read at a high level and, increasingly, on time per individual country standards. Our most recent results, from Laos, indicate that children in program schools are reading an average of 39 words per minute by the end of grade 2 compared to similar children at nonprogram schools, who are reading approximately 14 words per minute. Among Laotian children in program schools, 42% are reading at the 45 word-per-minute benchmark or higher,[7] the point at which they are reading fast enough that they can really begin to remember what they are reading and store that information for recall.

Fluent readers also enjoy reading more, in the same way we enjoy riding a bike more if we don't have to be consciously worried about balancing. In Sri Lanka, in our recent Sinhala assessment, children are reading an average of 59 words per minute, with 75% of children reading more than the minimum 45 words per minute. In Bangladesh, the average fluency rate is 52 words per minute. We are among the organizations that are "cracking the code" and starting to help large numbers of children from poor communities to develop critical foundational skills in reading.

Like our work in the Girls' Education Program, we still have a lot of work to do in literacy. We have had to streamline our content, hone what we offer, and integrate the various components of the Literacy Program to focus on the activities that have the most impact. Every day we are working to make our instructional materials easier to use and more self-guided for teachers. We are also becoming more rigorous about our coaching and support visits to schools to ensure that we are understanding how long it takes for a school to create a functional library or a teacher to become strong in reading instruction so that we can manage our staff time more efficiently. This information also becomes important to share with school systems so they have a better understanding about how to manage their own staff time when they start to take over these program activities at a provincial or national level.

Our highest priority is to have high-quality, consistent school support in our existing reading activities in classrooms and libraries before we consider reintroducing some of the other literacy activities that countries have tried implementing in the past.

The Right Approach at the Right Time

While Room to Read has maintained a consistent theory of change for reading and girls' education, our more detailed program design has evolved extensively over the past 18 years. The evolutionary process was not necessarily intentional or meant to be systematic. It resulted from our ongoing quest for the best results for the money we had available to invest. We characterize five main changes in Room to Read's program design over time (see Figure 4.4): (1) input, (2) output, (3) training and monitoring, (4) coaching and support, and (5) system-level change. Exact starting and ending dates for each stage are not precise, and there has been some overlap among the various focus areas. In addition, each focus builds on the last one. Room to Read has tried to incorporate the lessons learned and successes from each previous work effort into its next focus,

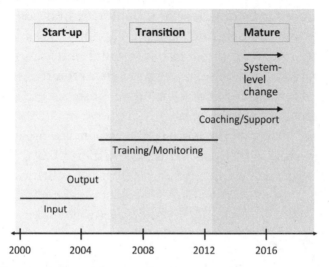

FIGURE 4.4 Stages of Room to Read Programming.

all the while trying to increase the impact more effectively, efficiently, and strategically.

Input Stage

Room to Read's focus in our early years was to ensure that communities had the financial and material resources to further its objectives for what we now call the Girls' Education Program. More complicated were the earliest Literacy Program activities. Between 2000 and 2003, Room to Read launched four separate programs to promote children's reading in schools: (1) Reading Room (Libraries) Program (2000), (2) School Room (Construction) Program (2000), (3) Computer Room Program (2001), and (4) Local Language Publishing Program (2003).

These programs required substantial oversight. They largely focused on distributing materials to schools. The Reading Room Program, for example, required shelving, flooring, and modest furniture in addition to the books themselves. The School Room Program required an initial commitment from communities for land on which to build new libraries or school blocks as well as tools and building supplies. Local Language Publishing required the logistics around international book donations and local procurement. It also required substantial work in book distribution, including customs clearance for international book donations.

Harmonizing all these processes was a major organizational focus and success in Room to Read's first few years. It was an essential first step before anything else was possible.

Output Stage

Room to Read entered a period of rapid growth. From an initial focus on Nepal in 2000, Room to Read expanded into Vietnam in 2001, Cambodia in 2002, India in 2003, and both Laos and Sri Lanka in 2005—still in the start-up phase of program work in which we emphasized program inputs. The reason for selecting each new country varied.

The first expansion, into Vietnam, for example, was because Erin had been working there for Unilever. Cambodia was a country of great need and came as an extension of our work in Vietnam. A key new investor who was passionate about India funded our early expansion there. We then conducted a more formal expansion study and identified Laos and Sri Lanka as key targets for future expansion to build out hubs in both Southeast and South Asia. We started working on an expansion into Laos next. The 2004 tsunami in Asia created a great need in Sri Lanka, and we expanded to the country in response faster than expected, ultimately launching into both Laos and Sri Lanka in 2005.

This is the time that we started to enter the transitional phase of Room to Read's programmatic work, the point at which we began to shift our focus from inputs to outputs. We measured success in several ways: the number of new girls served, the libraries and school blocks built, the books published, and the computer rooms established. As promised to our investors, every day we strove to support more children in more locations.

It was during this period that we began to monitor our work in earnest. Our staff began to chart the number of projects completed year on year as we advanced toward our goal of serving 10 million children. From 2000 to 2005, for example, Room to Read helped 1,700 girls stay in school. This grew from 10 girls in Nepal in the year 2000 to 1,757 girls in Nepal, Vietnam, Cambodia, India, Laos, and Sri Lanka by 2005. We also established 2,590 school libraries in the same period.

Training and Monitoring Stage

By 2005, with thousands of projects up and running relatively smoothly, our leadership had some breathing room to reflect on our first five years and what was to come next. Encouraged by the board of directors and others, we launched our first cross-national evaluation. Our question was, "How are we doing, and what more do we need to do to be even more successful?" The feedback we received from surveys and discussions with our country directors and field staff was that projects were already successful in many ways. We had built numerous school blocks and libraries, filled them with beautiful books, and granted thousands of scholarships and organized activities for local girls.

What was still not clear was the *quality* of what we were doing. We had ample evidence that planned projects were being completed in targeted villages and rural areas. But we also had some anecdotal evidence that our people on the ground were moving onto the next project without necessarily ensuring that the infrastructure they'd put into place was sufficient to achieve our ultimate organizational goals. In fact, reports from different countries indicated that the libraries we'd built were being underutilized and that poor girls were still struggling in school despite being given scholarships. That's when we realized that projects need more than bricks, mortar, and material support to be successful. We had to somehow get communities and school staff to understand and get behind the purpose of all the infrastructure and programs we had put in place.

Our programmatic focus—as well as our strategic approach—therefore changed accordingly. We needed to develop new programs and necessary training for activities such as how to most effectively use and manage the libraries, how best to teach reading to students, how to coach life-skills education, and how to mentor girls through tough challenges.

On the monitoring side, we realized we needed to visit the school more frequently and change the focus of the visits. Previously, school visits had focused on the development of the physical infrastructure. Were new library buildings or school blocks completed? Did libraries have the necessary furniture and books? Now, we had to track the extent to which new program activities were being implemented and sustained over time.

During the period between 2006 and 2012, we realized we needed to standardize best practices and other "nonnegotiable" aspects of our programs that everyone around the globe needed to adhere to and communicate those effectively throughout our entire organization.

Coaching and Support Stage

Changes in staffing and programming required a whole new way of working. By deepening Room to Read's program content and training local school staff and community members, we were spending a lot more money. Establishing long-term relations with staff in thousands of schools is very different from simply building schools and furnishing libraries.

As we hired more staff, our per-project costs continued to rise. Yet the actual returns on our investments were not clear. On the one hand, anyone who visited schools over the years could see program quality improving. On the other hand, these advances in quality were not consistent across countries—or even within villages and rural areas within countries. We saw large gaps between the strongest and weakest projects, and we did not have much insight into the reasons for those gaps.

Why were there so many disparities in project outcomes? We observed in school visits and in discussions with country leaders that the diversity in staff skills was the culprit. Some staff members were phenomenal. They were excellent trainers and knew their communities well. However, the skills our local staff members possessed seemed to be largely related to their previous experience—not to the training we were providing. We were somehow failing in our training to bring staff skills up to a consistently high level. Diversity also made our overall success rates difficult to monitor and evaluate. Although Room to Read had as strong a monitoring and evaluation system as any nonprofit organization that we knew, it was becoming difficult to monitor and evaluate multiple variations in the same core program activities.

As any good evaluator knows, the best way to evaluate an intervention is to hold everything constant in two situations except for a single variable. However, this kind of research was simply not possible for Room to Read in 2012. Although we had developed central organizational guidelines for each program, there were too many differences in actual implementation to know what truly constituted the "core" program approach. This diversity also made it difficult to hire and orient new staff. Each new hire had to understand the program variations for their geographical areas or country. In some places, new hires were fortunate to receive orientation materials developed by field-based or country office staff. Unfortunately, this was usually not the case. With such a wide diversity in program activities, it was impossible to develop a structured, high-quality process to consistently train new coaches, facilitators, and mobilizers in their jobs. Even more importantly, the rising staffing costs would price Room to Read out of the market as an efficient implementer of effective educational programming. Something needed to change.

We made a difficult decision in 2012 and 2013 to swing the pendulum away from local diversity and focus on creating innovative programs we could use across all countries. With core, worldwide program resources in hand, both the global and country offices could recontextualize the materials we created to be appropriate for each country's needs. The expectation was for teams to work together to translate new worldwide materials into local languages and modify materials as necessary to be culturally appropriate and administratively acceptable. The hope was that core materials would change as little as possible so that Room to Read could take advantage of the consistency for hiring and training new staff as well as monitoring program implementation.

The swing of the pendulum away from localized programming toward more centrally organized, consistent programming was also a big cultural shift for Room to Read. While most staff understood the logic of the change, it has not been easy for everyone to accept. Change is not easy, and people are often quite reluctant to move away from what they have done in the past—particularly if they were the ones who developed the original program activities for their communities or country.

The good news is that this transition in Room to Read's program approach has been a success. More than four years after starting the global content development, we have completed the core worldwide materials. Most of the content has been contextualized and is now being used in countries. Country staff have been trained in the use of the materials and are in turn helping school-level support staff in their roles as coaches. Staff in all parts of the organization have more clarity about the ultimate goals of our programming, the process for helping each community achieve its goals, and the steps along the way. Organizational materials have become much easier to use, and we have developed more meaningful research and evaluation activities.

Early evaluation results of schools that have used the contextualized worldwide materials are promising. There is still work to be done to ensure that all school-level support staff have the content, training, and skills that they need to provide consistent, high-quality services, but we are much farther down this road than at any other time in Room to Read's history.

In hindsight, we talk about this consolidation at Room to Read now as though it was inevitable. We forget that it was a difficult decision and not easy to execute.

System-Level Change Stage

Even as we continue to work on our standardized worldwide programs, we have entered a new stage of work: support for system-level change. This means work for change in laws, policies, and practices that apply to all schools in a provincial, state, or national school system. We have been flirting with this idea for more than 10 years but only now have the resources and experience to try it out.

Some organizations attempt to collaborate with authorities to create system-level changes early in their evolution, but we have been conservative, not wanting to get into it until we were ready. Moreover, system-level change requires another psychological shift, and we needed time to incorporate this new mindset into our organizational mindset and culture.

Historically, our staff has been driven—you could even say obsessed—by the goal of serving individual children. But incorporating a system-level approach shifts at least some of our focus away from individual children. Although we are still fully committed to every child and every family that we serve, some of our attention has now shifted to government engagement and, just as importantly, how we can organize program activities that can be sustained by the government system and other organizations.

This new emphasis means that we must make new choices. It could mean that we no longer have the same staffing resources to visit an adolescent girl's family multiple times if she is at risk for dropping out of school. Instead, we may instead share our "risk-and-response" tool in a more structured way with schools so that teachers and school administrators can be more aware of girls who are on the verge of dropping out. It is no surprise that this kind of a shift is uncomfortable. It is particularly so for Room to Read's school support staff in local communities. What is the right answer when deciding between supporting 100 children at 100% effort versus supporting 500 children at 75% effort? The trick is to figure out how much of our base programming is necessary to achieve our overarching program goals. What is that minimum threshold of success?

The honest answer, though, is that we do not yet know. Like everything else we do at Room to Read, answering this question requires hard work, good monitoring, honest reflection, and responsive program adaption along the way. Again, having the goodwill and trust of the communities in which we work helps tremendously. They know that we are acting in good faith and have been willing partners as we continue to evolve our programmatic approach.

Key Takeaways

In designing a compelling and impactful approach to developing programs, entrepreneurial social enterprises should consider the following:

- **Start with a clear approach linked to the overall theory of change that can be tested and validated over time.** This clarity is essential for your organization's success because it is the foundation that motivates staff and external stakeholders. The approach, however, does not have to remain static. There are great opportunities to test innovation over time if it does not overwhelm the core work.

- **Focus on a small number of programmatic goals**. Succumbing to scope creep can make work confusing and difficult to succeed, thereby devastating morale and work effort even among the most fervent staff members.
- **Recognize that it might be necessary to focus on different measures of success over time**. We do not regret our evolution from inputs to outputs to outcomes and system-level change. It was necessary for us to work through each of these emphases to grow the organization, its reputation, and its capability to achieve greater change each year.
- **Scale does matter**. An organization's program portfolio needs to be large enough and implemented in enough diverse contexts to be able to test the underlying program concept and prove that the model works.
- **A program can only be successful if it is grounded in the local reality**. It is therefore imperative that program designers listen to its local leadership and field implementers. They are the people who know best what is possible to implement and how participating communities will react. The best conceptual approach will fail miserably if it is not practical or responsive to local needs.
- **Over time, expect that the pendulum will swing back and forth between local and central approaches**. Local leadership is essential for program innovation and determining local needs. However, this must always be balanced by the organization's ability to implement efficiently, learn from its constituent experiences, and determine what parts of its programming are truly local versus more universal in achieving success.
- **Recognize that changes in program emphases require clear internal communications**. These changes have implications for how people do their work. Employees must be aware of the changes and the reasons for the changes to be able to be successful in their jobs.

NOTES

1. United States Agency for International Development, *USAID Strategy 2011–2015* (Washington, DC: United States Agency for International Development, February 2011).

2. United States Government, *United States Global Strategy to Empower Adolescent Girls* (Washington, DC: United States Government, 2016).

3. United Nations, "Goal 4: Ensure Inclusive and Quality Education for All and Promote Lifelong Learning," Sustainable Development Goals, August 2015. http://www.un.org/sustainabledevelopment/education/ (accessed January 2017).

4. Like our program content, program names have changed over time. So as not to confuse readers, we will be using the current program names to identify historical programs as well.

5. Erin Murphy-Graham and Cynthia Lloyd, "Empowering Adolescent Girls in Developing Countries: The Potential Role of Education," *Policy Futures in Education* 14, no. 5 (2015): 556–577.

6. Room to Read, *Global Monitoring Report 2015* (San Francisco: Room to Read, 2016).

7. The minimum 45-word-per-minute benchmark is based on research of English speakers reading in English. Room to Read is also conducting research to determine the appropriate minimum fluency in other languages for children to remember and recall what they have read.

5

Research, Monitoring, and Evaluation: What Gets Measured, Gets Done

Creating a Culture of Data Collection and Use

This was the day that we knew we had turned the corner. It was not different from many other days of site visits: the long car ride; the courtesy visit with the head teacher; observations in the grade 1 and 2 classrooms and school library; discussions with teachers, parents, and students about working with Room to Read. But there was also something special about the day. The schools we visited near Ajmer, Rajasthan, in rural India had a different feel about them.

On arrival in each school, Room to Read's local team rattled off very specific statistics about the schools that we would be observing. Discussions with school staff were more focused than usual. The head teachers had a sharp grasp of daily attendance and the progress in the children's reading. On the walls, interspersed with children's artwork and the colorful posters that you often see in classrooms were big sheets of paper that tracked the reading curriculum and children's reading scores. Writing and words were everywhere, and storybooks strewn around classrooms indicated that they were well used and that a culture of reading was well established.

Teachers had hand selected a girl and boy from each class to serve as library captains. These children were responsible for helping other children check out books and return them to the library on time. Book checkout registries in school libraries were detailed, well organized, and complete. Librarians had diligently recorded the large number of books that had been checked out and returned every day. Parent committees wanted to talk about reading outcomes, what they had seen since Room to Read had started working in their schools, and their expectations for their children's educational success. Throughout the school visit there was a high sense of productivity and accountability.

At one school, our visit overlapped with a group of Room to Read "enumerators." These are professionals whom Room to Read hires on a contract basis to collect our monitoring and evaluation data. On this day, the enumerators were collecting information about children's reading skills in grades 1 and 2. These are data that we collect on a periodic basis to chart children's progress. We collect information about children's ability to identify letters in their alphabets, read real words, read nonwords (to see if children can decode letters joined together instead of simply memorizing words), combine words into sentences, and understand what they are reading. We then compare the reading scores of children whose teachers participate in Room to Read instructional activities with children whose teachers do not.

We spent a lot of time with the enumerators that day, as there had been concerns in the past about potential bias in the data collection. There was suspicion internally that past scores were overly positive. Were enumerators conducting the assessment activities in a consistent, fair way? Were all children in grades 1 and 2 equally likely to be selected for the study, or were language-minority students and children with disabilities being excluded? Had schools instructed some children to stay home the day of data collection because they knew they would be less successful?

It was inspiring to see how rigorously the Room to Read staff had designed the study procedures. They had written very specific rules for every step in the process. For example, there were procedures to ensure that all children in grades 1 and 2 had an equal chance of being selected for the assessment. And if a selected child was absent that day, the enumerators would return to the school to conduct the assessment when the child was available. In addition, the assessment conditions were designed to give all children the best chances for success. The space for conducting the assessment was empty and as quiet as the external circumstances would allow.

Enumerators were trained to make the children as comfortable as possible—reminding them that the assessment would be kept confidential and have no effect on their grades at school—and the enumerators implemented the assessment procedures in the same way each time. The process also included both timed and untimed reading assessments. This was to ensure that we had a good measure of reading fluency but also maximized children's opportunities to comprehend the reading passages without the pressure of being timed. It was clear by the time we had completed school visits that day that our staff and school partners were truly using data to improve teaching practices and children's reading success.

That the Room to Read country office, school staff, and parents had begun to collect, track, and communicate about data as a normal course of the work was a big deal. It was evidence of a deep "culture of data collection" that we had been trying to achieve for years. In this ideal world, data collection is not seen as an afterthought or a way to police our school-based teams. Whether the results are positive or negative, there is always much to learn from it to improve programs and their replication.

Evidence is not something to hide but to shout from the rooftops and share broadly with internal and external stakeholders.

The India country team had been laying the groundwork for one of the key tenets of Room to Read's success: Investors tend to be more trusting in an organization if the organization is transparent about what is working and not working, especially if investors perceive that the organization learns from its failures as well as its successes. Too many organizations neglect project monitoring or seek to sweep bad results under the rug. This is not only dishonest but also creates superficial communications with stakeholders that can make even the most ardent supporters cynical. We have tried at Room to Read instead to engage investors transparently about ongoing challenges, explaining that if problems such as quality education in low-income countries were easy to solve, they would have been solved by now.

The attitude in the schools was a big turnaround from previous years. In the past, the country office was more reticent about collecting and sharing its monitoring data. In the Room to Read family of countries, India had always struggled to achieve expected project outcomes—and with good reason. As the second most populous country in the world, India has tremendous challenges in poverty and poverty alleviation. Any problem can be an order of magnitude more difficult in India than anywhere else on the planet. In many rural communities, children's schooling is often a lower priority than other basic needs, and trust in government schools is low. Independent reading is often not even taught in grades 1 and 2, when children are thought to be too young. Under these circumstances, it is also difficult to hire school-level staff members who have the skills to implement effective reading programs.

These are some of the reasons that the India team patiently explained each year why it was not achieving expected program goals. The country team asked the global office to consider lower expectations for our work there. However, we believed that all children deserve the highest-quality support and that expectations should not be set lower just because of contextual challenges. To the country team's frustration, planning discussions each year started with the question of how to improve the persistently low outcomes.

The statistical tables, which compared the India results to itself over time as well as to the results of other Room to Read countries, challenged everyone to think about ways to make our work more impactful. Perhaps we could reduce our geographical footprint and focus our work in a smaller number of states (which we did!). Perhaps we needed to think about different professional profiles for the school-level staff whom we were recruiting (which we did!). Perhaps we needed to think about aligning our program approach in India more closely to the worldwide approach, which was starting to show some very promising results (check!). Perhaps, too, we needed to rethink our approach to project monitoring so that it became a tool for learning and improvement instead of a way to call out bad performers (oh yeah!).

We used data as the fulcrum for communication, reflection, and change that allowed us to have frank discussions, transform a somewhat vicious cycle of negativity to a virtuous cycle, and help the talented India country office become one of the highest-performing countries in the Room to Read portfolio. In 2015, for example, grade 2 students in India's project schools were reading an average of 52 words per minute compared to 18 words per minute in comparison schools that did not have the Room to Read program. Knowing from the scientific literature and our own research that children need to be reading at least 40–60 words per minute to achieve modest comprehension, this is a hopeful result to achieve in just a few years at this scale of work. It was the highest average reading fluency score among Room to Read countries at the time as well as the largest difference between intervention and control schools. Again, a strong data system and commitment to transparency gave us the opportunity to promote success and a positive culture of data collection and use at the very end of what we describe in the next chapter as the "implementation chain."

Incentives and Disincentives for Creating a Culture of Data Collection and Learning

Although data transparency seems obvious—even when results are less than ideal—our long-standing experience is that it is not the norm in the nonprofit sector. Nonprofits do not have the same bottom line of profit as is the case in the private sector, so nonprofit organizations have a lot more discretion to determine and track their own metrics of success. Given competition among organizations for limited financial resources, the desire to put an organization's best foot forward by emphasizing positive results can be quite appealing.

Our long-standing experience is that the impetus to highlight positive results and downplay "bad" results is particularly strong in the government contracting sector. Large-scale projects funded by bilateral or multilateral organizations such as the U.S. Agency for International Development (USAID), the British Department for International Development (DfID), or United Nations agencies that are usually three to five years in duration are just too short to achieve the transformational goals that they seek to accomplish. Therefore, historically, the bilateral agency overseeing the project sets a relatively low bar for achieving results so that the project can be deemed successful, thereby justifying future requests from its own government funding source. This is perhaps an oversimplified view of the world, but we would argue that the incentives for robust project monitoring in bilaterally funded projects are not always strong. Financial costs are high, the challenges of collecting data in difficult country contexts are great, and the risks of failing to achieve project goals can be substantial for bilateral funders, host-country governments, and implementing partners.

More recently, though, we have seen the reverse situation. Substantial pressure has grown in the international education community, including the U.S. government, to help 100 million young children to become independent readers. This is a goal that USAID included in its 2011–2015 education strategy and one that other bilateral and multilateral organizations have taken on in recent years as their big challenge in international education. In setting this larger sector goal, we have begun to see huge expectations for children's achievement in recent USAID requests for proposals.

In a large-scale USAID reading project that we are helping to implement right now in Rwanda, for example, the expectation is that 65% of the more than one million children in grades 1–3 in the country will be reading fluently and with comprehension by the end of the five-year project period. Children must achieve a minimum of an 80% score on reading comprehension questions. This level of comprehension is a goal that no reading project has achieved at such a scale. Particularly daunting is the fact that a 2014 reading study in Rwanda found that 60% of grade 1 students, 33% of grade 2 students, and 21% of grade 3 students could not read even one word of grade-level reading passages.[1]

As the project partner responsible for ensuring children's reading success, Room to Read has a monumental challenge to help increase children's reading success across the country. We have never achieved such a goal but are working hard to rise to the challenge. This will be a true test of whether we can support children's reading development at such a large scale.

However, it is yet to be seen whether the value of learning and being open about problems will trump the need to show results. Funding agencies and their governments' budget appropriations bodies must set the tone.

Research, Monitoring, and Evaluation at Room to Read

We organize our work at Room to Read such that research, monitoring, and evaluation (RM&E) is integrated into everything that we do. This starts with a global RM&E team that is dispersed around the world: in the United States, Southeast Asia, South Asia, and sub-Saharan Africa. These people are responsible for setting the overall agenda for the organization as well as supporting country teams in their RM&E activities. Most country offices then have at least two related staff. These staff members are responsible for implementing annual worldwide monitoring activities, cross-national evaluations, and country-specific research. We conduct separate research, monitoring, and evaluation activities that feed into reflective discussions about program improvement and implementation effectiveness as well as much of our internal and external communications.

We built this full RM&E global structure eight years into the organization's history. This staffing represents a major investment of organizational time and resources, but it is one that we think is essential for the long-term success of the quality of our programs.

Monitoring

The worldwide monitoring process is a cross-nationally consistent approach to collecting similar data in every program country and charting progress over time. It helps us to track the extent to which we are implementing the number of projects that we have planned as well as the extent to which those projects are achieving their expected goals.

This means not only following the number of girls who are participating in our Girls' Education Program but also whether those girls are staying in school and participating in life-skills activities. It means we monitor not only the number of libraries that we have established but also how many books children are checking out from libraries. And we don't just count the number of teachers we've trained but also whether their children are becoming effective, independent readers.

Every year, we review the worldwide indicators, modify the forms and guidance, and monitor more than 4,000 project sites. We then input the information into an enterprise database management system that we customized off the Salesforce.org platform, and produce internal and external reports. The external report, which summarizes trend information, is published on Room to Read's website, while the internal report details country-specific information and cross-country comparisons. This information is used to identify successes and challenges, promote discussions within country teams as well as between country teams and the global office, and feed into annual country reviews and planning.

We have also started to collect what we call "program implementation monitoring" (PIM) data on a consistent basis. This allows us to determine whether schools are implementing projects as intended. PIM is early in implementation but is designed to answer key questions such as how long it takes for a school library to be set up and become fully functional, and how long it takes for a teacher to become proficient in reading instruction. With clear expectations for what we are trying to accomplish for each of our program areas, program implementation data also help us to determine which projects need additional help and which are doing fine without regular monitoring and coaching visits.

These data also help us to understand when we are implementing activities as intended but still not achieving our expected results. So, this information provides vital signals about when we need to review our overall program designs.

One of the biggest challenges in program monitoring is establishing appropriately collaborative relationships among program, implementation, and monitoring staff. Inevitably, staff members who are responsible for program design and implementation have some discomfort with project monitoring. After all, monitoring is a review of their work. It does not matter how often we talk about ourselves as a learning organization, or how much we say that we value transparent and open reflection— monitoring is equated with judgment, and judgment produces anxiety. Anxiety is then magnified if monitoring activities begin to feel like policing, and results of monitoring activities have consequences for people's job status, career progression, and compensation. We have experienced high tensions in some countries historically related to monitoring—particularly when program and implementation staff don't believe that the monitoring staff understand what they do or monitor their programs effectively.

For these reasons, establishing positive working relationships early in the process of designing program and monitoring activities is critical. Research, monitoring, and evaluation staff need to be full partners in program design to ensure that monitoring systems align with programs. If they do not align or are thought not to align, including a clear understanding of how results will be used to improve work and help children, monitoring efforts are doomed to fail. Efforts lose credibility and are not taken seriously when results are published.

It is also important that there be clear rules for engagement when implementation and monitoring staff are working in schools at the same time. Monitoring staff should not be intrusive and overbearing when they are in schools. They should not be perceived as controlling or patrolling the work of project implementers or school staff. The more unobtrusive they can be to blend quietly into the back of classes or conduct their assessment activities in a separate space, the better.

At the same time, it is equally important that there be at least some separation between implementation and monitoring activities. At Room to Read, school-level staff are often responsible for collecting some monitoring data. In fact, we have developed rubrics of data collection that implementers are supposed to use during each school visit. Some of this information just feeds back to their supervisors for immediate action, as necessary, while other information feeds into worldwide program monitoring systems.

However, there are times when we collect student assessment data in which we need to make sure that the people who are responsible for implementing activities are different from the people who are collecting the assessment data. Sometimes, the outcome we are monitoring even requires that we hire external data collectors to maintain real or perceived integrity in the process. Otherwise, there can be a concern about bias or conflict of interest.

The separation between monitoring and implementation also extends to reporting. Report writers need to maintain a clear distinction between analysis and advocacy. Analytical writing requires more of a neutral and fact-based approach ("Just the facts, ma'am"), whereas persuasive writing champions the results ("Our work is the best thing since sliced bread"). Both kinds of writing are important for an organization such as Room to Read.

One just needs to be clear, though, who is writing the reports and for what kind of a purpose. Regular monitoring reports should skew heavily on the side of analytical writing. Room to Read's annual internal *Global Results and Impact Report*, for example, focuses exclusively on results and country office reflections on the reasons their results in any year are relatively strong or weak, as in: "Country X exceeded its past success by 0.3 standard deviations this year. It tightened its monitoring visits and focused much more on helping teachers with instructional routines than it had done previously." This is substantially different from a blog that we might post with the headline, "Room to Read programming in Country X beat its previous outcomes for the third year in a row."

Evaluation

Evaluations are structured research activities that examine the extent to which program activities lead to expected outcomes. We try to understand why what we do makes a difference, and what we might think about doing differently to achieve better results. Unlike monitoring activities, which we consider integral to our regular project implementation, evaluations are special activities that are funded separately from our ongoing program implementation expenditures. A simple analogy to explain the difference between monitoring and evaluating activities is to compare cooking soup with eating it. Monitoring is like the chef tasting the soup along the way to adjust ingredients for best results. Evaluations are like presenting the soup to the diner and asking for feedback on the finished product.

We conduct some evaluations ourselves while we contract others externally. Evaluations usually require detailed planning, the hiring of temporary data collectors ("enumerators"), and consideration of comparisons. In some instances, we compare results in the same schools over time. In other cases, we compare results to control schools that are like the schools in which we are working but have not received Room to Read support. In all instances, we do our best to maintain the highest level of rigor in evaluation procedures while recognizing the challenges of working in difficult country contexts where schools can be shut down because of heavy rains or political instability, or where government permissions can be rescinded just before data collection takes place.

Room to Read also follows high ethical standards in the protection of personal data. We use international standards to make sure that we have people's permission to participate in research and evaluation, are clear with participants about the purpose of the study, and keep information about program participants confidential. Although educational research in general does not carry the same potential risks as drug-intervention studies, or studies about voting behavior in politically repressive countries, results can have implications for people's jobs or well-being. We are even more careful in research and evaluation involving our Girls' Education Program, in which our life-skills education and mentoring activities often do push the boundaries of cultural norms and can have implications for girls' standing with their communities.

Research

Research is the last component of Room to Read's "Research, Monitoring, and Evaluation" system. It includes the studies that are meant to inform our programming other than direct evaluation of our program models or implementation. Studies can be simple and short in duration or complex and extend one or more years. They can be initiated through the global office or any country office. In addition to larger research projects, one of the most exciting parts of our research program is country-initiated research. These are research questions that countries identify as important for their program improvement.

For example, why are dropout rates among girls higher in one country than in other countries? How does the creation of classroom libraries change implementation as compared to separate libraries? What is the relative value of hiring local organizations to serve as school-level support staff instead of hiring social mobilizers, library management facilitators, or literacy coaches directly?

Country and global office team members then work closely with each other to develop the research methods to answer the question, the research project is reviewed by the global RM&E director, and the project is launched collaboratively between the country and global office. Data are analyzed, results are written up, and reports are shared among all countries offices and the global office so that we can learn from countries' experiences.

Room to Read has been working on building the capacity of country offices to perform effective local research for many years. We tend to hire outstanding local research officers with strong academic credentials, but it is often difficult to translate academic experience into equally strong study designs and implementation capabilities. Some of the biggest challenges are in crafting focused research questions, linking research questions to appropriate study methods, summarizing study results, and facilitating discussions about how to use evaluations and research results to improve programs.

Every year, when the global office solicits research ideas from country offices, we receive long, enthusiastic lists of ideas. In almost every instance, topics are interesting and merit research. Questions such as "What are the major causes of poverty in a particular geographic area?" can be an important starting point for many new public and private initiatives.

However, the real question that we have to ask ourselves is "Assuming we find something interesting in research results, can Room to Read do something meaningful with the information?" This is the "So, what?" question. In the case of the "What causes poverty?" question, Room to Read has made the conscious decision not to pursue this kind of research. Instead, we maintain focus on our programming and do not try to tackle other important problems such as the broader reasons for poverty that communities might face. Of course, one can always learn *something* from high-level research questions that can improve program activities. The issue is whether we can learn something important enough to be worth the investment for us. Studies take time, money, and effort, and we need to be as strategic as possible in the use of these resources.

A second common problem with country-initiated research topics is that they are often redundant, covering questions that have already been answered elsewhere. Take, for example, the issue of girls' dropout rates from school. In most countries in which Room to Read works, extensive research on girls' dropout rates has been done. Do we then have good reason to believe that the causes of dropout in a region are so different from other parts of the country that they warrant special study? Perhaps. In Nepal, for example, the Kamlari system of indentured servitude in the low-lying regions is a unique historical phenomenon that is relatively limited to that part of the country. In most instances, though, differences across a country may not be as extreme, and new research might therefore not be warranted.

Before launching a new research study, we ask ourselves questions such as "Have we done a literature review to see whether a study has even been done on the area itself? Has Room to Read already conducted a similar study in a country nearby that could help us understand the issue in the first country well enough?" It is surprising how often we forget to examine whether a research question has already been answered well enough elsewhere.

Third, even after we have identified a meaningful research question, the proposed research methods must be effective and efficient. Take again the question of why girls drop out of schools. This really was a key research question in one country in which Room to Read was working. We did not feel as though we had enough information to understand unusually high dropout rates. However, the country team proposed a 20-page survey that was supposed to be used with scores of intervention and control schools. This design was completely out of scope with the basic question we were asking. Instead, what we really needed to do was interview a sample of girls who had left school early to find out about their experiences. These conversations would have given us much more information than an expensive, complicated survey design.

Finally, when conducting research or evaluation activities in complicated situations, it is important to anticipate and preempt problems with data collection to the extent possible. We have implemented some studies over time, for example, in which schools initially selected as "controls" later started to receive program support without the knowledge of the researchers. This was a big disconnect. The programs team was not in close enough conversation with the research team, and this simple act devastated our ability to study the benefits of our program over time.

For all these reasons, research and evaluation designs should be developed carefully, in consultation with program design and implementation staff, and checklists of problems to be avoided should be considered with any new study opportunity.

RM&E at Different Phases of Organizational Development

Although monitoring, feedback, and transparent reporting has been a fundamental part of Room to Read's culture from its inception, the way in which we approach this part of our work has changed markedly over time. Like many young organizations, it was important to us even in our very early days to document the number of books that we distributed, libraries that we established, and girls whom we supported with tuition scholarships. Now, 18 years later, we can still go back to those initial data and chart the number of projects that we have implemented since inception. We also know among those first scholarship recipients how many of those girls completed high school. However, it is also the case that in those early days we did not have many staff members, nor did we have a deep program outcome focus. Although we cared about quality programming, the immediate concern was in getting projects in place so that we could serve as many communities as possible, not launching a comprehensive monitoring system.

Perhaps the first major organizational shift in RM&E, from start-up to transition, came in 2004, when board members and management began to think about monitoring and evaluating the literacy and girls' education programs more formally. With a few years of implementation under our belts, and some momentum building from a growing investor and country base, it was time to think about what was going well and how to improve our work. It was at that time Erin reached out to Cory and Room to Read began to think about its first external evaluation.

Although it might seem like a small issue, the decision to invest in an external evaluation was a big deal. First, it meant diverting hard-earned funds away from direct program implementation and into evaluation work. This is not easy to do when you believe that all children around the world need urgent help and that every day and dollar matters. Second, it was risky to open ourselves up to external scrutiny. What if the evaluation identified major problems? Not only would this be a blow to our organizational morale, but it might also scare investors away.

Nevertheless, we took the plunge and hired our first external evaluators. This turned out to be a great experience. The evaluators were helpful in coaching us through the evaluation process and helped us think about longer-term systems for tracking our results. In addition, we were pleasantly surprised (and relieved) that the overall results were quite positive. Interviews with partners across countries and program areas indicated very strong appreciation for our work. The experience left us much more confident and bullish on M&E. It also left us craving more information. The 2006 evaluation largely focused on people's views about Room to Read programming. In retrospect, it is not surprising that partners and communities liked our work and believed it was making a difference. After all, who would not like new school libraries, books, or girls' scholarships?

Nevertheless, some of the feedback in the evaluation and from country teams, as we explained in Chapter 4, indicated that we needed to do a lot more work to ensure that our libraries were being used fully and integrated with school activities. This was the point at which we began to hire school-based field staff and develop more meaningful metrics for monitoring program quality.

The years from 2004 to 2009 were a vibrant transition time for RM&E at Room to Read. We hired a global director and country-based staff to oversee our monitoring and evaluation work in countries. We started to develop a comprehensive, worldwide set of indicators to measure program quality and outputs as well as country-specific indicators of program development and implementation. We completed our first external program evaluation, and we began to develop internal systems for incorporating lessons from the monitoring results into our annual planning.

Cory was not yet a Room to Read staff member at the time but was already a close advisor to the organization. It was Erin's straightforwardness and passion for transparent, data-anchored decision making that piqued his interest in Room to Read in the first place. He remembers being extremely impressed with the seriousness and thoughtfulness by which Room to Read began to grow its monitoring and evaluation function. The organization was fearless in its early efforts to try new approaches, and to be very up front about what was working and not working. Cory encouraged Room to Read even during this time to share its experiences with monitoring and evaluation as part of a larger discourse about education and international development. He felt that Room to Read was already on the cutting edge in study methodologies, and the field would gain a lot from hearing about its work.

However, this was not an easy sell. The organization was still reticent to share its experience broadly—not because it had anything to hide but because it was shy in feeling that it had not yet perfected its methods. It didn't believe that it had anything important yet to say. With gentle and persistent prodding, though, Cory was one of the voices that gradually persuaded the team to participate in international forums and workshops. And as staff began to present their findings—as preliminary as the findings were thought to be—other organizations began to take notice. And although Room to Read was not very well known at its first few conferences, its reputation grew rapidly, and it became quickly known for its deep program work and reflection.

The next big milestone in Room to Read's research, monitoring, and evaluation work—and the start of our transition into maturity in this focus area—came in 2009. Erin, along with the management team, was in the middle of developing the next five-year global strategic plan for Room to Read. We were eager to deepen the quality of our programs so we could have greater impact on the educational outcomes of the children and schools where we were working. Fortunately, we found a great supporter of evidence-based programming in the Bill & Melinda Gates Foundation. They signed on to fund our global strategic plan development as well as a host of follow-on evaluations and research studies. The Gates Foundation's generous investment launched a wave of internal research and external evaluation that has had a tremendous impact on our work, our credibility, and our visibility in the international development community, and our contributions to the larger literature. This was the time when we began to invest in country-based research and evaluation activities in addition to our regular monitoring activities.

Program Implementation Monitoring: Identifying Problems and Clues for Resolving Them

Today, research, monitoring, and evaluation continue to be integral parts of Room to Read's work. Our worldwide monitoring system is stronger than ever, with annual data collection, reporting, and reflection becoming smooth, regular activities deeply embedded in our systems. Each year we review the organizational indicators to determine their importance for our programs, operations, communications, and business development. We then adjust as necessary; update our data collection forms; train country leads, who in turn train enumerators; collect data; enter data into the Salesforce database; prepare preliminary statistical tables; reflect on findings and adjust program design or operations as appropriate; and publish our findings.

This design, implementation, and reflection process is illustrated in Figure 5.1, a workflow diagram developed by the program design team in 2014. This diagram has been a powerful tool for organizing our thinking. We have reproduced it in numerous internal and external documents and presentations, used it to reorganize our staff roles and responsibilities, and

FIGURE 5.1   Room to Read Workflow Diagram.

resurrected it to remind ourselves periodically about our overall approach to programmatic research and development.

The diagram shows how program content and related training that starts with the global office (though based deeply on experiences from our country offices) cascades through the system such that our intended approach becomes implemented at the school and classroom level.

Key to this process are the two feedback arrows that flow back into the system. They illustrate two important ideas. First, there is the recurring theme that monitoring feedback has consequences. When something is not going right in our work, we need to take stock and adjust accordingly. Second, the diagram shows that there are different ways that our work can go wrong and that each has a different effect on the workflow process.

For example, sometimes we have problems with fidelity. This means that the program is not being implemented as it was designed. There could be a problem in delivering furniture to school libraries. Or literacy coaches could be unable to visit their schools for three months because of a government strike or bad weather.

In other situations, the problem may not be with the implementation but with the design itself. We could find, for example, that teachers are doing everything that we ask in reading instruction or library activities, but children are still not learning to read or developing the habit of reading. These are situations in which we need to think hard about the overall design. What could be the problem? Perhaps adolescent girls are not achieving more success in school because they have more chores at home and therefore less time to do homework than do boys.

All this is to say that knowing *why* we are not succeeding in our work is the essential first step in identifying a reasonable solution. How do we do this? As we explained previously, we are in the early stages of implementing a worldwide system called "program implementation monitoring" (PIM). PIM is meant to help us understand the fidelity of program implementation. It includes our library rating tool, which tracks the physical elements of school libraries, library systems, and library activities; our reading instruction observation protocol, which helps us understand the extent to which teachers are implementing instructional routines and taking necessary corrective actions; and, although not an exact parallel, our girls' education risk-and-response tool.

Each of these tools helps us to track progress in implementing our programs as well as guidance for next steps. The library-rating tool, for example, is a paper-based checklist recording form that library management facilitators use when they visit their schools each month. They track a set of 15 indicators per library. Then, based on the findings, they work with school librarians on prioritizing and completing each element of library programming.

This tracking system is an invaluable tool for planning. It helps us to identify the projects that need additional help as well as the kind of help the projects require. It also helps us to determine when a school library is at the phase of development at which we can stop our support work and shift our school-based staff to another library or other priorities. We have seen incredible transformations in the focus of our field-based staff when this kind of tracking is in place.

We have also discovered that it does no good to use such a tool simply to list all the issues that need to be addressed at a library. When we originally created the tool, library management facilitators would debrief with librarians at the end of each monitoring visit by telling them the entire list of program elements they needed to work on. Without helping schools to prioritize the next steps, however, the overall project becomes overwhelming and progress is stunted. Teachers and librarians do not know where to begin. However, once our global RM&E team began to work with our programs team to prioritize the list of program elements, and our facilitators helped schools to prioritize their own work, the tool became much more useful.

Clarifying the implementation process is the first step. Like the development of any project plan in which activities need to be spaced over time, planners need to think about which activities must be implemented in a specific order. This is what the Project Management Institute calls "mandatory dependencies."[2] School libraries, for example, must have bookshelves before they have books, and the libraries must have books before librarians can start weekly reading activities. However, even in situations in which these dependencies are "discretionary"—meaning that there is no need for a specific order in implementation—it is still good to determine a specific order anyway. This helps the project staff and schools with a clear plan of action. It also focuses people's time, work, and other resources to be as targeted as possible. As the title of this chapter states, one of our favorite phrases at Room to Read is, "What gets measured, gets done."

Next Steps

The future is bright for Room to Read's work in RM&E. As we continue to grow our reputation for transparent monitoring and rigorous evaluation, institutional investors such as corporate and family foundations are increasingly coming to us to consider new research opportunities. They know that we have trusted relationships with governments and communities as well as long-standing programs and RM&E systems in place to test hypotheses about important issues in girls' education and literacy.

We are also receiving more invitations to participate in international education research and policy forums—not only in the United States but also in the countries in which we work in around the world. Room to Read's input into these discussions is particularly important as the world community grapples with the implementation of the Sustainable Development Goals that we are set to reach by 2030 and establish the kinds of metrics that will authentically track our collective progress.

One of our most exciting continuing RM&E projects continues to be program implementation monitoring. Although this might seem like a humdrum topic, it is one of the key tools enabling our ability to scale effective programming for ourselves as well as our ministry of education partners.

For example, as we wrote in Chapter 4, hiring school-based support staff was one of the most important steps that Room to Read took years ago to promote the quality of our programming. These are the people who monitor girls' success in school, the functionality of school libraries, and teachers' progress in reading and writing instruction as well as guide schools toward successful outcomes. At the same time, school-based support is expensive and difficult for Room to Read—much less ministries of education—to sustain in the long run. How can systems incorporate such an expensive yet vital function? PIM helps answer that question.

By understanding how long it takes to prepare a teacher, librarian, or social mobilizer in essential activities, and knowing how much support is necessary to master core skills, Room to Read and our ministry partners can become much more efficient in deploying school-based support staff.

Key Takeaways

- **Remember that targeted RM&E is a wise investment.** You will always be under pressure to invest scarce financial resources and staff time in program implementation. This, of course, is the reason you have created a social enterprise in the first place. But investing in RM&E, too, can help to ensure that programming is as efficient and effective as possible and that you can communicate effectively about it in the long run. It is difficult to raise funds for RM&E but important to help investors appreciate its value.

- **Understand that research, monitoring, and evaluation is critical** for the development of any entrepreneurial social enterprise, as it provides input into internal and external communication, improving operations and design, scaling your own organizational goals, and contributing to the larger field.

- **Think about RM&E at the earliest stages of organizational start-up.** This does not mean having a robust RM&E system from the get-go. However, thinking about RM&E early in an organization's development helps to focus program design and implementation, prove your theory of change, build an internal culture that values being a learning organization, as well as engage your key internal and external stakeholders in evidence-based programming.

- **Embed program monitoring deeply into program implementation activities.** Rating systems, observation protocols, and similar tools are essential to understanding whether program activities are being implemented in the way they were intended (program fidelity) and, if so, whether the activities are yielding the intended outcomes and impact.

- **Be curious about what the data are telling you.** Being a data-driven organization requires developing systems and processes that are actionable. It is important to collect, analyze, and then, most importantly, course-correct as necessary and make decisions based on the evidence.

- **Use data to help tell the story of impact and help communicate your own learning to key audiences** (for example, see Figure 5.2). We are not just data geeks at Room to Read. What we really care about are outcomes for children, schools, and communities. Data lead to insight and knowledge, which leads to action, which leads to better outcomes, which leads to greater scale and points in the direction of system-wide change.

- **Know that sometimes data don't tell a clear or full story**. Monitoring and evaluation data are never perfect. The mere creation of information systems can bias what implementers do and do not do. It is therefore important to determine which kinds of data are most important for which purposes. The postmortem discussions among your program and RM&E teams after data are collected and analyzed are therefore key to determining next steps. The experience, wisdom, and better decisions that come out of the team discussions are enlightening and help build capacity to make smarter and smarter decisions with data.

- **Always, always, always be honest with yourselves, your investors, and other stakeholders about what is working and what needs to be changed**. Acknowledging problems directly and clearly and then developing strategies for fixing them instead of hiding them builds trust, appreciation, and long-term support for your hard work. It is also important to remember that people can be quite sensitive about positive and negative findings. The way that results are communicated can have a big effect on what people do with the information.

- **Sing it from the rooftops!** Don't be shy in sharing your RM&E findings with external audiences in blogs, reports,

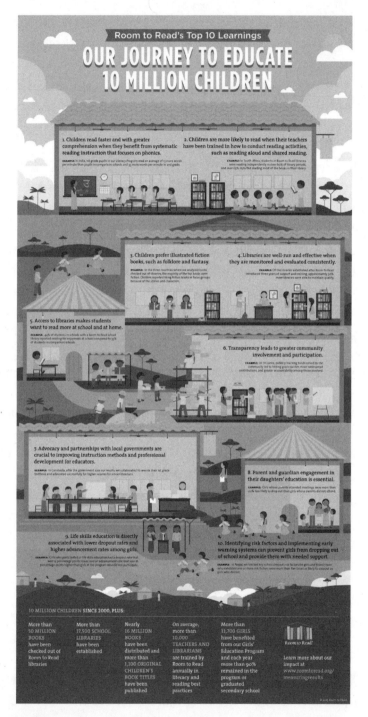

FIGURE 5.2   Infographic Illustrating Lessons Learned from Monitoring and Evaluation.

and public forums. Even if you think it may be too early in your organizational evolution to do so, there is a huge demand for information about effective programming at every stage of development. You can increase your visibility and brand, generate revenue, and contribute to the field by sharing your findings and lessons learned whenever possible.

NOTES

1. U.S. Agency for International Development, *Request for Proposals Number SOL-696-16-000005* (Washington, DC: Self, C-3, 2016).
2. Project Management Institute, *A Guide to the Project Management Body of Knowledge: PMBOK Guide, 2000 Edition* (Newtown Square, PA: Project Management Institute, 2000), 68.

How We Do It

6

Administration, Finance, and International Operations

Strengthening Operations and the Implementation Chain

A Tale of Two Libraries

We decided to make one last stop on the long ride back to the hotel in Dar es Salaam, Tanzania, after a great day of visiting schools. The schools we visited in the morning had been waiting for us. They knew we were coming and were prepared to show us why they appreciated Room to Read support. Despite its being late in the school year in September 2014, when students were busy preparing for exams, students and community members still took the time to welcome foreign visitors. Children waited outside to greet us. School administrators were dressed in their nicest clothes. Even parent representatives from the school management committee were at the school to answer questions, express appreciation, and gently request additional support.

Often district education officials are on hand to show they are actively engaged.

We always ask schools not to go out of their way. We know that everyone is busy with many more important things to do than greet international Room to Read staff. Yet the red carpet is rolled out (figuratively most of the time but literally in some instances, too), and so we often go through this ritual. In contrast, unannounced school visits give us a chance to see what really goes on in a school. There is no time for libraries to be set up or for children to practice responses.

It was easy to make unannounced school visits that day without being too conspicuous. We had just been in the area earlier in the week to facilitate an area-wide reading competition. The competition brought together children from communities throughout the region to participate in reading-themed sport activities (for example, a reading relay, in which children had to read a few pages of a book out loud before they could run down the field and tag their next team member), with hundreds of teachers and parents cheering the children on. Room to Read was a known quantity. We were therefore confident that we were working within the rules to stop at two adjacent primary schools off the main road that tracks the spectacular coast on the way back to Dar es Salaam.

What is interesting about these two schools is that Room to Read was supporting just one of them at the time. Another organization had been supporting libraries in the area, and we had agreed with that organization to focus our efforts on the schools that had not been previously been served.

We started our unannounced visit with the school that Room to Read had not been supporting. As is the custom, we walked to the office of the head teacher. She was happy to see us, as she knew Room to Read. Many of her children had participated in the reading event earlier that week. She took us to the room that housed the school library and tried to open the door. It was locked, so she excused herself to go find the key. It took some time for her to return; she initially did not know which of the teachers had the key. Eventually she found it and opened the door with a smile.

We entered a small room that did not seem to get much use. On one side was a series of dusty, dilapidated bookcases with a small number of books strewn about in semirandom piles on each shelf. Some shelves had taped, paper labels of the letters of the alphabet, presumably to alphabetize the storybooks, but there did not seem to be any real attempt at organization. Two other cases were blocked by a table on which there were precarious stacks of storybooks. The other side of the room was used as storage space for broken furniture. These included broken desks and chairs piled close together. Sharp, broken edges protruded dangerously from the pile. The only pieces of artwork on display were a few paper plates taped to the wall with colored animal faces on them and a painting of a large baobab tree on its side on top of one of the cases.

This was not what we would consider a child-friendly space, yet the head teacher was very proud of it. She appreciated the book donations and was happy to have a library. We asked about the school's ongoing interaction with the organization that helped set up the library. The head teacher said there was not much contact. The organization helped to organize the space initially and donated the books but did not help establish meaningful organizational or checkout systems or help school staff learn how to promote use of the books.

We thanked the head teacher and made the short walk to the second school. As we approached the second school library, the doors were wide open. Even though the formal school day had ended, there were still children and teachers milling about. The school librarian was busy attending to others but welcomed us with a nod. The space was three to four times as large as the first library. It was meant to accommodate frequent use by large classes of children. There were two big mats for children to sit on, with some pillows scattered on the floor.

Bookcases lined two of the four walls. They were painted brightly in blue, red, green, and yellow, reflecting the level of difficulty of books that were organized on each one. Shelves with neatly stacked books were labeled with photos of the animals that represented each book level: fish for blue, rooster for red, butterfly for green, and elephant for yellow. Colorful posters filled the wall space. These included the alphabet; maps of Tanzania, Africa, and the world; bodies and body parts; and health and hygiene. The wall also included a chart of the weekly class schedule for visiting the library. The librarian's desk included the checkout registry and registry of books. The space was clean, bright, and welcoming.

The point of contrasting these two libraries is not to cast aspersions on another organization's work or to pat ourselves on the back. We have been there ourselves! We've seen Room to Read libraries in the past that have resembled the first library described here. Focusing implementation in our early days on simply establishing libraries, stocking them with books, and moving on to the next school created a huge amount of uncertainty about what would happen to those spaces over time. Some of our earliest libraries were fantastic, while others were not. This had as much to do with school leadership and its interest in maintaining library spaces as it was a consequence of Room to Read's actions.

The difference between then and now is our implementation strategy. We decided many years ago that simply creating large numbers of libraries would not be sufficient. Nor would donating used English-language children's books. Nor would giving girls' families money for school tuition and school uniforms. It doesn't do anyone any good to have 100 locked libraries with broken bookshelves and dusty books if the same investment can support ten thriving libraries that are the focal point of school and community reading. We had to do something differently in our program implementation to increase the likelihood of achieving results. And we did! We were a young but rapidly growing organization, and we had learned a lot about what we needed to do better.

The differences between our old and new implementation strategies lay in how we structured professional development activities for school staff and hired school-level support staff. As described in Chapter 4, it was at this time that we started to create training workshops and ongoing monitoring support visits to prepare school staff to implement projects with quality and sustain them over time instead of just establishing libraries and filling them with books. This required hiring a new cadre of country staff members, including staff to conduct workshops and do school-level monitoring and coaching.

Overall Approach to Program Implementation

Our goal in evolving our implementation strategy has been clear from the start: growth with quality in everything we do. However, this is easier said than done, especially when staff are geographically spread out across time zones and oceans and speak multiple languages. As we fine-tuned our implementation over time, the pendulum swung back and forth between highly centralized to decentralized ways to improve the value we were delivering, but with one constant: All action is focused on the goal of providing high-quality educational opportunities for children. We knew that evolving our operational and implementation strategies had to be rooted in our organizational mission and theory of change but also aligned with the stage of development we were in at any given time. We also needed to be clear about changes along the way and the reasons for them so staff could understand and orient their own evolving functions appropriately.

Organizational Structure and Functions

Room to Read implements its historical country programs in similar ways in each of the nine countries in which we have country offices and full programs. These offices coordinate the work in countries and contextualize our global program content for local circumstances, manage program implementation, advocate, and negotiate with governments and other country stakeholders, and act as a communication hub for country staff. Field-based staff then have the most important job of all: delivering high-quality programming and support to schools and communities. Staff in regional offices throughout countries are responsible for facilitating training activities and managing school-based program activities. We then have staff who support the work in schools themselves. This includes staff members who monitor and coach the literacy work happening in classrooms, manage the library, and work with girls and their families. Finally, each of our country offices has staff members who are responsible for research, monitoring, and evaluation. These staff develop study designs and data collection tools, as well as oversee data collection, processing, and analysis.

The country office structure is meant to scale. In countries with fewer projects that are less geographically dispersed, we hire fewer program officers, program associates, and school-level staff. However, for countries with large portfolios, we hire the appropriate number of staff members for oversight and support.

Operational Structure at Room to Read

From an operational perspective, Room to Read is divided into two core operational units: the global office and the country offices. Figure 6.1 below shows the main functional areas as well as reporting relationships. Each country office has its own programs and its own finance and accounting, research, monitoring and evaluation, human resources, technology, and administration teams.

1. **Global office (darker shaded boxes in Figure 6.1):** Room to Read's global office works collaboratively with all countries to design programs; develop and oversee worldwide policies, standards, approaches, and guidelines; raise funds; and drive awareness of Room to Read's programs and their impact. The global office supports the country offices so that local programs are consistent, yet contextualized, and are operating with the efficiency and effectiveness needed to ensure the best results for the children we serve.

2. **Country offices (lighter shaded boxes in Figure 6.1):** Room to Read's country offices work to contextualize and implement high-quality worldwide program packages based on Room to Read's global office approach. Country offices operate using clear, consistent, and actionable program materials to achieve the desired outcomes set by each country office in partnership with the global office. The country offices are responsible for reporting local results to the global office to improve programs and share with stakeholders.

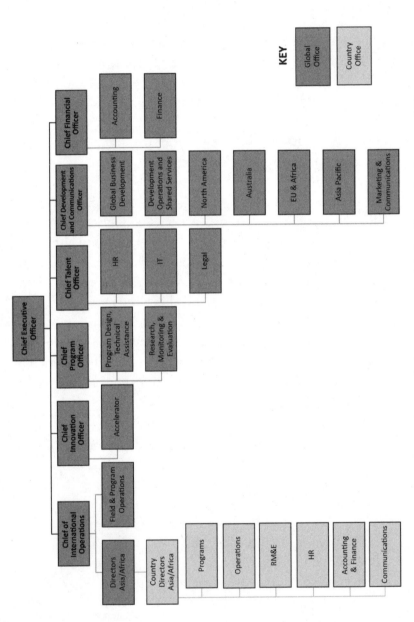

FIGURE 6.1 Example Staffing Structure for the Room to Read Global Office and a Country Office.

Implementation

Room to Read's implementation approach combines periodic workshops with ongoing coaching and support visits. This is true for the Girls' Education Program as well as for the Literacy Program. In the Girls' Education Program, our school-level social mobilizers work directly with girls. We train these women in workshops. Program associates then conduct periodic school visits to observe and support the mobilizers. Similarly, in the Literacy Program, school administrators, librarians, and teachers participate in periodic workshops. The workshops explain program concepts and how to implement program activities. Regular school visits then allow library management facilitators and literacy coaches to monitor program implementation and offer guidance and support.

One of the most important aspects of our implementation approach is community coinvestment and the gradual transition of responsibility from the project team to schools and communities.

Room to Read's initial interactions with leaders in any new community in which we are hoping to work involve frank discussions about roles and responsibilities. We then negotiate with leaders to decide whether they would like to coinvest in a long-term project with us. Not only does Room to Read choose its communities, but they choose us, too.

After 18 years of work, we have a good sense about what Room to Read programming can achieve. Successful programming, though, relies on substantial community buy-in and partnership. This is an essential step to the longer-term transition of project ownership to communities and schools after projects end. It is one of the prerequisites for Room to Read's investment in new projects. Geographical targeting is another critical aspect of program implementation. Decisions about which geographies to target, for example, have huge consequences for logistics and costs. Transportation costs in particular can be high, and the logistics of coordinating travel to disperse geographies can also be challenging.

Strengthening the Implementation Chain

Key to Room to Read's progress in evolving our implementation systems is constantly reminding ourselves about our implementation chain (see Figure 6.2). The chain starts with a global design, which, in the case of Room to Read, is based on years of country experience. The global design is then translated and contextualized for each country but then changes more as the content moves from the country office through the cascade of staff members all the way to school-level implementation. As Figure 6.2 shows, the original design inevitably changes and becomes less like the original as it cascades from the start to the end of the implementation chain.

The goal of a functional implementation chain is to maintain as much fidelity as possible to the original program design as appropriate for the local context. This requires being very clear about the roles and responsibilities in the organization, from the people responsible for program design, to those responsible for contextualizing the programs in each country, to the people implementing the program activities in every school. It also

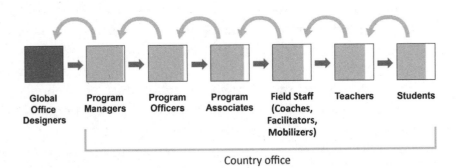

Global Office Designers — Program Managers — Program Officers — Program Associates — Field Staff (Coaches, Facilitators, Mobilizers) — Teachers — Students

Country office

FIGURE 6.2 Room to Read's Implementation and Feedback Chain.

includes the feedback loop at each step along the way: defining the processes by which staff members at each point in the implementation chain provide feedback to staff members from the previous step about what is and isn't working.

Clarifying roles, responsibilities, and communication processes is critical for understanding when one or more links in the implementation chain is weak or broken. Anyone who has played the children's game of telephone knows that any original message inevitably becomes distorted, sometimes wildly, as it cascades from one person to another. In an international organization, in which communication regularly jumps thousands of miles and is filtered through different cultures, languages, and individual biases, relaying expectations and intent is even more difficult. It makes it that much more important that messages are clear and communication strategies are explicit from the outset.

As shown in Figure 6.2, you should always expect some loss of fidelity in any original program design or contextualized program design. A social mobilizer implementing girls' education life-skills discussions in a school will never have a complete understanding about what was in the mind of the person who originally designed the activity. However, fidelity should remain a priority because, as we discussed in Chapter 5, it helps you identify whether any specific problem is due to program design or project implementation.

The Three Phases of Program Implementation

It should not be a surprise that an implementation strategy is core to the success to any organization that provides goods or services, including organizations in the nonprofit sector. It is essential for Room to Read. Ultimately, as summarized in Table 2.3 and reproduced in Table 6.1, the ultimate goal of any implementation strategy should be to provide targeted, high-quality goods

TABLE 6.1 Phases of Program Implementation

Theories of change	Phase of development		
	Start-Up	**Transition**	**Maturity**
Implementation	Emphasize local experimentation	Consolidate lessons from local implementation, with focus on program quality	Target support to enhance program outcomes efficiently and with more impact

and services on time, on demand, and in a way that is scalable. The way that an organization accomplishes its goals, though, can differ markedly depending on its phase of development. It can be difficult to achieve your targeted goals at the early stages of program implementation, especially in an organization that focuses on underserved communities in low-income countries. It is certainly not likely overnight. Thinking strategically about implementation is just as important as designing your programs. At Room to Read, we still have a long way to go to achieve an on-demand implementation strategy, but we are continuing to work hard to get there.

Like the program development cycle, you should plan for a period of experimental development, followed by a consolidation of lessons learned, before assuming that it will be possible to target support in an efficient way. Of course, this bird's-eye view does not happen in an orderly way. There are always mini cycles of centralization and decentralization, particularly when developing new products and services. However, we have found it helpful to keep track of the larger trend of organizational maturity as Room to Read has worked through its various phases of development.

Implementation During Start-Up

Like the evolution of Room to Read's program models, we experimented with many different program implementation strategies during start-up. We tried everything. Each country implemented differently and had different implementation chain structures. Erin recalls the first worldwide country management conference in 2004, when the worldwide leadership came together for the first time in Kathmandu, Nepal. There were heated debates about the best way to implement program activities, the only common elements among countries being "books" and "girls." In the Literacy Program, some countries had installed bookshelves in each classroom while others moved library books around schools in mobile carts. Still others kept books in central school libraries. The India country director advocated strongly for teacher training and capacity building while the Nepal country director wanted to focus on developing guidance manuals that could be dropped off at schools.

In the Girls' Education Program, some countries had begun to pay boarding fees for girls to attend distant schools. The belief was that this was going to be the best way to support a quality education. Other countries thought it was culturally inappropriate for girls to be so far away from their families.

These meetings were exciting because of the creativity and problem-solving that took place. Some of our early decisions were deeply rooted in cultural norms and countries' geographies and administrative systems. Others were based on country directors' own experiences or ideas. Everything was on the table. Do we hire our own staff to implement project activities or do we contract services to local organizations? Do we concentrate our work in a small geographical area, or do we try to spread our visibility and influence? How much do we expect local communities to contribute before we commit to a new project in a geography?

One of the innovations that came out of the 2004 Country Management Conference was new language about implementation and the concepts of "nonnegotiables" and "preferred ways of working." Nonnegotiables were the implementation strategies that would be required of all countries, whereas preferred ways of working were more about promising practices that countries were advised to consider but were not required to adopt.

An example of a nonnegotiable in our Literacy Program was that libraries must have books in the local language, whereas a preferred way of working was they could also have children's books in English if they felt these would be useful to the school library. In our Girls' Education Program, we decided early on, as a nonnegotiable, that only women would be hired to work directly with the girls. A preferred way of working would be that different kinds of financial or material support could be provided to the girls to support them, depending on the community and family situation, ranging from paying school fees to providing uniforms, a bicycle, or bus fare for girls living far from school.

Our worldwide leadership began to grapple with the question of how much of Room to Read's work could and should be standardized across countries and how much should be left to local leadership. It can sound quite democratic and enlightened to talk about freedom of choice and local control. However, as we described in Chapter 4, you pay a price—sometimes quite high—for using diverse approaches. At the same time, given Room to Read's penchant for close observation, reflection, and revision, we did learn from this diversity that there were better and worse ways to implement program activities. And although local preferences are important, organizations must be open to the lessons that they are learning from actual experience, be as objective as possible in their analysis of the empirical information, and adjust implementation as necessary when they identify better ways of working.

The principle, as summarized by a board member with a strong background in international development, is for ESEs to think about central policies and local management. That is, ESEs should consider more centralized oversight for activities that have strong proof of success, are expensive to design or require global technical expertise, are necessary for ethical or moral purposes or to promote equity, or are needed to maintain organizational cohesion across countries (for example, human resource policies). At the same time, organizations should emphasize local approaches when subtle local information is too expensive to gather and track centrally and in a bureaucratic manner or local approaches are critical for generating buy-in by empowering local staff and partners as codesigners.

Implementation During the Transition Phase

One of the clear lessons that came out of the start-up phase is that we needed a strategy for ensuring program quality. As described in Chapter 2, it was no longer merely enough to establish a new library and fill it with books, or to give a girl a scholarship to pay for school fees. It was too easy for schools to express appreciation for the work and then forget about it, as we saw from the first Tanzania school at the beginning of this chapter. The sad state of some of our early libraries was never because of bad intent. Schools simply did not have the knowledge and experience or, in some cases, the motivation, to make our services work for them. We needed some mechanism to ensure that schools could use the libraries and books effectively and that girls were progressing in school and at less risk of dropping out.

We began to crave hard evidence about the actual impact our work was having. We needed new strategies to capture that information. Access to regular, concrete information to improve project quality was a critical missing piece in our process to improve our programs.

It was therefore during the transition period that Room to Read invested heavily in school-level support staff and country-level monitoring systems. We institutionalized these positions formally into the implementation chain. This decision transformed our implementation approach. We needed to think about what these staff members would do and how often they would visit schools. We needed a system to train and supervise school-level staff. We needed to build a project-tracking database to house all the school site- and girl-specific information our staff were collecting to inform the quality of our implementation and program design.

Key to success was customizing the database and using it consistently over the years to track our program outputs and outcomes. That required investing in mid-level country staff members: program associates, most often, who would oversee and support the school-level social mobilizers, library management facilitators, and, later in our evolution, literacy coaches. We also had to agree on global indicators, map out the kinds of data we wanted to collect, and then customize the database to house the relevant information. Given the growth of our project portfolios in countries, we also needed a certain number of program officers to oversee the program associates and report to program managers.

On the monitoring side, we also began to hire monitoring and evaluation associates and officers who would visit schools at least once per year to collect our annual program indicator information and verify the regular monitoring information that was coming from the mobilizers and facilitators. This staffing structure was becoming complex and expensive. But it was what we believed—and still believe—to be the necessary infrastructure to sustain quality outcomes.

These new investments in school-level support and monitoring, though, exacerbated some of the tensions that we were just beginning to understand during start-up. For example, it is much more difficult to implement school-level support when projects are spread over a large geography. This was less of an issue in setting up projects initially, as costs were limited largely to projects' set-up expenses. However, ongoing school visits over the course of years require substantial planning. Then there are the costs for transportation, lodging, and daily allowances (*per diems*) when staff members stay in remote areas overnight, and additional considerations if some areas are less accessible in rainy seasons.

Another tension that became more acute during the transition period was determining how we were going to structure implementation at the school level. In Africa and Southeast Asia, in most instances, we did this directly by hiring Room to Read employees as school-level support staff. In South Asia, most school-level implementation was done through local partner organizations. In these situations, Room to Read still staffed most positions in the implementation chain. It was just the very last link of school-level support (that is, social mobilizers, library management facilitators, and later, literacy coaches) that would become the responsibility of local partners. The logic for working with partners in South Asia was that these community-based nonprofit organizations had direct relationships with communities. They would be able to mobilize quickly with high levels of trust and respect. In addition, helping local organizations implement Room to Read programs was a great way to build their capacity and increase the likelihood of sustaining programming even after Room to Read left a geographical area. Local organizations could then continue to support schools and even expand the work to new areas with their expertise.

Room to Read's transition phase was a time of high growth. We were implementing more than 1,000 new literacy projects per year—an average of three per day! We established projects, trained staff and school personnel, and monitored not only the new sites but also all our other literacy projects and girls already in the programs. This was a serious logistical challenge, but visiting remote schools in places from Salavan in Laos to Kafue in Zambia, to Chitwan in Nepal was highly motivating. We would arrive at a school and find children running toward the library at recess time to grab a book or listen to a teacher reading. We saw new authors and illustrators winning awards for the quality of their children's books. The work felt vibrant, dynamic, and fulfilling—and completely exhausting. After spending years in the transitional phase, though, we were ready to evolve into a more mature organization.

Implementation During the Mature Phase

As we reflect upon on the growing maturity of our implementation, we should say that Room to Read is perhaps still not as mature in this dimension as in other aspects of our work. We did not invest as much in our operational systems early in our history as was necessary given our rapid growth. We do have a clear vision for implementation success and have begun to execute our plans in some ways, but we still have far to go. Operating in two major program areas on multiple continents requires hard work and patience. However, we are starting to see the fruits of these efforts and believe that innovating implementation is one of the most promising and exciting aspects of Room to Read's future.

The biggest difference in implementation in the mature phase is that it needs to be more demand driven and focused at increasingly higher levels of impact. During the transition phase, Room to Read structured its program implementation around a core approach. We worked with ministry of education officials and other partners to identify potential partner communities, became smarter about how to select geographical areas in which to work, established working relations with targeted communities and schools, and regularly conducted workshops and ongoing monitoring and support visits.

The problem with this approach is that it emphasizes our own schedules and doesn't necessarily align to schools' actual needs. How do we know, for example, that four years of ongoing school support is the right amount of time to sustain long-term teacher success in reading instruction? Could this require substantially more time? Perhaps a lot less time? The truth is, we still do not know. Nor does anyone else. However, as we explained in Chapter 5, we are starting to analyze the classroom observation forms from reading lessons to answer these questions. This information will enable us to be much more responsive to the actual needs of teachers instead of merely following a rigid plan, albeit in a more structured and strategic way than in the past.

Tools for Operational Accountability

In our mature phase, we also created tools to clarify operational responsibility and accountability. We have found that having tools to ensure clarity in operational and implementation roles and responsibilities goes a long way to building an aligned and highly functioning global organization. One of the most important tools we have created is our performance implementation management system that we discussed in-depth in Chapter 5. Two other tools that have been particularly helpful at Room to Read are management dashboards and our delegation of authority matrix.

Management Dashboards The ethos of "What gets measured, gets done" that we use in our program operations applies throughout Room to Read. In our more mature stage of development, we have created a series of dashboards for each country of operation and, in a slightly simplified form, for each technical-assistance project. These dashboards roll up to a global management dashboard, which is a key monitoring tool for our management team. Results of the global management dashboard in turn feed into quarterly reporting to our board of directors.

One of the challenges of building dashboards is trying to streamline them while still serving the needs of multiple audiences. Our dashboards cover all critical functional areas of the organization (outlined in Figure 6.1) and generally include 6–12 metrics for each department. Each metric then includes an annual target and a quarterly flag for progress in reaching that target (green for tracking well to target, yellow for slightly off target, and red for major issues in meeting target). For example, for our human resource department, some of our performance metrics are the percentage of positions that are vacant, turnover, percentage of staff who are female, percentage of management who are female, and staff satisfaction. Our goal is to have a visual snapshot of the health of each country operation and our global office departments at our fingertips. It is important, though, as with all data collection, not to make the dashboard too complex or lengthy to avoid overloading users.

Delegation of Authority Matrix   We developed our global delegation of authority matrix at Room to Read to help alleviate the tensions that inevitably occur in a growing organization around "Who gets to make what decisions at what level of the organization?" During times of dynamic growth, it's important to embrace decentralization of authority so that decisions can be pushed to the lowest appropriate level in the organization. By doing this, you can be nimble and fast-moving. The tricky part, particularly in an international organization working across multiple geographies and in multiple languages, is communicating clearly what types of decisions specifically can be made by what level of employee. Thus, we created a delegation-of-authority policy that ensured consistency and clarified who had authority for approving actions at different levels of funding. This matrix also specifies who may sign various contracts. Like our management dashboards, the delegation-of-authority matrix covers every functional area of our business. For example, our HR delegation-of-authority policy clearly states who can approve new headcounts, adjust salaries, award benefits, give promotions, and approve professional development budgets. We review and update our delegation-of-authority matrix annually as our organization continues to evolve.

Specifying this level of detail may sound tedious, bureaucratic, and perhaps overkill. It's certainly a far cry from our start-up days when we made many of these decisions through phone conversations or e-mail. However, we have found that at our current mature size of more than 1,500 employees, we would otherwise face huge bottlenecks. Before we created the matrix, we were making many decisions on an *ad hoc* basis, criteria were being applied differently across different teams and country operations, and we were spending more time trying to solve internal challenges that arose from this ambiguity than focusing on our work. After we developed our delegation-of-authority matrix, we regained precious time to focus on activities that added value to our mission.

Developing and managing systems and processes are not always the most fun part of the job, but some investment up front can allow you much more time for higher-level, strategic activities as you grow.

External Technical Assistance

One of the most exciting, demand-driven implementation innovations we made during the mature phase of organizational development was to begin offering "external technical assistance." This is a new kind of service delivery for Room to Read that goes beyond our full-country implementation. Rather than implementing project activities ourselves or through partners, we train government officials and professionals from other organizations in Room to Read programming.

This approach allows us to move up the implementation chain from directly supporting girls (in our Girls' Education Program) and teachers (in our Literacy Program) and enables us to work at district, provincial, or national levels to increase system-level support for our activities; or simply leverage the interest of others, such as governments or other nonprofit organizations that have shown interest in undertaking work in line with Room to Read approaches. The ability to offer external technical assistance builds our system-level capacity to have a sustained impact in a much more profound way than we could do in the past.

Government implementation chains are not very different from ours at Room to Read. They are just at a completely different order of magnitude, and in some cases, may be constrained or helped by existing policy (for example, decentralization policy). Governments and other organizations, too, need to figure out ways to translate program designs into local action. In most instances, as with Room to Read, the closer a government's implementation is aligned with the original design, the greater the impact—and more likely the impact will be sustained. Figure 6.3 shows how Room to Read activities are intended to influence governments' implementation chains.

The figure illustrates the various levels in the cascade. The goal of effective technical assistance is to promote fidelity of successful implementation from the beginning to the very end of the chain. With the start of our external technical-assistance work, Room to Read's implementation activities are now interjected into government implementation chains at different entry points.

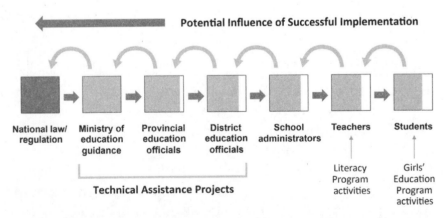

FIGURE 6.3 Level of Influence of Room to Read Implementation.

Our direct implementation works primarily at the classroom level while our technical assistance works at higher levels of the educational system. The goal, of course, is to do such a good job at whatever point we are working in the government system that news of our efforts trickles up and influences ever-higher levels of the government implementation chain. This is how we attempt to strengthen our impact and sustain our efforts.

The launch of Room to Read's technical-assistance practice was the result of our 2015–2019 strategic plan objective to be more strategic, accelerate our impact, and to "do more with less"—a common goal for any scale-up effort. As we had been evolving our programming to that point in time, we had a new set of worldwide implementation packages that had been tested extensively and validated in different countries, as well as a growing set of organizational skills to contextualize the packages for individual country use. We also continued to receive regular requests from other organizations and governments to share our knowledge and approach. Still, we had no mechanism to do so other than our full-country programming.

We therefore launched "Room to Read Accelerator" in January 2015 as our new technical-assistance practice area to meet these needs. The goal was to promote technical-assistance services as a way to have strategic influence on educational implementation chains to complement our school-level direct implementation. This was an exciting proposition but also a complex one that had tremendous implications for our organizational infrastructure and approach to implementation.

Incorporating Accelerator into Our Program Implementation

Even during the earliest days of planning for the Accelerator, our management team realized that we would have to think differently about various issues. For example, our programmatic approach for literacy and girls' education was based on the idea that schools needed a comprehensive set of approaches for children to benefit. Either Room to Read, other partners, or the school itself needed to implement a specific set of activities well if they wanted the children to succeed. Deciding to prioritize technical-assistance projects could put us in situations in which only pieces of our programs would be implemented and most likely be implemented by others instead of Room to Read staff. We therefore had to be comfortable with the possible trade-off of more children receiving services but perhaps at a more limited level of intensity or comprehensiveness.

In many ways, we covered our eyes and peeked through our fingers in starting our technical-assistance work. We dipped our proverbial toe in the water. We acknowledged that adding this new complex capability to our organization would be a risky experiment. We would want to reflect on the experience at specific intervals over time to make sure that it was worthwhile. The first reflection point would be a 2017 review. This would be in the middle of our five-year strategic plan period and a good time to re-examine our assumptions, reflect on challenges and successes to date, and be rigorous in learning about what was working and what need to be improved. To what extent have the investments in technical-assistance projects contributed to our organizational goals? The results of the review would then guide Room to Read's future investments in technical assistance.

Another important consideration in any decision to pursue technical-assistance projects is their opportunity costs. Again, we realized that project activities will be at least somewhat different from our core programming and potentially less comprehensive than what we might otherwise recommend to ensure children's success. So, a big question for our review has been, "What have the opportunity costs been for accepting these kinds of projects as compared to what would have been an alternative investment in regular program implementation?" In other words, is implementing technical assistance worth it?

In addition, the spirit of most of our technical-assistance project activities is that we share our ideas with others but that they must make the decisions about what they will do with that information themselves. This is also very different from Room to Read's direct implementation, in which our staff are directly responsible for program outcomes.

Equally as important, we decided that we would only pursue technical-assistance projects that would contribute to our organizational mission. We did not want to become more of a traditional government-contracting organization that geared itself to respond to a wide range of issues. The decision about how close a technical-assistance request is to our organizational mission is close enough is extremely subjective. We are already opening ourselves to substantial risk of mission creep by choosing to do technical assistance in the first place. Even with the best of intentions, it is possible for different people to interpret the same funding opportunity differently. However, the intent of the global management team is to be hypervigilant in considering the efficacy of "go/no-go" decisions so that we can be as true to our mission as possible.

Last, the global management team uses other criteria as well when deciding to pursue any new technical-assistance project. For example, we decided that any new project must bring enough funding at least to cover all expected direct project costs. Although Room to Read does have some discretionary funding at its disposal, we would not be able to keep the organization alive for any length of time if we were to spend more money over time than we raise. This is a very difficult message to convey. After all, as people working in a mission-driven educational organization, we all want to ensure to we can help as many children as possible. We never want to say "no" to any request that could serve this interest. However, we need to continuously remind ourselves that providing services without the requisite funding behind this decision diminishes our overall organizational capacity to do good work.

The other major consideration for any specific "go/no-go" decision is our overall capacity to pursue a proposal and, subsequently, to implement the project. Do we have adequate staffing resources and experience to write a successful proposal? Have we worked in the area previously? If so, with what success? Do we currently have the staff, or can we quickly bring on the necessary talent to make the project successful without robbing resources from our existing activities? Is the government receptive to the work?

Our experience in implementing technical-assistance projects thus far has been quite positive. We have completed two successful technical-assistance projects, started nine others in five existing Room to Read countries and four new countries, and have one new project ready to begin in the next few months. We also have multiple opportunities each year so far to bid on new projects. We have secured approximately US$21 million of new funding and estimate that the current set of projects will benefit at least six million new children. However, as we describe in later chapters, incorporating this new approach into our overall work continues to be a challenge, and we have a long way to go to ensure smooth processes and systems.

The Pendulum Swingeth

As we have discussed previously, one of the ongoing challenges for any implementation organization—particularly for organizations with an international focus—is about control. Who designs and implements programs? Is it the central organization or the satellite offices? As described in Chapter 4, Room to Read's path to programmatic excellence began with its openness to innovative local experimentation. It was through this diversity that we learned what works in each of our countries and how to structure our program design and implementation to meet the needs of as many children as possible.

As we moved deeper into the transition phase, Room to Read's implementation became more consistent across countries. We became more efficient and delivered more consistent quality. This has been important for us to be able to manage implementation on a larger scale. While fully appreciating differences in local contexts, we've found that the advantages of consistent programming and implementation have far outweighed those of diversifying our portfolio based on local needs. We've benefited substantially by maintaining largely consistent staffing structures, implementation chains, hiring practices, and standard operating procedures.

Do we expect to be as firmly consistent in our implementation in the years ahead? Probably not. Developing consistency has been an important part of our evolutionary process, but it is not the final state. Even as we begin to relax our standard approaches somewhat, though, we will want to do it differently than in the start-up phase of our work. We now have much more clarity about what we are trying to achieve and how to achieve it.

Rather than promoting broad diversity, we will experiment more systematically and strategically, providing a much tighter set of options for demand-driven implementation and a more focused research and development process for new services. These require collaboration between the global office and the individual country offices to identify possible deviations from or enhancements to our core approach; to develop clear expectations for how this would work; and to monitor implementation so that we can understand what is working and what is not.

In addition, introducing our technical-assistance projects has offered us a new route to local experimentation. While these projects are still rooted deeply in our core approach, they are also tailored to meet client needs and not simply to replicate our direct implementation. Even now, we're able to incorporate lessons from direct implementation into our technical-assistance work as well as share our experiences from technical-assistance projects with our full country teams.

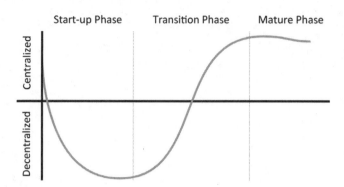

FIGURE 6.4 Wave of Centralization and Decentralization in Room to Read's Overall Program Implementation.

Moving from one phase of organizational development to another does not necessarily mean a unidirectional change exclusively from decentralized to centralized implementation or vice versa. Room to Read's experience is that the overall implementation strategy is more like a wave (with the continuation of many smaller waves as we potentially conduct research and development for new services). Figure 6.4 summarizes Room to Read's own experience in negotiating this balance. Will this change again in the future? Perhaps there will be a move toward more decentralization. Someone can update the story then.

The underlying message is that entrepreneurial leaders should be aware of their organizational needs at different times, be very clear with their teams about the reasons for shifting roles, and be ready to shift the wave in another direction if the organization can benefit.

Key Takeaways

Organizations live and die by implementation. You can have the best idea in the world and have a brilliant program model, but it is only through consistent, high-quality implementation that social enterprises can achieve their missions and achieve impact at scale. To summarize:

- **Help staff to understand your organization's implementation strategy at each stage of development**. Doing so makes it easier for people to orient themselves and implement program activities in a consistent, high-quality manner.

- **Take your time progressing through the start-up and transitional phases of development**. Honor the fact that you need to grow in your knowledge and experience about what works over an extended period before trying to progress too quickly into mature implementation. Try various approaches, and experiment extensively along the way to learn as much as possible. The quality of your long-term approach will be higher and your relationships with partners and the communities that you serve will be stronger for taking the time to implement at each phase with care, thoughtfulness, risk, and reflection.

- **Plan for the fact that implementation during the transition phase of development could be substantially more expensive and complicated than during the start-up phase**. The shift in focus from simply "getting projects done" to "getting projects done with quality and impact" can require a layer of staffing, quality control, and system building that can require additional staff and processes that increase the challenges of the implementation approach substantially.

- **Throughout all phases of development, remember that scaling effective programming is the ultimate goal**. Knowing that your long-term goal is for communities, other organizations, and governments to adopt your most compelling program elements will help you design your implementation approach. You will be able to not only maximize your impact but also make it easier to understand, easier to implement, cost effective, and more easily transferable to others.

- **Seek a balance between developing consistent, streamlined, effective execution at scale and creating space for continued learning, improvement, and innovation.** Not all programs and countries will be at the same stage of development, particularly as organizations promote research and development of new services. Organizations need to build structured flexibility into their operating systems to accommodate this diversity.

7

People Management: Changing the World Is a Team Sport

C ulture is the fabric that bonds people in an organization together. The shared values, solidarity to a cause, comradery, and repeated jokes make the long days working together more meaningful. Even in the most difficult circumstances, humorous moments are sometimes what you remember most.

Erin recalls being in Sri Lanka a few months after the December 2004 tsunami hit. She was visiting some of the first communities we were partnering with to rebuild schools. It was a challenging time as Erin and the Room to Read country director of Sri Lanka witnessed firsthand the devastation and ongoing suffering. Reconstruction efforts were slow. In one small, predominantly Muslim community on the eastern coast of the island, we held a groundbreaking ceremony to lay the foundation of a preschool we were rebuilding with the community.

In the speeches being spoken in Tamil, Erin heard Room to Read being referred to as "Room to Breed." The community thought our mission was to encourage families to have more children. In Erin's speech, she had to correct the name to Room to Read and clarify that Room to Read's mission was about ensuring all children were educated and developing a lifelong habit and joy of reading. This experience turned into a shared joke among

165

the staff for years that rippled throughout the worldwide team of different names for Room to Read: Room to Work, Room to Travel, Room to Eat, Room to Party, and so on. Room to Read's culture has always been one of hard charging for the best results, but it has also always had a heavy dose of fun.

Promoting fun has also been an important part of organizational leadership, and great leadership is, of course, key to building a world-class team. One of the most challenging aspects of rapidly scaling an organization is evolving one's own leadership style and supporting other leaders throughout the organization to do the same. Every entrepreneur is trying to build the best team possible to deliver on his or her vision. Probably the most succinct and useful advice Erin was given was from one of her board chairs who had been the CEO of Yahoo! when it went public and had many hard-learned lessons to tell about scaling a company. During one of Erin's monthly check-ins with him, he shared his philosophy about the role of a leader. To create a durable organization, leaders must anticipate skill gaps in the organization and fill them with other great leaders. They must be committed to giving everyone a path to grow as far as they can, and give them the professional development opportunities and training to get there. He summarized his advice about how to successfully manage a team as follows: (1) hire the very best you can; (2) set a clear vision and expectations; (3) get out of way, delegate, and give them the space to contribute their talent; and (4) check back in regularly to ensure they are succeeding and to provide support that might be needed.

This management advice struck Erin as simple but elegantly summed up. The only additional challenge she faced as a social entrepreneur is that she had do it on a shoestring budget. Non-profits are obviously different from private companies in the fact that there are minimal incentives for attracting and retaining top talent other than satisfying people's passion to change the world for the better. It's wonderful when a social enterprise can leverage people's desire to work hard for a mission. And it can also create an even more challenging work environment to manage. Expectations are high when staff members give up other opportunities to work in the private or social sectors, and they often have deep-seated beliefs about how the work should be done.

Because an entrepreneurial social enterprise has limited discretionary resources, investing in management systems and people development is difficult. Yet the greatest asset of any organization—and certainly those that have service-based program delivery models—is its people. As we say at Room to Read, world change is a team sport. The conundrum for the ESE sector then is how to attract, retain, and develop a world-class team on a limited budget.

In this chapter, we share some of the key lessons learned that have worked for Room to Read in four key areas of people management: (1) building a strong organizational culture, (2) attracting top talent, (3) building the capacity of a diverse talent base, and (4) evolving senior leadership through dynamic growth.

What Is Really Core in Your Core Values

Building and sustaining a strong organizational culture is essential in creating a successful ESE. When we attempted to write down our core values for the first time, we were in our fifth year and developing our first five-year strategic plan. This first strategic plan was an attempt to spell out our beliefs, our goals, and our strategies to accomplish them. Key to this plan was a set of 12 core values that we felt represented how we worked. Of course, 12 values were an overly ambitious way to start and proved to be too many to remember. The idea of "core" was clearly lost on us at this first attempt. But the exercise was motivating and empowering for a young organization as we set the tone for and created our organizational culture over time.

We focused in future strategic planning on whittling the 12 values down to three truly core values: (1) passion for education, (2) focus on action and innovation, and (3) commitment to collaboration. We tried to answer the questions, "What is most important to us at Room to Read?" and "What is unique about working here?" Starting in that first strategic planning process and refined several times since then, we also defined operating principles that support our core values. These statements together guide our decisions and actions.

Perhaps more difficult than developing core values is living them every day. Every organization has its explicit culture represented in its core value statements. However, the way we act as leaders says as much about organizational culture as the words in a core value statement. It is only when what we *say* on paper (our explicit culture) aligns with what we *model* in our behavior (our implicit culture)—when we "walk the talk"—that trust is high. When there is a wide gap between an organization's stated values and what staff feel are the real ways decisions get made or people are encouraged to behave, an unhealthy organizational culture develops.

At Room to Read, we've seen the gap between our explicit and implicit organizational cultures vary over time. We can see how well they are aligned in our annual staff satisfaction surveys (translating the survey to ensure our global team can fully understand and respond meaningfully in their first language) as well as informally from "water cooler" conversations in the office.

One of the most notable gaps occurred in 2010. We had experienced a decade of rapid growth, and our employee base globally had grown to approximately 500. We had not devoted the time to focus on developing strong internal communication systems. Although we had hired many new staff members around the world, we had not yet established great ways of onboarding them or developed robust performance-management or professional-development systems to support them.

We hired a new chief talent officer around the same time. As part of his onboarding, he did a "listen and learn" tour of many of our offices. By then, our staff were spread out across a wide geographical footprint. Our new chief talent officer identified many Room to Read cultural behaviors that were not supporting our organization any longer given our larger size and the need for more professional and structured processes to manage the additional complexity. He then led the management team through a process to identify ways to adapt these old organizational cultural behaviors to newer ones. We decided to evolve 24 behaviors in all. (Who knew we had so many explicit and implicit behaviors?) This was when our get stuff done (GSD) mentality became get stuff done right (GSDR) to transition our start-up mentality from one focused on speed to one that embraced important and strategic matters, too. "Cheap and cheerful" became "cost effective." We moved "taking the time to supervise" and "conduct regular one-on-one meetings with your staff" from a secondary responsibility to a primary responsibility. We also placed a greater value on management and established clearer organizational structures, roles, and responsibilities.

Identifying that we had to shift our organizational culture led to a three-year human resource long-range plan. This plan committed us to invest in better systems and processes to support our growing staff. It focused on onboarding new employees, developing positions and appropriately managing workload, and improving our performance-management system. We began to focus more on helping supervisors develop their management skills, especially since we had many first-time supervisors, as well as aiding staff members to enhance their skills and achieve business goals.

These human resource investments in many ways are still a work in process. We didn't accomplish everything in three years, but we have evolved our work culture to one that focuses on supporting and sustaining an engaged employee base. From defining core values in our early start-up days to investing in our staff as a more mature organization, we have prioritized building an organizational culture that reflects what we want to be.

Another complicating factor in growing our ideal organizational culture is that we work across numerous country boundaries, languages, and cultures. Our worldwide staff work in places with different languages, work habits, traditions, and practices. As a result, culture is something that we think about a lot. We try to simplify the language we use internally to be friendly for nonnative English speakers and work to celebrate the diversity in our organization. But there are also the unspoken aspects of the dos and don'ts in any given culture, and the norms of acceptable behavior vary widely. These are harder to navigate.

Take the issue of how openly authority can be challenged. In the entrepreneurial cultures that many social enterprises cultivate in the West, leaders want to encourage a nonhierarchical structure in which new ideas and innovations can come from anywhere in the organization. This is harder to do in Asia, for example, where hierarchy and respect for status is highly valued. Another issue is expressing anger and frustration. Many Northern cultures like we have in the United States express these feelings relatively openly. If a conversation gets too heated, people apologize and are generally forgiven afterward. In many of the Asian cultures we work in, however, it is never acceptable publicly to show these emotions. Bonds of trust can be broken that are very hard to repair.

Room to Read has not figured out all the nuances of working globally. What we have done worldwide, though, is realize and place a high value on in-person meetings. We feel this builds a level of trust and collaboration that has allowed us to traverse many misunderstandings. We try not to assume we understand what another colleague is thinking or perceiving. We spend a great deal of time building a sense of community in the greater Room to Read global family. We often say a staff person must wear both her country hat ("I work for Room to Read Bangladesh") as well as her global hat ("I work for

Room to Read") and understand how her decisions and actions impact both parts of the system. Functional teams from different countries meet periodically in person.

Team bonding is another way we've ensured we have a strong Room to Read organizational culture that crosses country barriers. Investors and partners who travel to our country offices often tell us how amazing our country staff are and how much there seems to be a sense of what it means to be a "Room to Reader" that translates across cultures.

At one of our country management conferences, in 2012 in Vietnam, we asked each country team for a short phrase or word that described what it is like to work at Room to Read. There was amazing consistency in what people said, and this consistency has persisted over the years. Common phrases were that Room to Read was a learning organization; that people were cooperative; that we had energetic and dedicated staff; that we had the freedom to express ourselves; that we were fast paced; that we had lots of deadlines; that we were not bureaucratic; and that we were like a family. As we have scaled Room to Read to more than 1,500 full-time employees and more than 16,000 volunteers, maintaining this strong sense of organizational culture has helped us build an amazing global movement.

Leadership in the Social Enterprise

Bill Draper, one of the founders of the Draper Richards Kaplan Foundation, which invests in social entrepreneurial organizations, says that the three characteristics that set social entrepreneurs apart are their empathy, energy, and vision. We couldn't agree more. These are the characteristics that make social entrepreneurs see injustices around the world in the first place and seek solutions.

People who join social enterprises also tend to be mission driven. Perhaps more than corporate leaders, who can use a variety of financial and status-oriented incentives to motivate staff, nonprofit leaders rely extensively on "influence management." This requires the power of personal persuasion to affect the actions or decisions of staff members, investors, and partners to commit people to a collective goal.

Of course, every executive's job is to set vision and strategy as well as manage teams and deliverables; but to tap into the emotions and passions required to sustain a social movement, the investment is particularly high. Erin in her own leadership development has often reflected on the truth of the Maya Angelou quote: "People will forget what you said, forget what you did, but will never forget how you make them feel."

For more than a decade now, Room to Read has held an annual country management conference (CMC) in which country directors—the senior leaders from each of our countries of operation—join our global office headquarters management team for a week-long offsite to set priorities and align leadership for the coming year. We rotate the location every year to a different country so that leadership can see and experience the different contexts firsthand. One of the primary purposes of the CMC is to build a supportive environment for the worldwide leaders to share and learn from each other, as a global movement requires great leaders throughout our network. Our country directors, each in his or her own way, encompass the empathy, energy, and leadership vision to inspire country teams that make up 90% of our worldwide staff.

At this conference, Erin delivers an opening talk, jokingly referred to as the State of the Union address, summarizing the strengths from the past year, the current challenges, and the strategic vision for the way forward in the coming year. She also selects a book each year to give to the leaders that represents a key issue of focus for the organization. Topics over the years have varied from change management to scaling to organizational development. But the topic that most frequently reappears is leadership.

One of Erin's favorite books from the early days of Room to Read is Jim Collins's *Good to Great*. As Collins writes, everything begins and ends with great leadership. His model for what he terms "Level 5 Leadership" touches on an aspect of leadership that is not discussed enough in the social sector: Charisma is overemphasized. To drive profound and lasting change, a leader needs to have the mix of personal humility and professional will. Personal humility, Collins says, is about inspired standards, not inspired charisma. The leader focuses on the organization more than the self and apportions credit for success appropriately. Professional will, Collins describes, is about a commitment to superb, long-term results, apportioning responsibility for poor results adequately, and looking inward rather than outward.

By heeding the insight into the Level 5 leadership style Collins highlights in *Good to Great*, ESEs can become less reliant on these charismatic characteristics and instead focus on leadership skills that lead more enduring collective movements. Scaling world change is a team sport, and it is not just about the leader or even the leader's ideas alone. Organizations need to make room early in an organization's life cycle to build, value, and recognize a world-class winning team.

Selection of recommended reading from our country management conferences

Good to Great by Jim Collins
Built to Last by Jim Collins
Forces for Good by Leslie Crutchfield and Heather McLeod Grant
Five Dysfunctions of a Team by Patrick Lencioni

(continued)

Selection of recommended reading from our country management conferences (*Continued*)

The Oz Principle by Roger Connors, Tom Smith, and Craig Hickman

Managing Transitions: Making the Most of Change by William Bridges

Scaling Up Excellence by Hayagreeva Rao

Beyond the Idea by Vijay Govindarajan and Chris Trimble

Attracting Top Talent

Collins also came up with the bus analogy of organizational development that we frequently referenced in our early start-up years. "The Good to Great organizations first got the right people on the bus in the right places and then figured out where to drive," he wrote. Good executives we knew focused on strategy, managing teams and deliverables, and always, always, always keeping an eye out for talent to attract the best and brightest to their organizations.

To this day, even with more than 1,500 full-time employees around the world, we spend an enormous level of effort attracting top talent. Many staff comment after joining the Room to Read team that our recruiting process was one of the lengthier and more extensive processes they have endured. We used to question whether we should change this. Several organizational development consultants over the years have advised us to shorten our recruiting process to get people in the door faster. We have chosen to stick with our practice, however, and now it has become a source of pride and a hallmark of how we have built an incredible team.

At our global office headquarters, we follow generally recommended best practices in recruiting. Those include clear job specifications; a wide sourcing of candidates, particularly drawing on outreach to our networks for referrals; screening of candidates by our human resource department to ensure candidates meet minimum criteria and demonstrate a close cultural "fit"; surfacing red flags (often salary, title, or relocation issues) that may be deal breakers; at least two rounds of interviews; and thorough formal and informal reference and background checks.

We do two things consistently that have helped us immensely to make good hiring decisions. One is to prioritize organizational culture fit. We always have at least one colleague outside the hiring department participate on the interview panel to provide input into that fit. Second, our final-round interview is an intensive, eye-opening day. Candidates who make it to the final round all have the minimum qualifications for the listed job, so at that point we are more interested in determining who we think will best fill the role and fit culturally into Room to Read.

Additionally, the day is about giving the candidate the opportunity to get to know us and make sure they understand our expectations. We want them to be enthusiastic about joining the team. The final-round day starts with a presentation the candidate delivers to the entire interview panel. We give the candidate a presentational prompt several days earlier that represents a real, on-the-job situation or strategic activity that would be typical for the position. We ask them to walk us through how they would develop a solution.

Often the interview panel will play different roles as part of the session, acting as demanding government officials or skeptical potential investors and asking tough questions. This part of the interview process can be intense, but it gives us the opportunity to really get to know the candidates and evaluate how they strategically approach problems, conduct research, think through solutions, and articulate their perspectives. The candidate then spends the rest of the day in interviews. If a candidate makes it through the end of the day and is still energized and excited to work for Room to Read, we know the person will be a good fit for our dynamic, fast-paced work environment.

We put a lot of effort into recruiting at Room to Read and created our recruiting process early in our organizational history and have used it consistently throughout the different stages of growth. It is one of the few things that has not changed much as we have matured.

When we do hire the wrong person for a job—which can sometimes be the case since interviewing is a very artificial situation—we try to part ways quickly. This is rare and tends to be because people don't cope well with our demanding work environment rather than to any shortcomings in skills. We try to be up front in our interview process and screen for strong organizational cultural fit, but it can be difficult at times to separate the "talkers" from the "doers" until they are on the job. Preserving the strength of our culture is key, and allowing poor performers to remain brings down the whole team. Hire slowly and, when necessary, part ways quickly, has worked for us as a basic principle.

This recruiting process is for our global office headquarters. In Asia and Africa, the employment markets and talent pools can be very different. Local country staff members who are experienced and have the capacity to guide and inspire change in the educational system in their country are even more key to our success. Although the global office is often involved in hiring senior country management positions, country management teams have a lot of latitude in hiring as they are best placed to assess talent in their markets.

This process of recruiting locally works efficiently and effectively. Over the years, we have built a strong reputation for being a preferred employer in the nonprofit sector. In India, for example, for three years in a row from 2015 to 2017 we placed in the top 10 in the nonprofit category of the "Great Place to Work Award," which is determined by anonymous surveys of organizations' staff. India is a country with a very competitive nonprofit sector. Given that Room to Read India is our largest country operation, this has been a great honor.

To align our various Room to Read office hiring practices, we focus on three areas. First, we have a collaborative hiring process for senior staff in country offices to ensure we are getting a person with the best technical skills for each position as well as someone who can successfully work in a global organization. Second, we have always remained committed to hiring local nationals to staff our country offices. This practice ensures we are building local capacity, demonstrates our trust in and respect for our local staff, and promotes great in-country relationships with our government and local partners.

Our third area of focus in recruiting is onboarding new hires. Building a quality onboarding process across all offices is challenging due to differences in language and work practices. However, we have tried to develop a process that recognizes the key information every employee needs to know irrespective of location (such as mission, strategy, program overview, global structure, key worldwide policies) as well as the office- and job-specific information they must understand (for example, country program overview, local operational guidelines and policies, local application of information technology systems, and office customs).

Although people management is still a work in progress for us, many of our investors and partners who visit our country sites say that they are most impressed and surprised with the quality of our staff, and that the same passion and dedication was in evidence everywhere in the organization. As one investor said after witnessing Room to Read's work in Laos:

> I was blown away by how hard-working, extremely driven, and motivated the Room to Read Laos team was. Each had a personal

story for why they cared so much about ensuring children had more educational opportunities in Laos, many relating to the fact that they were the first person in their family to gain a higher education. And given the bureaucracy and frustrations I experienced traveling in Laos, I found myself wondering how Room to Read managed to find staff that had a can-do approach.

Retaining and Scaling Top Talent as You Grow

In countries with more developed economies, people make a deliberate choice to go into the nonprofit sector. Employees are (usually) forgoing higher salaries and have other options. However, expectations are also high that they will be doing meaningful, impactful work. In countries with lower-income economies, where top talent is often looking for financial opportunities, generally to pull their families out of poverty, it can be hard to attract the most capable people. You simply can't compete with the private sector on salary. In both situations, retaining talent is difficult.

Interestingly, research has identified that the talent gap is one of the few things that gets worse as social enterprises mature. At the 2016 Global Entrepreneurship Summit, the Silicon Valley–based foundation RippleWorks revealed that access to talent and funding are by far the two toughest challenges for social entrepreneurs, but talent is the lone challenge that gets tougher as companies mature. The RippleWorks Human Capital Crisis Report in 2016 captured perspectives of more than 600 social entrepreneurs and investors in 59 countries. A full 63% of young, unfunded companies and 75% of funded, early-stage companies believe the inability to access the talent they need will have high or critical impact on their businesses. This talent challenge eclipses funding as the number one challenge as companies mature. RippleWorks found that 45% of later-stage entrepreneurs find accessing talent to be very or extremely challenging, up from 25% of early-stage entrepreneurs.

In our start-up years, we were simply focused on just getting the right people on the bus and building our founding team. However, in our transition years, to build the larger global team, we prioritized retaining talent as long as possible.

Our human resource long-range plan identified several principles that helped us create a more sustainable, productive, and healthy work environment as we grew.

Never Lose Focus on Culture as You Grow   Keeping your finger on the pulse of the organization is important to ensure you are continuing to nurture a dynamic, thriving culture. At Room to Read we use annual staff satisfaction surveys to get regular feedback. We analyze the results and ask each country office to pick areas to work on based on staff feedback. Some years it is related to benefits, or access to and communication with management. Other years it might be requests for more team-building activities or career-development opportunities. For the sake of transparency, we share a summary of the staff-satisfaction survey with everyone in the organization. We ask for their ideas on how to address the areas of greatest need and take ownership in the solutions. Organizational culture can be led from the top but needs ownership by all to be sustainable.

We have also found over the years that creating a sense of community in the office requires time and space. Since the earliest days of Room to Read, we have scheduled regular "all-hands" staff meetings at the global office (see text box).

We know our efforts of building a strong culture pay off when former staff members check back in with us after working at other places. Receiving messages like the one below makes it all worth it:

> Erin!
>
> I truly appreciate and am grateful for my Room to Read experience. It is the gold standard by which I compare all organizations

I've worked at before and since. I've worked with incredible people doing all sorts of important work but Room to Read is such a unique and special sauce. The values—knowing our numbers, getting the right people on the bus, asking for forgiveness rather than permission, treating "nos" as "not-yets"—are ones I continue to incorporate in my work, no matter where I am or what I am doing.

Jenny

Always have a Hiring Plan in Mind for the Next Growth Phase As entrepreneurs, our mindset is often to hold back from hiring, conserve resources, and try to stretch the team as much as possible because we never know when funding is going to run out. It took us a long time at Room to Read to realize we were on a sustainable growth path, that we weren't going to go out of business next month, and that we needed to plan so we weren't constantly overwhelming and burning out the team. As one of our early board members told us regularly at board meetings, "Organizations scale; people don't." He would ask us what is the next set of key hires we would make if money were no object. In our high-growth transition phase, we were often doubling staff worldwide annually, and it was important to have a plan for how to bifurcate roles and keep up with our growth.

Create Time to Manage As leaders, a big part of our job is getting the best out of people. Yet, it is often the reality that this just adds to one's workload, without acknowledgment of or appreciation for how much time it takes. At Room to Read, we have developed staffing models to analyze each staff member's workload. A staffing model is a tool that clarifies the major activities in employees' jobs and how much time it takes to complete those activities. This tool then allows employees to discuss with their supervisors whether this is a reasonable workload or whether expectations of the role need to be defined differently.

We have by no means solved the heavy workload problem, but the staffing model process is helping us set clearer and more realistic expectations of the duties of each position. Staffing models allow managers to reprioritize or eliminate tasks that are no longer necessary or have as high an impact.

Power of One-on-One Meetings   One of the best ways to prioritize management responsibilities and hold people accountable (in a supportive way) is to conduct one-on-one (1:1) meetings regularly between managers and the people who report directly to them. Room to Read sets the expectation with all managers worldwide to conduct regular 1:1 meetings with each direct report to support employees in their work activities, address concerns, and deepen relationships. This may seem obvious, but we've found that management practices vary widely around the world. Creating the expectations of frequent 1:1s is a simple management practice that promotes the very important relationships between managers and their team members. In fact, surveys indicate that the relationship between team members and their supervisors is one of the highest determining factors of turnover risk.

We provide guidelines for conducting effective 1:1s. The key is to reserve a time for an uninterrupted, high-quality discussion between the manager and the employee. They discuss project updates and deadlines, troubleshoot any challenges, recognize the employee's accomplishments, and discuss professional-development opportunities. As needed, 1:1s can also be used to check in on individual employees' wellness, morale, and career goals. It is the hope that these regular meetings ensure periodic performance reviews do not contain any surprises but are just a continuation of a great ongoing management relationship.

Tool for building your organizational culture: All-hands staff meetings

A simple but effective way to engage your staff and build a strong organizational culture, sense of team, and connection to the mission is holding regular "all-hands" staff meetings. We have done this at our global office headquarters since the early days when we could all fit around one table until the present—when we are spread out around the world. Nevertheless, the need still exists (maybe even more so today) to be aligned in our priorities. A meeting like this goes a long way in sustaining staff morale, optimism, and motivation. Here are a few tips to make this meeting useful:

Frequency: We used to meet weekly when we were small, then every other week when we grew bigger. Now that our global office includes more than 140 people across multiple continents (with approximately 70 in our San Francisco office), we have monthly meetings. We vary between mornings and afternoons to offer staff members in different time zones the ability to call in at convenient hours for their locations. We also record the meetings so people can listen at their leisure and send out notes by e-mail of the highlights of the meeting.

Structure: Our meeting lasts an hour and a half (now that it is monthly), and the general structure is:

- **Welcome and introductions to any new staff.** The hiring manager introduces the new person and provides a high-level overview on his or her background; the new hire shares a "fun fact" we wouldn't know from reading a résumé. Fun facts can be very enlightening about a person's personality, such as they are a triathlete, speak six languages, or once competed in a national rock-paper-scissors competition.

- **General updates.** We try not to make updates a laundry list of what every department is working on but instead keep it to key updates from management on larger, cross-departmental initiatives that impact a lot of people. Each department has its own regular meetings where topics can be discussed in more depth.
- **Deep dive into a key topic.** These are 20- to 30-minute presentations that educate the team about important elements of our work. Examples would be training on a new computer application, overview of our newly updated website, or sharing of our annual monitoring and evaluation metrics.
- **Stories of inspiration.** These stories are kept to five minutes and focus on programs (someone shares photos and talks through recent visit to a country office), fundraising (share results from recent event or anecdote of a family raising money for us), or an exciting media/social media win. The goal is to connect us to why we do the work we do.
- **Shout-outs.** We close each meeting with "shout-outs," in which staff can recognize someone who went above and beyond the call of duty on a project. We also like to highlight great cross-departmental collaboration. This is how we reinforce our core values and recognize the behaviors that make Room to Read a special place to work.

(continued)

Tool for building your organizational culture: All-hands staff meetings (*Continued*)

Tips: Remember, an all-hands staff meeting represents a large amount of time when you multiply the 60 or 90 minutes across all the staff members who attend it. It also requires a great deal of planning. An administrative assistant runs our meetings, and part of that person's role is to ensure any presenters are well prepared. We also try to mix it up. Sometimes we play team-bonding games for people attending in person, or invite in guest speakers on a topic. One of our most popular all-hands meeting activities is to invite a panel of three or four of our investors to join us. We ask them why they invest in Room to Read, and what we could do better to engage and involve them. Their insights are always interesting.

As we have entered a more mature stage of development, we have continued to emphasize the importance of investing in a sustained and engaged workforce. Some current practices that seem to be having promising results include the following.

Grow Leaders from Within Our long-range human resources plan included developing a series of tools for building capacity faster. In addition to job descriptions and staffing models, we have integrated an individual development plan process into our performance-management system. Staff members set business goals each year, which are evaluated during performance reviews. Individuals also establish goals for developing skills the organization has identified as important for their positions.

We call these skills "organizational competencies," and they include attributes like adaptability, team leadership, analytical thinking, being results oriented, or leading and managing change.

One of our biggest challenges has been building the skills of our junior staff members so that they're less dependent on more senior staff members. Our goal is to have trained and empowered employees at all levels so we can drive decision making down to the lowest possible level. This is challenging globally. We are constantly hiring across a wide variety of staff levels, and local labor markets can be thin on talent. Growing leaders from within has become our best option for building the qualified, high-performing teams we need.

Luckily, the chair of our emeritus board and one of the longest, most generous investors in Room to Read is a big believer in supporting our teams. She has funded the building of these systems, as well as the designing and facilitation of mandatory supervisory training for all supervisors. She calls this management training program the "no whining" program, because we give managers all the support and resources they have requested. This is a far cry from the early complaints we received about not investing enough in our staffs' professional development.

Focus on Accountability   One aspect of management that is not discussed enough is accountability. Much of what we have talked about relates to an organization adequately supporting its staff. But this is a two-way street. Managers must hold staff members accountable for delivering results. The culture must be high-performing. Central in doing this is creating an environment in which staff members understand the idea of "functional conflict," where healthy, constructive disagreement between groups or individuals is encouraged. Leaders also must address underperforming staff members directly and in a timely fashion. We have found this very challenging but worth it.

Our experience is that nonprofit leaders often go to great lengths to avoid conflict. Possibly this is because we are all working to "do good." Presuming good intentions all around, it is sometimes hard to promote functional conflict. And cross-culturally this is also difficult for the reasons we have mentioned previously about cultures varying in how direct and open they are at dealing with disagreement. We have persisted, though, at trying to create an open environment where we set goals and expectations, are transparent when they are not met, and reflect and discuss solutions. Keeping debates respectful and focused on the specific work at hand helps to move away from the personal or cultural and stresses accountability.

Don't Forget Internal Communications If supporting an engaged staff seems complicated and time consuming, rest assured that it is! Unfortunately, as any leader knows, and as the research supports, growing one's talent base is one of the hardest tasks you face running an ESE. Yet it is necessary, as you can't simply keep asking your people to do more with limited time and resources. As we put these human resource systems in place during our transitional phase, we realized we also needed to communicate how the pieces all fit together, and how they were of value to staff members, particularly managers. We didn't want these tools and training to become just another check-the-box exercise that creates unnecessary bureaucracy. We needed an internal marketing plan—an internal communications function—to help Room to Read's management communicate better with all staff members around the world.

We first developed an annual calendar of how often and in what ways the global office management team wanted to communicate with the staff members in the individual countries. We focused on taking a thoughtful, considered approach to communications with staff where we shared the right amount of information at the right times to keep them informed and engaged in key organization-wide initiatives. We agreed on a monthly e-mail from the global office to the country management teams. We also created a quarterly internal newsletter that would go to all staff members. We call the newsletter the "Yak Bell," referencing our founding in Nepal where you can hear yak bells when trekking in the mountains.

The monthly e-mail enables our global office to give each country office management team updates on key events. Each country management team can then communicate the information to staff members using the language and in a manner that is best understood locally. The newsletter focuses more on celebrating accomplishments in each office, sharing best practices and fun facts and stories that build a global sense of being a part of the Room to Read family. In recent Yak Bell issues, we have featured the following stories about our amazing country teams:

- Room to Read's Bangladesh Girls' Education Program participants recently shattered the national pass rate for the country's secondary certificate exams. The pass rate for the 110 girls was 85%, while the national rate was 72%.
- Room to Read Cambodia recently conducted a "Writing Storybooks for Early Grade Readers" training course, which brought together writers from all over the country to learn the technical skills required to write various types of stories, and how to be creative to capture young readers' interest.
- Room to Read Nepal colleagues recently celebrated National Library Day with a "Drop Everything and Read" campaign across four districts to highlight the importance of libraries in shaping the culture of reading in school communities. Students read more than 10,000 books during the event.
- One of Room to Read Tanzania's social mobilizers, Neema, was highlighted for attending the London Room to Read Gala as a presenter. She was proud to represent her country and said, "I am helping girls to overcome challenges that

might have otherwise held them back from being competent and confident individuals. I am thankful to Room to Read for giving me a chance to live my dream and, most importantly, for helping all these young girls to take a step in achieving their long-term dreams."

The Yak Bell also introduces new staff hired around the world and provides links to recent blogs, newly released videos of our work, and media stories. After reading any given edition of the newsletter, it is hard not to be in awe of all that is happening in the Room to Read world and excited to be part of the team.

Founder's Syndrome

Founder's syndrome. What is it and what can be done about it? With Room to Read headquarters in the San Francisco Bay Area, arguably the start-up capital of the world, this is certainly not a problem for social enterprises alone. It is a popular term you hear to describe the difficulties that can be encountered by an organization when its founders retain so much power and influence that they risk holding the organization back from evolving into a more mature one. It often afflicts nonprofits to a greater degree, however, because nonprofit leadership can be so personality driven. In addition, founders can sometimes stay involved longer than is ideal because there are no clear financial metrics that boards can use to ask a founder to step aside.

Founders provide vision, strategy, connections, and motivation in those critical start-up years when many organizations struggle to survive. Your founding story serves the organization by building momentum that is necessary for growth and development. However, it is important to evolve your organization's story as you grow. At Room to Read, as we built a strong, diversified team globally with a full management structure and local country leadership—a team that learned and innovated as we evolved—we could have done a better job sharing our more complete and complex narrative.

The challenge then became that we were victims of our own success. People saw Room to Read as "that organization that builds schools and libraries." We struggled to move beyond those early associations to ensure people understand the depth and breadth of our approach. We trained teachers, worked with governments to increase the quality of their early-grade literacy instruction, and the strength of our Girls' Education Program was our life-skills curriculum. It has been harder for people to get as excited about the many, many years of attempting new things, failing, iterating, and identifying methods that worked. That is the real story of most successful organizations that make it past the initial start-up stage. So, we've received benefits from our founding story, but there have also been other needs.

The greatest need was making sure everyone felt valued and part of our success. Even as a founding team, we did not do a great job of recognizing our own unique combination of complementary skills. Dinesh demonstrated strong local leadership in the field, which built respect and trust that is now core to our organization's approach. John envisioned big goals, and he attracted other people to the cause. He tirelessly focused on building a global network to support our work. Erin was the systems and process person. She was a team builder and motivator, detail oriented and highly focused on quality execution.

As we evolved, we should have done a better job recognizing the incredibly dedicated early team that worked beyond their limits to heroically build Room to Read. Many of our first key hires stayed with the organization for years. They became our "cultural whisperers" who created and spread our organizational culture. They were a positive magnet for new hires and a model for how to succeed at Room to Read.

As we realized we needed to move beyond our cofounders' initial ideas to grow and evolve, we worked harder to share the story of our team effort. We wanted staff members to push back at us—even though we were the founders, with new ideas or suggestions for improvement. We feel strongly that staff members should be encouraged to innovate. We try to have the team feel rooted in the founding values of Room to Read but not constrained that they should act in any specific way.

Some may ask why this is a problem if the founders are still dedicated to the cause. One simple answer is the "hit by the bus" test, meaning that if anything were to happen to the founders, would the sustainability of the organization be at risk? Perhaps the greater issue, though, is that the founders can't do everything. If they attempt to, the organization would not be able to evolve and grow to its maximum potential. It is important to create space for new leaders to come into the organization and be given increasing levels of authority to avoid bottlenecks as the organization grows.

What do we recommend doing about founder's syndrome? Some of the ways we at Room to Read have tried to address it, sometimes messily, have been as follows.

Employ the Principles of "Adaptive Leadership" Being a good leader throughout the different stages of organizational development means figuring out how to embrace, adapt, and even thrive in a challenging and ever-changing environment. Adaptive leadership is a model that emerged from more than 30 years of research at Harvard University by Dr. Ron Heifetz and Marty Linsky. Founders and ESE leaders need to improve their leadership skills continually and adapt different tactics as their organizations evolve. At Room to Read, we have long related our experiences to a child's development from baby (start-up years) to pretween and teen years (transitional stage), to adult maturity. Just like a child growing up, leaders must adapt their behavior and assume different responsibilities at different stages. Many of our key leaders have worked with executive coaches and have undergone 360-degree feedback assessments to ensure they can adapt. Since the passion and enthusiasm of the founders is important fuel for the organization, the roles of the founders over time can move from visionary entrepreneurs to motivators of the team, and, ultimately, to being keepers of the organizational culture.

Value Everyone's Contributions from the Beginning   It is important to deeply understand the value of the team effort and how vital strong collaboration is to successfully scale an organization. Always strive to make it less about you and more about the team.

Build a Strong Management Team   As early as possible, hire senior talent that is independent minded and brings new skills and fresh perspectives to the organization. Then—and this is the hard part—truly empower them by giving them responsibility to run important aspects of the organization. Create an environment that values learning and organizational evolution. It is key to not just give this lip service and dictate that as founders, "this is what we want." Instead, you must allow senior talent to change things and make decisions that are different from what the founders would have done. And as founders, be open to your role, responsibilities, and title changing to create space for new senior-level talent. This will set the organization up for moving beyond start-up mode into the mature phase.

Discuss Founder and CEO Succession Planning Openly
At the board-of-director level and with the management team, discuss succession planning for the founders, CEO, and any key senior positions. Several of the social entrepreneur networks estimate approximately 40% of their organizations are now managed by CEOs who succeeded the founders. It is likely to happen eventually, so planning for it transparently is best. We regularly discuss the idea at Room to Read that the goal is to have more leadership in more places. This messaging needs to

come right from the top, so we discuss succession planning for all the senior-most roles. If you don't focus on it, you won't be prepared for it, which will make it infinitely more difficult when senior staff members leave. And discussing it helps to minimize the perception that anyone is indispensable to the organization.

Check in Regularly to See How Much Fuel Is Left in Your Own Tank One of the dark secrets of social entrepreneurship is that no matter how hard you work, the world will still never be a perfect place. Social entrepreneurs must pace themselves and find an ebb and flow in their work. Just as life is not a sprint but a marathon, so too is world change. Don't give up your life. Nothing replaces being present for your family and for yourself. Burn-out is an epidemic in the nonprofit space. Learn to recognize the signs when you hit it. It is better to leave your organization on a high note than to stay too long and hold the organization back. As a founder, Erin also says it feels reassuring to think about and plan for your exit strategy. Being the key person in charge of an organization is hard, and envisioning how and to whom you might transition leadership makes it feel less so.

When leadership, succession planning, and everything else that leaders of ESEs must do seems simply too overwhelming, then seek out your tribe of other social entrepreneurs who have lived through similar experiences. They will have great suggestions about how to build resilience, remain curious, and remain engaged in the work.

Key Takeaways

- Setting clear **core values** and building a strong **organizational culture** are central to a productive and sustainable organization. You need to **evaluate your organization's culture** continually and make necessary changes as the organization evolves.

- A key area to focus on in sustaining a vibrant culture is **internal communication** at all levels: one-on-one meetings, management communications, "all-hands" staff meetings, and worldwide staff communications.
- **Organizations with global operations** have an even harder job developing consistent organizational cultures, but when done, this helps a lot in terms of collaboration.
- Leaders of ESEs should tap into their **strong empathy skills** and develop ways to use their personal influence to **inspire and motivate** a team effort around their cause.
- Great leaders need a balance of personal humility and professional will to succeed, as Jim Collins stated in *Good to Great*. This combination will ensure the focus is on **developing more enduring collective movements**.
- **Hire slowly and part ways quickly**, if necessary. Develop a **customized recruiting process** for your organization that selects the best candidates to fit into the work culture, and use it consistently to build **a strong, cohesive team**.
- Develop a **long-range plan for managing human capital** that prioritizes where to invest to support a more sustainable, engaged, and healthy work environment. It is important to put systems and processes in place for managing human resources while being conscientious to not create too much bureaucracy. Remember that **organizations scale; people don't**.
- Maximize the power of your founding story and founder(s), but also recognize when their contributions begin to diminish. Address the issue **of building strong leaders beyond the founders early and openly** to create a culture that can innovate and accelerate beyond the initial programs and structure. Founders and **key leaders need to adapt their leadership and hire in new talent continually** to meet the evolving needs of your organization.

8

Fundraising: Defining and Selling the Value Proposition

The room grows quiet. The lights dim. We have 15 precious minutes to motivate this crowd of more than 250 people gathered at the City Club in the Financial District of San Francisco on this warm April evening to become Room to Read supporters. Most people have come from directly from work. Approximately half the people in the room have already invested in Room to Read and are eager for an update on our progress. Many have brought friends and colleagues along to introduce them to Room to Read. The anticipation is high that this will be another successful evening raising much-needed funds for our work, which means that pressure is also high for Erin to deliver an inspirational presentation.

She starts with the need: Approximately one out of every seven people on this planet cannot read or write. Two-thirds are women and girls. More than 60 million children woke up this morning and didn't go to school. The world is not set up to be fair to children, and many lose opportunities at very early ages as they do not have access to quality education in their local communities. Erin drives home the point that at Room to Read we believe education is a basic human right. There is no way to reach one's full potential in life without it. There is no way for a community to break the cycle of poverty without ensuring that the next generation is educated. Many in the crowd vigorously nod in agreement.

After we get the audience fired up about the issue, we explain that Room to Read has a scalable, replicable solution. We describe our programs in literacy and gender equality in education and share the impact we are having both in terms of data as well as powerful and emotional anecdotes of the children, teachers, and families with whom we are partnering to transform schools. In every presentation, we focus on the efficiency and effectiveness of what we do. We share that we have strong local leadership managing each of our countries, that we partner with the government in each country to ensure our programs are sustainable, and that we run ourselves like a local nonprofit to ensure most of our funds are going directly to high-quality programs. We seize this opportunity to tell the Room to Read story by engaging people's heads and hearts. And then we ask for their partnership and support. In many of these presentations, we quote visionaries like Nelson Mandela, who said it best: "Education is the most powerful weapon which you can use to change the world."

We go through this case for support in one form or another at fundraising events and in boardrooms or coffee shops with individual investors, whenever and wherever the opportunity presents itself. We have been telling the Room to Read story for more than a decade and a half, hundreds of times a year across multiple countries, raising awareness and resources for our cause. We do it because it works. We raise more than $50 million annually. On that evening in San Francisco, we raised more than $450,000, the equivalent of funding more than 9,000 children in our early-grade reading program, or 1,500 participants in our Girls' Education Program for a year.

We focus relentlessly on growing and engaging our support base because we know that nothing gets done without active investors who care just as deeply about our mission as we do. We call them "investors" at Room to Read instead of donors because we believe they should feel fully vested in the organization and our work. Since day one at Room to Read, cultivating, engaging, and stewarding our investors is one of the most important things we do. In the past several years, more than 75% of our funds have come from nearly 275 individuals, corporations, and foundations with whom we interact regularly. They are a key part of why Room to Read has been able to grow.

As every social entrepreneur knows, unlocking financial resources to support one's mission is essential to operating a social enterprise. Yet it is one of the areas we all struggle with the most. It is also one of the most difficult activities to scale.

Fundraising Is *Not* a Dirty Business

It is surprising to us how many people ask, "Do you like fundraising?" They say it with the same disdain, as if they were asking, "Do you like getting your teeth cleaned?" or "Do you like eating Brussels sprouts?"—something they know they are supposed to do because it is good for them but dread it all the same. In many organizations, fundraising is considered the evil business of asking for money to do the fun part of implementing great programs.

We need to change our mindset and come up with a new paradigm around fundraising. We need to embrace it as the fuel that feeds our engine to change the world for the better. Fundraising is *fun*. Seriously. Think of it like this. Let's assume we all want to have a positive impact on the world. Many of us think about the legacies we want to leave behind at the end of our lives. We all see things in the world every day that we wish we could change for the better. Investing and supporting the work of great nonprofits is one very efficient way to have that desired impact. Not everyone can be so lucky to have a full-time job directly working in a nonprofit solving social problems every day (although we highly recommend it!). But by asking people to invest, you give everyone the opportunity to be part of a social change movement in some way.

When we go into fundraising meetings, we think of ourselves as solution providers. Solving problems, building partnerships, and focusing on solutions is fun and empowering, right? In fundraising, we say that everyone has the "Four T's" (their time, talent, treasure, and ties to their networks) to contribute. Investors want to direct those Four T's toward a cause that has meaning for them. We as fundraisers are here to partner with investors to figure out how to do that through a well-managed organization that is doing quality work in an impactful way. That is a win-win for the investor and for the nonprofit.

We consider fundraising and program delivery part of everyone's job at Room to Read. A strong culture of fundraising has been a central part of our success. We tell everyone in the organization that they wear two hats, a program one and a fundraising one, and should thus feel ownership of both. Every person in the organization should be able to understand how he or she is helping to reach more children with better education efficiently and effectively. And, likewise, everyone should be able to articulate with passion and clarity why Room to Read is a great investment.

Our country staff host investors regularly at Room to Read field offices to directly discuss the impact and value of their financial contributions. Our development staff members also visit our work so they can have firsthand examples to share with investors of the quality and effectiveness of our programs. We encourage each staff member to think, "How can I ensure in my role that I am doing everything I can to further our work for the communities we partner with and the investors that support us?"

When we were smaller, we went through times when all headquarter staff members helped in fundraising efforts, especially in the fourth quarter of the year when charitable giving is at its peak. Staff members from all departments were part of "Thank-a-Thon" sessions in which we would make appreciation phone calls to investors or write thank-you notes. In our staff meetings, we shared stories about successful fundraising events and read letters from our investors to personalize who they are and why they care about investing in our cause. We rang a yak bell from Nepal, our first country of operations, in the office when we received a sizable gift in the early years. And now, even though we are larger and spread out in offices around the world, we e-mail news about investors' commitments across offices so the whole team can be aware, learn from each other's wins, and celebrate.

How did Room to Read build such a strong, private base of investors? In this chapter, we summarize our fundraising history into three phases and share our essential fundraising tips in each of them. These different phases are primarily differentiated by the size of our fundraising budget and the resulting complexity in our staff, fundraising activities, and the barriers we needed to overcome. The first phase is the lean-and-mean start-up years. The second is the rapid year-over-year transitional growth phase. And the third is the maturing and stabilizing phase.

Phase I Fundraising Best Practices: The Lean Start-Up Years (Approximately $0–$3 Million)

Key Strategies

If you have less than $3 million in your annual operating budget, we would define your entrepreneurial social enterprise as a start-up. Our experience is that organizations function quite differently with this size of operations. The start-up phase comes with great cachet, and it is important to capitalize on the enthusiasm and excitement investors have for supporting visionary leaders and the new, bold ideas that they bring with them. Following are some initial building blocks that Room to Read found important to put into place at that time.

Leverage the Passion of the Founders As social entrepreneurs who founded the organization, we were our greatest fundraising asset. Everyone wanted to hear directly from us: our vision, what we had accomplished so far, and what high mountain we planned to tackle next. We worked hard to inspire everyone we met to invest. In this phase, fundraising and networking should take at least 50% of the founding team's time to obtain the kind of breakthrough funding required to fuel a start-up.

Engage Your Personal Networks We found it important to become comfortable with tapping into our personal and professional networks and asking for money. People invest in people, not necessarily causes, in the early years of an organization. It is necessary to find ways to approach one's friends, family, old colleagues, school and professional association alumni networks, and so on. We honed our pitch with any audience that would host us and then kept widening the circles. And we had to remember not to just tell our story but to be sure to close with an "ask" for them to invest in Room to Read. The number one mistake made in fundraising is that people don't directly ask for contributions.

Focus on Fewer Types of Funding One of the best things we did during this phase was not to spread ourselves too thinly by going after many different funding sources. Like other aspects of

Room to Read, we focused on where our potential for impact was greatest. Most organizations in their first year or two find a type of funding that is most closely associated with their mission and organizational approach. At Room to Read, we broadly define the types of funding sources as individual investors, corporate investors, foundations, and government/institutional investors. Each source requires a different way of soliciting, engaging, and reporting. Even the "individual investor" category can be broken into subcategories of major gifts or smaller annual fund investors. Early on, we developed a strong skill set in soliciting individual major gifts greater than $10,000. As a thinly staffed start-up, it is stressful to go after too many types of funding streams simultaneously, as the organization doesn't have capacity to steward them all well. We found our sweet spot: On average, in our first decade, 70% of Room to Read funding was from individuals.

Have a Clear Plan   It was essential to have a well-thought-out theory of change accompanied by a business plan. Investors want to understand the intended impact an organization is striving to achieve and how that impact will be measured. They also want to understand the business plan for how you will grow the organization to maximize the impact over time. A road map for scale is thus essential. One of the things that Room to Read did well was to create a simple, compelling, well-articulated pitch for what we were doing, why it mattered, and how to measure our progress and success. We stuck to our initial model of establishing school libraries and keeping more girls in school in low-income countries long enough to build a large and enthusiastic base of supporters.

Underpromise and Overdeliver   This has always been a key rule at Room to Read. As we set goals—programs, organizational growth, financial projections, and so on—we tried to be realistic yet ambitious. Pie-in-the-sky goals without a clear ability to achieve them can lead to disappointed investors. Likewise, slow progress doesn't inspire a movement to gather behind your cause. Bold goals attract bold people, as we often say at Room to Read. The trick is to be bold and realistic at the same time so the organization can inspire and deliver at the same time.

Connect Investors to the Impact   We created an "adopt-a-project" model in which investors could directly support programmatic work in a country of their choice. This was the hallmark of our success raising support for our work in our early years. We realized we needed to find a way to connect our investors personally with the results of their contributions and to do a good job reporting those results. When investors supported a school library or the construction of a school block, we sent them, within the year, at least one written report on their project—the specific school or library, with pictures and some details of the change that their investment made possible. Videos, stories from beneficiaries, site visits, and events (if engaging individual investors) are also good ways to connect people to the work they are supporting. All investors want to know that their dollars are being spent successfully. The second biggest mistake in fundraising, after not making the ask, is to not report back to investors often or adequately.

Leverage the Power of Volunteers   One of the best things Room to Read did was leverage the power of volunteers in innovative ways. Early in our history, we started a volunteer chapter model. Given our work overseas and our desire was to engage local communities, we did not need volunteers to help directly in implementing our programs. However, we did need to create a global movement behind Room to Read's work to build public awareness and get sufficient financial support. We encouraged chapters to form in different cities, to hold events and outreach activities, and to essentially be our "feet on the street" to build a network of supporters. In our first decade, our chapters collectively raised about a third of our annual operating budget.

Keys to Room to Read's volunteer chapter model

Our chapters lead and organize local fundraising events, participate in global Room to Read initiatives, and build awareness about our mission and programs in their local cities. They primarily focus on two issues: raising funds and building brand awareness. Keys to success of this model are as follows:

- They are geographically based in cities so volunteers can meet and collaborate easily.
- The chapter model is an organic, opt-in model. Individuals come to us to join a chapter or set up a new one in a city that doesn't already have one. Thus, volunteers are self-selected, self-starters, and highly motivated. They have an entrepreneurial mindset that matches Room to Read's own culture.
- Each chapter has usually at least two chapter leaders who act as the liaisons between staff and the other volunteers. Every chapter defines its annual plan: the number of events, what the revenue goals are for the events, and what other activities it is planning. This planning helps drive accountability.
- Our most active and dynamic chapters largely specialize in fundraising events for their locale. Their events run the gamut: large-scale events, such as galas; medium-size benefits for young professionals; or in-home small salon gatherings. They hold grassroots

events, such as film screenings, or come up with their own themed events. Creativity and fun is part of what makes the chapter model thrive.

- Chapters are key to broadening the Room to Read network and building our exposure to new investors. The number one reason people give to a nonprofit is if someone they know introduces them to the organization. We were able to raise funds with individual investors relatively fast and diversify our revenue base internationally because of this model.

- We try to encourage volunteers to know their "super power"—the specific talent they can bring to add value quickly to the collective effort. Maybe it is finding a great venue for an event, or getting donated wine, or making connections to caterers that will donate their services, or soliciting silent auction items, or helping with media outreach. All volunteers are encouraged to engage their networks to get involved and donate.

- We celebrate our chapters when they meet their goals. We hold a chapter leadership conference regularly (every year or two) where we bring the leaders from various cities together for a few days to celebrate their achievements, inspire them, update them on new initiatives happening, and set goals together. We also host special chapter treks to see Room to Read's work and connect them to the mission.

Our chapter model has evolved over the years to connect with the growing trend of peer-to-peer fundraising. We still have chapters that are geographically organized, but now groups have also organized around other themes like bikers in the technology sector or marathon runners.

Connect with Your Peer Group   Room to Read was also lucky to tap into the social entrepreneur funding networks. In an organization's beginning years, it is beneficial to apply for support from foundations that seek to build a network for social entrepreneurs. More recently, there are several great ones, such as Ashoka, the Draper Richards Kaplan Foundation, Echoing Green, New Profit, the Skoll Foundation, the Schwab Foundation for Social Entrepreneurship, and others. We gained valuable, unrestricted funding, skill-building opportunities, credibility, and introductions to attract other funders, as well as a network of like-minded peers going through similar growth pains as us. Our first large investor was the Draper Richards Kaplan Foundation (DRKF). Room to Read was the second organization it funded using a venture philanthropy model of giving $100,000-a-year unrestricted grants for three years as well as joining our board of directors. It absolutely changed the trajectory of Room to Read to be a DRKF-selected social enterprise organization and to have its support and network help us grow and thrive.

Development Department Structure

In this start-up phase, roles overlap, and everyone always has more to do than time to do it. We pulled program staff regularly into investor meetings to help our programs come to life. We trained our in-country staff members to play critical roles in writing investor reports and hosting investor visits. In addition to this team effort, it is important to hire one to two staff members in these early years entirely dedicated to fundraising. Staff members are needed to work with executives, boards, advisors, volunteers, and the most supportive investors to tap into networks to expand the investor base. We found that our best early fundraisers didn't necessarily have professional backgrounds in fundraising, but they were passionate about our mission and skilled in engaging our investors.

Tools and Metrics

Despite our revenue growth at this early stage, we did make the mistake of not asking our earliest investors systematically to make introductions to their networks. It is surprising how rarely this is done. We did have the foresight early on, though, to set up a database to track investor information. This resource has paid dividends over time. We kept it simple but collected and organized basic data. Now there are so many great customer relationship management tools. Some, such as Salesforce, are free for nonprofits for a small number of users, so social entrepreneurs have no excuse not to do this right from the start. Our early investor database was a map of our entrepreneurial lives: "Erin met on shuttle going to the San Francisco airport" or "John sat next to on flight to London." Erin remembers how we celebrated when our first investor spreadsheet reached 1,000 entries. Now our quarterly e-mail newsletter is distributed to more than 110,000 people.

Part of good investor relations is also the appreciation of the natural fundraising cycle. Unless you track an investor's data, it is hard to develop a meaningful stewardship plan. The basic fundraising cycle is meet or be introduced; engage a prospective investor in your cause and organization; solicit that person for a contribution; thank them; stay in touch and report back on progress; ask again for another investment, hopefully increasing support; and repeat cycle. It is not magic, but it requires disciplined work that needs to be recorded and re-evaluated before each new engagement.

The critical metric to track in this first phase of growth is the top-level revenue goal for the organization. At Room to

Read, it didn't matter so much in the early days which fundraiser got credit for which investor's support. The whole team, and organization for that matter, focused on ensuring we made our annual goal … and in most instances, blew it out of the water every year. The team's success was more important than any individual's, and this team culture is one we have maintained ever since.

Phase II Fundraising Best Practices: Rapid Growth Years ($3 Million–$30 Million)

Key Strategies

Rapid growth raises its own challenges. For many years, we were annually doubling our program targets, staff, and (almost) revenue raised. We were excited to have the resources to expand our programs in each country of operations as well as add approximately one new country each year. Our volunteer chapter model was organically expanding into new cities and countries as well. Many of our investors would tell us they continued to give to Room to Read each year because of our focus on results, the quality of our programs, the transparency in sharing our monitoring and impact data (good or bad), and how we were run like a business in terms of operations and financial integrity.

However, the rapid growth for many years prevented us from always being as efficient or strategic as we could have been. In hindsight, here are some of the things we wished we had done better.

Focus on Retaining Investors During our high-growth years, we did not at first focus on keeping our current investors engaged as much as we did on finding new ones. Fundraising is a long game. You must look at every opportunity to keep people engaged in the cause and develop a solid partnership. Often at Room to Read we focused on bringing in new investors through events and outreach, but we didn't spend as much time ensuring we were keeping our current investors informed about our progress.

Later, as we continued to grow, we did start to place a higher priority on retaining investors. We had a loyal and generous base of annual investors, and we focused on reporting back to them on the impact of their investments. This also gave us a key opportunity to discuss with them whether they would like to renew their gift for the coming year, or, hopefully, even increase it. We learned it is much more efficient to continue to energize your existing support base than constantly seek out new supporters.

Diversify Geographically   This was key to our growth and spreading revenue risk in any given year. We diversified globally, largely due to our chapter network's organic growth. When raising money internationally, we learned firsthand there are many cultural differences in fundraising. We have found it important to hire staff locally to help navigate this. We have been in investor meetings in Europe where you never really ask for a gift directly, so "the ask" is done in a much subtler way when following up after a meeting. Of course, Erin was also in a meeting in Hong Kong, where business is conducted quite rapidly, when an investor wrote us a $10,000 check to end the meeting early because he joked he could make more money to give to us if he were trading rather than sitting in a meeting.

Keep Communication Crisp and Clear   At times, we let complexity overtake our core salient messages. As many organizations grow, their story becomes more difficult to explain, but investors have limited time and want to understand the strategy as quickly as possible. Investors expect social entrepreneurs to be able to clearly and succinctly articulate their theories of change, business models, and pathways to scale and impact. We led with what we wanted to accomplish—the big, hairy, audacious goal, as Jim Collins says. And we always also tried to understand investors' desired outcomes and how we could partner to help achieve their goals. The trick is doing this in short meetings and within a few succinct pages of a proposal. Most funding decisions are made by teams that include families, foundation staff, and corporate executives. This means that we must provide investors with compelling information that they can use to do internal sales jobs within their own structures. Providing them with crisp and clear proposals allows them to help make your case. At Room to Read we did not always do this well. We often talked at people, rather than with them. We told them why they should care and invest in us rather than listening for what motivated them to give.

Don't Succumb to Program Creep   On the positive side, we didn't stray too far from our core programs during this growth phase. Often organizations feel they have to be all things to all people to unlock funding. But we have found the exact opposite to be true at Room to Read. What investors like about us is that we are clear about what we do and what we don't do. We are obsessively focused on excellence in our program areas. To be world class in a few key areas takes great effort. To be mediocre in various ways is a lot easier.

Many nonprofits fault investors when they fall into this trap of mediocrity with a story of "The donor asked us to do such and such," or, "We were offered so much funding to do an extension of our program that we just couldn't say no." The reality is one must say no to funding opportunities to be best-in-class in one's field. And the best way to increase one's funding base is to be exactly that: best-in-class in one's field. We worked hard not to veer from our strategy. The cost was too great to our efficiency and effectiveness.

Organizations are made up of people. In the typical nonprofit, you never have enough talented people to do all the things that need to get done. Room to Read is certainly one of the most fast-paced and dynamic places that most of our team has ever experienced. People come to us and want us to do all sorts of requests for "small" extensions to our programs. Can you help us vaccinate children? What about nutrition programs or solar energy at the schools? Can we extend your literacy work to teach adult women? And so on. The answer to whether these are all great, viable ideas in the abstract is probably, "Hell yes!" The answer, however, to whether Room to Read is the best organization to take on the initiative is generally no. It doesn't feel good to say no, but say it on occasion we must if we want to have any hope of achieving excellence at improving literacy and gender equality in education for children.

Use a One-to-One Fundraising Model   Our adopt-a-project fundraising model worked well for Room to Read in these high-growth years. This allows major investors to invest in the organization at a relatively high level, for example $20,000 to $50,000, and see very clearly the school literacy project they are directly supporting, even commemorating their investment with a dedication plaque. They receive a personalized report with the specific name of the school, number of teachers and children impacted, an outline of what materials and training were provided by the organization, and, if they choose, they can even travel and see firsthand the impact of their investment.

The challenge with this model is that we trained our investors to only give at that certain level. Because they were so satisfied with the impact of their investments, we had a hard time upgrading their giving levels year over year. We now have gotten better at providing a vision for larger, transformational gifts in the six-figure annual level for those investors who want to help us with bigger goals. For example, they might fund us expanding into a new geography, or support an important organizational development initiative like a new information technology project to streamline operations or a human resource project that provides customized supervisory training programs for our worldwide staff members. We want our investors to see that at higher levels of investment they can support even broader activities and drive even greater impact.

Development Department Structure

It is also necessary early on in an organization's development to invest in a fundraising team. Most entrepreneurial social enterprises underinvest in building a large enough development team and then wonder why they can't raise more revenue. At this transitional stage of Room to Read's growth, we expanded our development staff to more than 20 people. This was important because fundraising with individuals is staff intensive if you want to manage numerous investor relations properly across multiple geographies.

As another fundraising professional once told us, "Talent is not half the battle; it is the whole battle." Finding and retaining great fundraising staff is one of the hardest things to do in the nonprofit sector. The average tenure for fundraisers in an organization is approximately 18 months. Here are a few tips for what Room to Read looked for when hiring at this stage.

Hire People Who Are Great at Building Relationships and Trust   Giving away money is a very personal decision. We did not hire professional fundraisers as much as people we thought had passion for our mission and desire to inspire others about our cause. Many investors are stressed out with work and life, and we wanted interacting with Room to Read around their philanthropy to be their happy place! We also sought people whom we thought would connect well with our investor base. Can you picture your fundraisers in the office with your investors or socializing in their homes? If you got stuck on a long bus ride with them, would you have a good conversation?

Hire People Who Are Disciplined by Nature and Skilled at Follow-Up Fundraising requires developing a stewardship plan for each investor and running that playbook well and consistently over time.

Give Time to Be Fully Functional When a new fundraiser is hired, we find it takes them time to get to know the portfolio of investors and build a pipeline of new investors. We do not expect to see major additional revenue coming from a new fundraiser for at least 12 months.

Leadership We have learned the hard way that one of the most difficult positions to fill is the head of your development team. Our most successful chief development officers have been promoted from within after proving themselves superior fundraisers when part of the team.

Once a development team is on board, it is important to empower them to manage investors. We call our fundraisers "relationship managers," or RMs for short, because they are the primary architects and drivers for all interactions with the investors with whom they work. We explicitly discuss how they are the main point of contact for their investors as well as the rules of engagement for how they plan to partner with other executives, board members, and staff members to help steward and inspire those investors. Too many people interacting with investors in an unmanaged way can be confusing. But if you can execute a well-planned journey based on investor interests and facilitated by the RM, it will generally end with the investor giving at their maximum potential and developing a trusted relationship with the organization and its people.

We also found it necessary to have a clear system of how to hold RMs accountable. We would define their revenue goals, specify the number of investors they needed to engage, describe the new investor pipeline they needed to build, and articulate the upgrades in giving we sought with current investors. Plus, an RM should always know where investors are in the journey and what the next action should be. Does the investor need a report on how an investment has been spent or a deeper dive on a special topic of interest? Would a site visit be worthwhile or time for the next ask? We set up systems that tracked investor journeys so there is visibility, transparency, and predictability that taken altogether drives accountability.

As you start to hire more staff members to focus on fundraising, the founding team must create space for these fundraisers to manage investor relationships so RMs are not seen as glorified support staff for executives. This does not mean the founding team or key executives don't have an important role in interacting with investors. They absolutely do. But we found that keeping up with our growing investor base required our fundraisers to be the main relationship managers. They needed to develop and drive a clear plan for how the rest of the organization (including founders) should be involved in engaging, inspiring, soliciting, and thanking investors so that all aspects of the relationships are aligned and coordinated.

At Room to Read, we were often too slow at doing this. The founders became bottlenecks to many relationships. The result was that as our investor base grew rapidly, we had too many relationships to manage well, and the development team staff wasn't empowered enough to take the lead. Investors started to fall through the cracks, which is the worst thing that can happen.

Although development staff members need to build their own credibility with their own portfolios of investors, they also need to realize that it can be hard for the founding team to let go. Founders have worked incredibly hard to build a base of support and care deeply about many of these relationships. After all, many of these investors gave money to the organization because they believed in and trusted in the leaders at the outset.

Tools and Metrics

At each stage of our organizational growth, we picked several aspects of our fundraising systems to improve. During our years of rapid growth, we focused on proposal and report writing as well as our investor research capabilities. We customized a project-tracking database so that we could send those well-received, specific adopt-a-project reports with inspiring and informative photos back to investors about the schools they helped support. We also improved other investor communication tools such as our website and annual report and created an annual *Global Results and Impact Report* that shared regular findings from our monitoring and evaluation data for external audiences.

Many companies such as Wealth Engine, Relationship Science, and Foundation Center provide tools to research investors. Doing more research has helped us tailor our requests to potential investors much better. We have also been able to understand which investors in our database had the highest potential to contribute and concentrate our staff time and energy more effectively.

Our fundraising staff members have individual fundraising goals based on their portfolio of investors, the types of investors they work with, and the market they work in. Generally, a midlevel fundraiser raises $1.5 million to $2.5 million per year, and a senior one $2.5 million to $3.5 million. The other metric we watched at this stage was our overhead ratio as we grew our development staff. The age-old debate about overhead in the nonprofit sectors continues. Does it help or harm nonprofits to be evaluated by this metric of how much their fundraising and general administrative costs are as a percentage of their overall spending?

Most people who have worked or invested in the nonprofit space for some time realize that one single measurement such as one's overhead ratio is far too simplistic to quantify the efficiency and effectiveness of an organization. However, those newer to philanthropic investing still often seek out this measurement as a quick and easy way to assess an organization. We think the best way to approach the situation is to not shy away from conversations about overhead but instead to take the opportunity to engage with investors around how the work of the organization is managed.

We tell funders how much our overhead is and ask them directly to build it into their investment in us. Then we share other metrics about the effectiveness of the organization, including output and outcome metrics of our programs, so that the conversation is not just about efficiency but instead is broadened to include our effectiveness in having an impact with our programs.

The key is to communicate to investors what resources are needed to run the organization effectively. We believe we do ourselves a disservice and hold back the development of the nonprofit space in general if we don't communicate what it takes to support and grow an organization in a healthy and sustainable manner.

In our early years, Room to Read didn't do this very well. We tried to survive with a very low overhead, promising to keep our overhead under 10%. Quite frankly, we burned ourselves out. We then realized social change is a marathon, not a sprint. We had to fuel ourselves to last through the marathon. It takes adequate staffing to make an impact and systems and processes to be efficient. When we shared with key investors this conundrum of how to fund our "overhead" and put forward specific areas for which we needed funding such as for a new senior hire, information-technology system, or staff professional development initiative, it allowed our investors to fund our general support and administration in a way that felt tangible and transformational for the organization. Currently, we operate at a 16% to 18% overhead rate in any given year and always strive to remain efficient by keeping it under 20%. This allows us to invest in managing a healthy and sustainable organization.

Phase III Fundraising Best Practices: Maturing and Stabilizing Years ($30 Million–$100+ Million)

Key Strategies

What no one ever tells you about successful fundraising is that it only gets harder. There is a "valley of death" phase in the nonprofit sector as well as the corporate world, a revenue-related aspect of the sophomore slump that we discussed in the introductory chapter. Being based in Silicon Valley, we commonly heard venture capitalists warn about the period when a for-profit start-up company receives an initial financial capital contribution to when it begins generating revenues as the "valley of death," where additional financing is usually scarce. This leaves businesses vulnerable to cash-flow challenges.

As the name implies, being in the valley of death carries with it a high probability that a start-up might die before it can establish a steady stream of revenue. Similarly, as a start-up nonprofit, you can find a lot of interest from investors as an organization is celebrated as the cool innovation. However, as you start to scale your work, establish new geographies, hire more staff, and invest in more research and evaluations, your cost structure increases. Yet it can be challenging to find additional streams of revenue fast enough to cover your increasing operating costs. There is a long stretch where you are no longer the attractive start-up and yet the organization also doesn't have an endowment or secure streams of regular funding. You know you are in the valley of death when you start to hear things like, "You may be too big for us now," or, "You seem so successful, I am not sure my investment will matter as much to you."

No one warned us about the valley of death for nonprofits. We thought that since our programs were higher quality and more efficient and scalable than ever before, we would continue to be able to grow our revenue year over year in the double digits. In almost every way, investors get a higher return on their investment per dollar now in Room to Read than they did in our chaotic start-up years. But philanthropic investing is not always economically rational. In many ways, decisions are made for emotional reasons, and investors like to be part of the start-up trajectory of an organization. It is key at this stage to find ways to stand out at this more mature phase and stabilize your fundraising team and systems to provide sufficient funds year over year to meet organizational needs. Room to Read is still in this phase, and some of the key things that we are doing now include the following.

Diversification of Type of Revenue One of our biggest mistakes earlier in our growth was not diversifying our portfolio of investors so we were not overly dependent on one type, geography, typical gift size, or industry for funding. In our first decade, we found our niche market of major-gift individual fundraising largely tied to the financial sector and went hard and fast at it. When the financial sector encountered challenges in 2008—which led to restructuring of corporate giving as well as reducing salary and bonuses for several years afterward— we felt the pain as well in terms of our ability to raise funds. We picked the type of funding most like our sweet spot to leverage our existing network. For example, we asked individual investors to introduce us to their companies' foundations. We also started an annual fund program (defined as investors who gave less than $5,000 annually) in which people can introduce others in their networks who can give at lower levels. We now have many more investors, individual and corporate, in the technology industry, retail, beauty products, luxury goods, travel, entertainment, and so on.

Brand Building   We focus even more on communicating and building a world-class brand. We spend more time and energy now on thought-leadership activities, public speaking, blogging, and social media to build toward a recognizable, household brand name. Our aim is to be a trusted leader in international education. This focus on raising our profile has inspired our investors to increase their levels of support as well as attract new investors. We have been fortunate to win many awards over the years as well, which has helped provide cachet and credentials that validate our model.

Identify Ambassadors   We work to identify people in our organization and broader network who can be great ambassadors for Room to Read. These ambassadors are our "fund whisperers," or people who can inspire other funders with great stories of how our organization is having impact. There is nothing more important in fundraising than a robust network. We have created regional development boards, for example, of some of our most committed and significant investors in Europe, Asia, Australia, and the United States to build a sense of community and com- mitment to Room to Read.

Technology Investments   We are investing more in technology than ever before. Technology has revolutionized fundraising. Online giving has grown double digits every year for several years now. Crowdfunding and peer-to-peer fundraising are standard models that most organizations employ. We have invested a lot more heavily in technology to support our global fundraising and investor communications at this stage.

Tailor Your Interactions for the Investor   We have
started to segment our different types of investors into categories defined by what motivates them to give to our organization
so we can tailor our interactions and communications while
also building scalable systems. We have broad categories of
the key motivators for our investor base, such as people who are
motivated by social change, or public leadership and recognition
within one's peer group, or family philanthropic activity. This
allows us to continue to take investors on a journey with the
organization as we discussed previously based on their interests,
but also allows the organization to chart out certain common
journeys for our investor base.

Evolve Reporting   We have also found that we needed to be
prepared for savvier investors. As our investor base grew, we met
more investors with a deeper knowledge of our content space.
Particularly with foundations and institutional funders, there
is a certain "technocratization" in which investments are made
by people with deep technical knowledge in a field. They tend
to focus on impacts and theories of change and desire volumes
of data and details. It can be challenging for an entrepreneurial
social enterprise organization to supply all the information being
requested. It requires more sophisticated and formal reporting
systems to be put into place. As philanthropy has become much
more systematized, our start-up entrepreneurial organizational
culture has had to adapt to this.

Development Department Structure

An organization's development team needs to continue to grow
in the maturing and stabilizing years. Our highest paid staff
members at Room to Read on the development team are our

out-the-door fundraisers who directly interact and work with investors. To leverage their time for greatest revenue generation, we have also hired other functionally specialized staff to enhance their success. A well-established development team needs grant writers, gift-processing data processors, annual fund managers, event managers, and employee and investor site-visit managers. Many of these roles can be organized into a central support structure leveraged across geographies and types of funding streams for maximum return on the investment.

We have also found that staff turnover is higher than expected in fundraising than in many other areas of the organization, and you need to build in training to grow your development team's capacity and quickly onboard new staff. We have found it best to hire staff with the right soft skills, competencies, and passion for our work and then enhance their fundraising skills on the job. Here are some of the key areas we train our staff on for interacting with investors.

Approach Every Investor with Respect   Investors are busy people with many competing priorities. They often have different stakeholders to engage with, and response times can sometimes be slower than you desire. The difference between sales and fundraising from individuals is that securing an investment quickly doesn't generally lead to the best investment. The first "get to know you" meeting is often not the right time to bring up making a financial contribution, as you might just get the polite, small gift in which an investor gives the minimum instead of the maximum, or, worst case, the potential investor feels you have rushed them and your organization is not a good fit.

Learn as Much as We Can   In the first few meetings, we try to talk less and listen more. Are investors motivated by a commitment to social change (in education, healthcare, alleviating poverty)? Or by finding organizations that can scale? Do they have a geographic focus, such as Southeast Asia? Do they want their whole family to be involved in the philanthropic decisions? Do they have a family connection to India, or did they hear about us from a friend they trust? Or, for corporations, are employee engagement opportunities and media exposure key opportunities they are seeking? The list goes on. What motivates the person's giving is fundamental information for fundraising. Good fundraisers ask a lot of questions and build strong relationships with their investors such that they learn the answers to what matters most to them.

Be Prepared to Answer a Lot of Investors' Questions, Too   Every funder usually asks the following in some form, so be prepared to answer questions such as, "Where do you want to go? What are your big goals?" "What are your biggest challenges and barriers?" "What do you want to accomplish next?" "How can we help you get there?"

"No" Should Never Be Taken as an Absolute End of the Conversation   We always like to think of a "Sorry, we can't fund you" at Room to Read as a "Sorry, we can't fund you YET . . . " with a crack in the door always open for possible funding or an introduction to another investor later.

Finding the Right Level of Communication   It is important to not undercommunicate or overcommunicate, so we always ask what amount of communication each investor prefers.

Trust and Transparency   Many of our investors have told us that what they appreciate the most about interacting with us is how transparent and candid we are. We will share what is not working and what our challenges are. Whenever we share bad news, we share what we have learned from the situation and what we are going to do to fix it. One of our proudest moments, oddly enough, was when a few former employees misappropriated several thousand dollars in our Africa operations. We could have kept quiet and absorbed the loss, as all program deliverables were still achievable. However, instead, we decided to personally call each major investor to our Africa operations at the time and explain the situation as well as the new financial controls we were putting into place to prevent this from happening again. We did not lose a single investor, and, in fact, many said they had a greater respect for the operational challenges we face.

Fundraising from Foundations and Corporations Can be Different Beasts Altogether than Fundraising with Individuals   Every foundation or corporation has a different history for why it was established and rationale for what change it desires to support. Some operate off tight guidelines; others are more fluid. A program officer at a corporation or foundation, in any case, is that organization's advocate. That person often has many constituencies to please. It is important to become familiar with the strategy of the foundation and analyze how your work can fit into that strategy best. Program officers want to be good partners. Foundations can be slow to change their priorities or approach. They are driven by the founding family, their history, and goals under which they were set up. It is more common now for foundations to reject unsolicited proposals, so building a network with staff members who work in corporations and foundations is a key part of the job of any nonprofit leader or fundraiser.

Tools and Metrics

As an organization's annual budget grows, more accurate annual revenue projections are important as well. At Room to Read, we

set up a system where all key fundraising staff members estimate the size of gifts, the percentage probability of acquiring
gifts within the year from individual investors, and the financial
quarter in which the gifts are likely to be received. We also track
whether revenue comes in restricted to certain programmatic or
operational areas, or is unrestricted, and set annual goals of the
amount of revenue we hope to raise unrestricted. This allows
for an estimate of the annual revenue and the cash flow projections throughout the year. We generally count prospects in our
projections in which the probability of an investment is 50% or
greater.

In our first decade, we did not do bottoms-up revenue
projections by relationship manager and geographical market.
Instead, our board of directors and management team estimated
an expected growth rate based on historical revenue growth
trends that were in the double digits year over year. However,
as our fundraising team and structure became larger and more
complex, we found it necessary to have a ground-up revenue
projection process in place so that the development team felt
ownership over its individual and departmental revenue goals.

We also had to develop a process to help us evaluate where
to put additional staff members and other resources within our
fundraising structure. This was necessary to identify the biggest
return on each additional dollar spent. Should we build out
capacity for more major gift fundraising in the United Kingdom,
focus on corporate fundraising in Japan, or invest more heavily
in building an annual fund base of support in the United States?
Some years will be good years in a market, and some will be bad
years due to various externalities out of our control or because
of staff turnover. We always try to accept the bad years as part of
the learning process, not simply as failures, and understand what
we need to do to grow back in any specific market.

Special final note: Top 10 tips for investors

If you are a philanthropic investor supporting nonprofits, thank you! Whether you give a lot or a little, thank you for giving. If we may be so bold, we would like to give a few suggestions on how to be the most supportive in your relationships with nonprofits:

1. **Invest in fewer organizations, but invest larger amounts** and spend the time to really get to know the organization. You will likely get more out of the experience as they will have more communication and interaction, and feel a bigger part of the solution if you employ this strategy.

2. **Consider sticking with an organization longer and offer multiyear grants if the organization is demonstrating adequate progress.** The inefficiency of having to start over with nearly zero dollars in the bank every year and race to a deadline 365 days later to raise one's full operational budget is challenging. We believe that investors would rather have a larger portion of the staff's effort go toward programming. Foundations in the United States that simply focus on giving away the minimal 5% of their assets, as they are required to do each year by U.S. tax law, may be missing an opportunity to deploy their resources to address social issues faster. If the goal is to support real social change, don't fall into the "shiny new object" syndrome, whereby investors

(continued)

Special final note: Top 10 tips for investors (*Continued*)

are constantly looking to support start-ups as their sole focus. Stick with organizations that you think are having real impact through the "valley of death" march that many great organizations are slogging through.

3. **Always ask the nonprofit what its biggest challenges are, and seek to find ways to support it in breaking through those barriers.** Challenges are likely not just related to funding. Maybe the nonprofit is looking for people to introduce them more widely in their networks. Maybe it is looking to hire new employees and you can help promote their positions. Perhaps it needs a key investor to be willing to be a reference for others. Maybe it needs introductions to experts in a field you work in, or *pro bono* support.

4. **Be clear and specific in what kind of reporting and communication you as an investor would like.** State your timelines upfront. It is always easier for the nonprofit to be successful in engaging an investor appropriately if it understands what is ideal for the investor.

5. **Be understanding and ask clarifying questions when a nonprofit might need to communicate to you a missed goal or objective.** The work of a nonprofit doesn't happen in a linear fashion. Big change often means taking calculated risks. The pathway to achieving any mission is likely paved with potholes, so see the experience as a journey and be a positive travel partner.

6. **The reality is if you believe in the organization and its ability to have impact, the absolute best way to invest is by giving an unrestricted gift** so the nonprofit can determine the area of greatest need. If you cannot give unrestricted due to guidelines, the next best thing is to add a portion of funding to any grant made to cover the organization's overhead. The idea that nonprofits can miraculously scale their impact while having to raise funds for every line item in their budgets independently is not realistic. Does anyone buy a corporate stock and ask to just invest in the search engine portion of Google (without supporting any staff or research and development costs), or ask to invest in Johnson & Johnson in the United States only and not any international markets? No, of course not. Yet we are engaged in these conversations every day in the nonprofit sector: Investors ask only to support programs but no overhead; or, worse, only one component of a nonprofit's program, not the holistic approach being employed.

7. **Give thoughtful, individualized, constructive feedback** to nonprofit organizations whenever possible about what they are doing well and where they can improve on all aspects of your relationship—their programs, their leadership, and their reporting and communication—with you.

8. **Make your investment in the first half of the year, if possible.** Most organizations receive much of their funding in the latter half of the year, which can result in cash flow issues, lack of visibility to annual revenue, and an inefficient fundraising cycle for staff.

(continued)

Special final note: Top 10 tips for investors (*Continued*)

9. **Tell organizations early if you don't plan to renew their funding.** Don't avoid the conversation because you hate to deliver bad news. Hearing bad news is always better early than late as it enables the organization to plan.

10. **Make the effort every so often to visit the work firsthand**, even if it is in other countries. You will have such a deeper understanding of the context of an organization's work if you experience it up close.

And, finally, be encouraging. Leaders in entrepreneurial social enterprises hear a lot of "No" or "That will never work." They are doing hard work of disrupting the *status quo*. Be there as a sounding board, and give them positive encouragement to continue the fight.

Key Takeaways

- **Focus on a building a positive fundraising culture.** Cultivating, stewarding, and growing your investor base is one of the most important things you can do to build a sustainable organization that has great impact.
- **Everyone in the organization should feel a part of the fundraising team.** Each person should help engage investors as directed by the fundraising team and think about creative ways to have the power of the organization's work come alive for supporters. A strong fundraising culture is essential to any successful nonprofit.

- **Different phases of organizational development require different fundraising strategies**, staffing structures, investments in tools, and support systems. Know where you are in your organizational growth trajectory and plan for what you need to do next to continue to build your fundraising momentum.

- **Play to your strengths, and don't diversify too quickly.** It takes time to build skills and processes to manage different types of funding streams and raise revenue from different geographical locations. At the same time, don't diversify too late. As you grow, think about the next type of funding you could start to attract.

- **Harness the talent and energy of volunteers.** Direct them to help in the areas in which you are most underresourced. If you play to volunteers' "super-powers," you can get extra value.

- **Simple, clear, and transparent messaging is key to stand out in a crowded field.** It is not as easy to achieve as you might think.

- **People invest in people first.** Focus on building long-term relationships based on trust. Philanthropic investments are often very personal decisions, and you want to engage both the head and the heart of your investors.

- **Build wide networks of ambassadors**. This includes investors, board members, advisors, and partners who can be "fund whisperers," sharing your work with new supporters and inspiring them to give.

IV

Scaling for Global Change

9

Strategic Influence: Growing Our Impact

The flight from Dar es Salaam to the capital city of Tanzania, Dodoma, in the fall of 2014 felt surreal. It had not been a part of the country-visit plan until just a few days earlier. The suit Cory was wearing on the flight was too big, but he had to make a last-minute purchase in the downtown market in Dar es Salaam because he had not planned for a formal meeting. No time for tailoring. The prime minister had summoned us.

Dodoma seemed to appear out of nowhere. It was an urban oasis in the middle of an arid region, dusty and dry just before the rainy season. What were we doing here? What did the prime minister want?

Security was tight as we entered the grounds of the National Assembly. That day was the end of the legislative session, and we could see on the close-captioned television in the prime minister's office that the debate on the assembly floor was vigorous. Cory and his two colleagues waited for a short time before the minister of education and vocational training at the time, Dr. Shukuru Kawambwa, entered the waiting room. We had met previously, so it was nice to see a familiar face. We engaged in the niceties of polite conversation and updated Dr. Kawambwa about recent successes in our literacy and girls' education programs. We could tell he was a bit distracted, as his eyes continued to divert to the floor debate on television, but he remained cordial and engaged. At the same time, he did not offer any clues as to why we had been invited.

At last, Prime Minister Mizengo Pinda entered the room. He was all smiles and radiated charisma and gravitas. He spent more than an hour with us. He was a gracious and funny host, even making all of us laugh, nearly to tears, at one point in the meeting. It turned out that although he had some questions, he really just wanted to express his gratitude for the work that Room to Read was doing in Tanzania. Cory kept waiting for him to express displeasure with some element of our programming or to request a larger or more targeted investment. It never happened.

The prime minister had simply heard good things about Room to Read's work from the minister of education. The minister of education was also a member of parliament from the district of Bagamoyo, where Room to Read had been working. He was particularly impressed with the school libraries there and had put in a good word with the prime minister. The prime minister said that he believed strongly in the importance of books for young children and had established a library in his home village in western Tanzania. He even said that after hearing of our great work in eastern Tanzania, he had renamed his village library "a Room to Read."

What was most amazing about this meeting is that Room to Read had only been working in Tanzania for three years at that point, since 2011. Tanzania was the newest country in the Room to Read portfolio, and we were relatively early in our organizational development and program expansion. It is also a large country with a population of nearly 52 million people. Our work was just a drop in the bucket. Yet we had obviously made enough of a positive impression for the leader of the country to request a courtesy meeting on the busiest legislative day of the year.

The goodwill that we generated could not have hurt when we bid two years later as part of a larger consortium on a USAID education project in the country. Our consortium won the project, and Room to Read is responsible for developing the supplemental reading materials that are being used in six major regions of Tanzania.

In many ways, this unplanned meeting with Prime Minister Pinda was the exception in our collective professional experiences as Room to Read emissaries. However, the lesson we learned is that an organization does not need to have worked for many years in a country nor possess a huge national footprint to make a good impression on political, business, and community leaders. We had even achieved a strategic influence on policy and practice in the country! Some of our other country teams have worked longer and on a wider scale but have not been able to achieve the same level of national influence as we had in Tanzania.

Scale and Influence: Defining the End Game

The term *scaling for global impact* is thrown around a lot these days. A key question, though, is "Scale what?" Is scaling about the organization? Or the program? Or the outcomes? These are three different things.

We believe that a variety of paths can lead to achieving global impact. Over the course of Room to Read's history, we have had to grow the organization enough to test our models, gather evidence, and develop robust implementation systems. As we have matured, though, the organizational growth has slowed somewhat as we have begun to experiment with ways in which governments and other organizations can replicate and scale our programs without needing as much ongoing support from us.

A second set of questions when thinking about scaling is, What is your end game? How do you want to affect the broader system? What is your ultimate exit strategy to ensure that your good work doesn't lead to dependency? These big decisions affect program design, organizational structure, budget, marketing, and fundraising, to name just a few. The answers to these questions need to be baked into your organizational theory of change. As we discussed previously, though, as your theory of change evolves, so too may your end game.

The point of having an end game is to guide the organization to take the right actions, at the right time, and in the right way to change larger systems and achieve lasting social change. The system can be the government system or the commercial system. As we discussed in the first chapter, the challenge for the "third sector," civil society, is the lack of sustainable recurring revenue sources. The best way—and only option—for broader system-level change is to have your program or invention be incorporated into the public or private spheres. Building your organization is a key first-order business to make larger adoption possible. Of course, social entrepreneurs are ultimately not in the business of building organizations. We are in the business of social change. A commercial enterprise can define success as an ever-growing customer base. A nonprofit must define success by change for the end user.

The irony (and often frustration) of our work as disruptors is that we must then shift tactics and figure out how to integrate our products and services with government bureaucracies and capital markets. But integrating social solutions into existing systems is an essential part of the scaling process, for better or for worse.

The key to strategic influence is to pick your pathway to scale with a clear end game so you determine how you will influence private and/or public stakeholders to create the greatest sustainable value for the communities that you serve.

The Unique Role of ESEs in Scaling Social Change

As discussed in Chapter 1, the role of nonprofit organizations in communities and countries is to provide services that are not otherwise offered through governments or private companies. But what is the difference between a regular nonprofit organization and an entrepreneurial social enterprise? We think about ESEs as a specific subset of nonprofit organizations that share a few characteristics. They are pushy and disruptive—usually in good ways! They use rigorous data and analytics to continuously improve services, aspire to scale their work broadly, and seek strategic opportunities to extend their work into the more traditional public and private sector spaces. This could be the difference between a community group that comes together to build and support a few school libraries in their town and an organization that has helped to establish thousands of libraries in multiple countries so that millions of children can learn to love reading.

ESEs play an extremely important role in the international development space. They not only provide direct services but also create models for solutions that can be replicated in hundreds and thousands of communities. They seek big changes and are bold in their approaches and communications. They highlight gaps in government services and show products and services that could have commercial value. They have deep knowledge about what seems to work from one community to the next and what must be adapted to specific local circumstances.

At Room to Read, for example, some parts of our girls' education program are universally applicable. We ensure that all girls in life-skills activities have the chance to learn about ways to communicate effectively with families and friends and better manage their time. At the same time, the kinds of specific challenges that girls face and the ways that social mobilizers help girls work through those challenges vary quite a bit across countries.

This is the kind of information that entrepreneurial social organizations can use to advocate forcefully with governments and other organizations and promote broader social goals. ESE leaders can host or participate in policy forums, consultations about national programs, or industry events that showcase new products and services. ESEs passionately promote the value of social causes. They change minds and demonstrate viable paths to improve lives in big ways. ESEs plot their change strategies and execute plans methodically but also take advantage of strategic moments when circumstances unfold. This could be a change in government officials, an exposé in the national news, or, unfortunately, and too often, a disaster that highlights the importance of their work.

We distinguish between ESEs and the industry of government contracting organizations that has grown over the past 50 years. Governments, as well as bilateral and multilateral organizations, often hire contractors to implement large-scale social projects for three to five years per project. This is a completely different approach to achieving social goals. Compared to ESEs, which often work over long periods of time and develop long-term relationships and solutions, government-sponsored social projects are often short and result in focused shocks to a system.

Short-term projects can be transformative and impactful, particularly when projects build in a plan for transferring responsibility and long-term sustainability of efforts to others when projects end. However, they can also be quite risky for longer-term development, as they shift attention and resources overnight in a way that is often unsustainable over time. Projects can distort labor markets by providing jobs with high salaries for project employees that can then disappear when projects end. In addition, intensive, short-term projects create huge expectations in countries about long-term change that is usually difficult to sustain after the three- to five-year project period.

ESEs with longer-term commitments and relationships in countries can play key roles in promoting stability and continuity even in the wake of short-term project shocks.

However, there are other ways to promote strategic influence, too. This includes sway in the private sector, where ESEs can influence the development of commercial products and services. For example, in many countries, Room to Read is one of the biggest publishers of children's storybooks. And although we do not sell books commercially, creating school libraries and advocating for children to borrow books and take them home has enhanced the "culture of reading" in many countries and inspired commercial publishers to create content for this new market of early-grade storybooks. As we explained in Chapter 4, the children's book publishing market grew substantially in several countries where we work grew markedly after Room to Read began its publishing work in the early 2000s.

We have also initiated projects over the past few years to train commercial publishers to create children's storybooks. We've had huge success with this, as evidenced by the Room to Read–facilitated commercial children's storybooks that won awards at the 2016 Samsung KidsTime Authors' Award in Singapore. An ESE can also exert strategic influence at the school and community level. The entire point of Room to Read's programming is to create a new vision for children's learning that can transform the way that communities think about the issues. Community commitments start with some monetary or in-kind contribution to the projects themselves, but they also include commitments for new practices and behaviors: getting parents or guardians to agree to keep their daughters in schools; ensuring that all children in an elementary school participate in one library period per week; ensuring parent or guardian participation in periodic community meetings to discuss reading and girls' education; and getting parents or guardians to commit to making time and space for children to read their library books at home. Although not all agreements are upheld in every instance, creating these expectations and promoting them over what is often a four-year period or even longer helps establish new cultural norms that extend beyond the time that Room to Read works directly in a school or community.

Expanding Room to Read's Role as an Influencer

Like other aspects of our work, Room to Read has evolved its role as a strategic influencer as we have matured as an organization. Our starting point, and what we would argue is the critical starting point for any ESE, is to deliver innovative and excellent products and services consistently on time and on budget. When you do this over many years, governments and private organizations will take notice. You can then more easily advocate for your issues as you earn both trust and expertise.

Strategic Influence During Start-Up

In the first decade of Room to Read's work, our primary organizational focus was to bring educational services to the next child, the next class, or the next school. This was our start-up mindset and an ambitious and important-enough aspiration to drive our passion and hard work. Although we had the support of local and national governments to work in schools and tried to integrate our work into normal school processes, our work was mainly in parallel to that of school systems. In these early days of Room to Read, we focused on survival. We didn't feel particularly confident that we had much to share to influence other international education professionals or government policies. The one thing we did do at this phase was develop a programmatic model that assumed our end game was local government adoption and adaption. With scale and sustainability in mind, we decided to work exclusively in government schools and to have a fixed timeframe for our program interventions. We shared this information openly when negotiating with governments and schools as potential partners.

Then something interesting started to happen. Host governments started to seek Room to Read's input into national policies and practices. In 2010, requests started to come from many countries. As one example, the Ministry of Education in Bangladesh invited Room to Read to join a committee tasked with overhauling the national educational curriculum. This was the first time that nonprofit organizations were invited to join the government curriculum revision process, and we were thrilled to have an opportunity to influence Bangladesh's national literacy textbooks and teachers' guides. In another example, Room to Read Cambodia launched a literacy instruction pilot to improve the way Khmer literacy skills are taught in early grade Cambodian classrooms. The pilot was a huge success, and the Cambodian government invited us to help rewrite their Grade 1 literacy textbook so all children in Cambodia could benefit from our program's best practices.

Over the past several years, these requests and Room to Read's contributions have continued to snowball. At present, for example, Room to Read's grade 1 and 2 reading curricula are being used as the basis for the national curriculum in Nepal, and our grade 1 curriculum is being used as the basis for the national curriculum in Grenada. We are leading in developing supplementary reading materials for a large-scale reading program in Tanzania that is reaching all grade 1 and 2 children in six regions, and we are leading the overall early-grade reading curriculum in Rwanda.

Government officials have begun to take notice of our work. Room to Read has proved itself to be a productive and loyal partner. The statement by a Sri Lankan educational official that we referenced in the introductory chapter, that Room to Read is "the quiet organization that does not say much but gets things done," is a huge vote of confidence.

We also started to see in some countries that classroom teachers were using our student reading workbooks instead of government reading textbooks. That was not the plan. Our workbooks were meant to close gaps in the reading curriculum, highlight key concepts, and provide children with more opportunities to practice their reading and writing. All of this was to support the core textbook and not replace it.

However, many teachers felt that even though our workbooks were not meant as a complete curriculum, they were easier to use and served as a more effective teaching resource than the regular textbooks. This dynamic became awkward in some early instances because government partners did not appreciate this insubordination. More enlightened governments, though, embraced this teacher interest and sought Room to Read's counsel for larger educational reforms. It was at that point that we started to work more closely with governments not only on supplementary instructional materials but on the core textbooks and teacher guides.

Strategic Influence in Transition

Gaining a higher profile and having more influence turned out to be a double-edged sword. It created somewhat of an existential crisis of identity that we still discuss today. On the one hand, it was flattering to be invited to policy forums and to participate in consultations about educational reform. We had become confident in our approach, and clear about what we were doing well and what we still needed to improve, and felt we could add real value to these policy discussions. At the same time, any energy that we put into policy discussions, conferences, op-eds in newspapers, or academic journal articles took time away from our direct implementation. The more our opinions were sought, the more we began to question what Room to Read was doing. Were we about helping that next child or community with the absolute highest level of service and compassion, or were we more about influencing larger systems but perhaps not at the same kind of depth or intensity? This was a real question and, in many ways, a long-term organizational struggle that drove to the heart of our vision and mission.

We had casualties along the way. Staff members who joined Room to Read to work directly in schools could not fathom how we could allow even one child to slip through the system without learning to read, or one adolescent girl to leave school for work in a clothing factory. They were uncomfortable discussing trade-offs. They were not interested in discussing "maximum benefit," such as whether investing all our money and person-power into a small number of children and their families was fair to all the other children we were serving, or whether we should pay attention to reforms that would help all children in a region or country.

It was also during this turbulent transition phase that we started to grapple more with the issue of phaseout: When should we stop working in a country or region? This issue played out much in the same way as the issue of child- or system-level focus of our work. It was uncomfortable because it is never easy to end a long-term relationship, and there are always more children to serve in any geography.

India was at the epicenter of this struggle. By 2010, we had developed a wide footprint across the second-most-populated country in the world. We were working in a relatively small number of projects given India's size, but our work was spread across many states. Some staff believed that we needed to spread our resources widely so we could show governments that we were serving children throughout the country. Other staff believed that by spreading ourselves so thinly, we were hurting our efficiency and not providing the highest level of service in the communities in which we were working. The latter view won the day, and the India country leadership team had the unenviable responsibility to work with some states on closeout plans.

When education officials in affected states learned the plans, they were most unhappy. They had appreciated Room to Read's support and believed there was more work to do. One compromise in these delicate negotiations, though, was that Room to Read would train state educational officials in Room to Read's program activities. This process, initially under the radar and a side project initiated by the India leadership team, turned out to be an exciting model for a new way of working—technical support for educational officials and others—that was part of the inspiration for the new Room to Read Accelerator unit that we described in Chapter 6.

It was also during this transition phase that Room to Read began to see its strategic influence on commercial book publishing. As described earlier in this chapter, this includes assisting in developing new commercial children's book markets, advocating for higher-quality children's books from the private sector, and supporting ministries of education that create and oversee approved book lists. This last activity is a sensitive and often politically charged issue. Commercial publishers can make a lot of money selling their books to government schools. Having books selected for approved book lists is therefore a lucrative prize, and the process is often fraught with nontransparent and corrupt processes. In this situation, an ESE such as Room to Read can be in a strategic position to work with ministries on more transparent approval processes. It can also provide technical support to help ministries, as we are now doing in South Africa, to develop selection criteria for approved books that yield higher-quality books and, therefore, more opportunities to promote children's love of reading.

Strategic Influence as a Mature ESE

Room to Read's strategic influence as an ESE has grown substantially as we have deepened our work in countries over the years and demonstrated the follow-through and success of our programs. We have developed long-standing, excellent relationships with governments and business leaders around the world. However, it is only in the last few years that we can say that we have been moving into a more mature phase of strategic influence.

The difference is in becoming more proactive instead of reactive in our influence. It is only in the last few years that we made strategic influence a formal part of our work as we actively searched for ways to help incorporate our lessons into larger country systems. We have sought meetings with government officials and private sector leaders. We have hosted policy forums. And we have negotiated projects specifically designed to systematize our approaches. In our 2015–2019 strategic plan, we call this "doing more with less." It is the way to support more children even though we stay a relatively small organization.

Could we have made this shift earlier in our organizational evolution? Perhaps. Every ESE must decide timing for itself. However, the timing was right for us. In 2016, for example, a small Room to Read team traveled to Myanmar to scope out a new project. A private investor who had business interests in the country was prepared to fund it. We'd heard that it was extremely difficult to collaborate with the Ministry of Education, as the government had historically been closed to outside engagement. Nevertheless, a prominent business leader in the country who had known Room to Read by reputation was eager for us to bring our expertise to the country, and set up a rare meeting with the new minister of education.

This short presentation was sufficient for the minister to support a memorandum of understanding about how the ministry and Room to Read would collaborate pending the success of project funding. Neither the opportunity for this kind of meeting nor the enthusiastic support of the minister could have been possible if Room to Read had not already established itself as a mature ESE elsewhere in the world.

Influencing Governments

Planning is essential to an organization's ability to influence systemic social change. For many ESEs, the focus of that change is government and its public programs. In Room to Read's case, our goal is for governments in the countries in which we work to adopt, adapt, and then scale the most important elements of our programming. In Chapter 7, we described world change as a team sport in which we work hard to engage many people to create the momentum for change. Extending this metaphor, engaging governments is definitely a contact sport. Government staff members want to feel heard and recognized. They want to feel supported, not undermined. We at Room to Read know that for our school-based programs to succeed we must gain trust as well as help them build their knowledge and skills. Often that requires us to disrupt their normal ways of operating and convince them of new ways of working that can be more impactful.

Planning for Government Adoption

What is the difference between a reactive and proactive approach to strategic influence? It is in the planning. Room to Read's 2015–2019 strategic plan gave us a mandate to share our lessons, experiences, and approaches more broadly. This means building opportunities for strategic influence into our annual planning cycle, devoting staff time and financial resources to it, and monitoring our progress in achieving strategic goals. This does not preclude us from shifting our goals over the course of the year as new opportunities present themselves, but it does help guide us and set reasonable expectations for what we want to do. It also helps us put boundaries around how much time we set aside for this aspect of our work. It lights a bit of a fire under us and gives guidance to country teams that are reluctant to go beyond our direct project work. It also taps into the enthusiasm of country teams that perhaps want to spend too much time wheeling and dealing with government and private-sector partners.

Room to Read has developed a framework for helping country teams maximize the likelihood of system-level adoption of key program elements. We've also created a tool for focusing our strategic influence activities. We describe these below.

Setting the Stage

ESEs can create disruptive change in a variety of ways. Yes, we can all give examples of disruptive ideas that have caught like wildfire and have changed the world overnight. The Arab Spring is one example. The spark of democratic fervor in Tunisia in December 2010 spread to many other countries in the Middle East over the following year, forever changing the landscape of the region. However, most technologies that we would classify as "disruptive" require time to take hold and become part of the social fabric of any society: mobile phones, the Internet, or even driverless cars take years, not months, to go fully mainstream.

Often, the technology itself must change and adapt to its user base for it to be successful, despite initial excitement and enthusiasm about it. This takes time and good planning. Someone we admire a lot is Atul Gawande, who goes so far as to say that people tend to romanticize the one-off disruptive successes in the health sector and undervalue the painstaking process of "incrementalism."[1] It is through long-term, iterative trial and error that some of the best innovations evolve. And it is often through a longer engagement with communities and larger social systems that ESEs can disrupt historical ways of working. It is a mistake to think that disruptive change can just be turned on like a light switch.

In Room to Read's work, our goal has been to improve the policies and practices of large educational systems. In most countries, government ministries of education are the authorities that oversee elementary and secondary schools. Although some private or religious organizations sometimes develop parallel systems—often competing with governments in the large numbers of schools they manage—this is the exception. Governments are the most likely partners to sustain core program elements after individual school projects end. Governments are also positioned to scale core educational program elements to serve many more children than would be possible for any ESE to do alone.

Anyone who has worked with large government-led education systems, though, knows how difficult it can be to affect larger change. Political appointees come and go, but many government employees work in systems for years. They are acculturated to ways of working that are very difficult to change. In many ways, it is good that governments remain relatively stable over time. An unpredictable government that is too responsive and adaptive would cause anxiety and confusion.

As we illustrate in Figure 9.1, the bigger, the more complex, and the higher cost of a proposed change, the less likely governments will be to adopt that change. This is the lightly shaded triangle on the left. This contrasts with the triangle on the right, which shows the disruptive potential of a truly innovative educational reform idea. The assumption in the right-hand triangle is that the further away the new reform idea is from what the government is currently doing, the greater the benefit. The question is how to reconcile these differences: making an effective new reform palatable to government (or other system-level) stakeholders. We want to grow the overlapping triangle as much as possible.

The answer (see Figure 9.2) is to make the slope of the left-hand triangle more gradual and the slope of the right-hand triangle steeper. In this way, the overlapping area under the two triangles becomes larger, and governments are more likely to adopt new policies or practices.

How do you do this? Let's start with the right-hand triangle. The way to make the slope steeper is to improve the quality

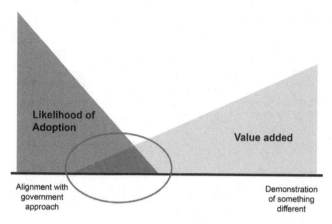

FIGURE 9.1 Program Alignment and Likelihood of Adoption.

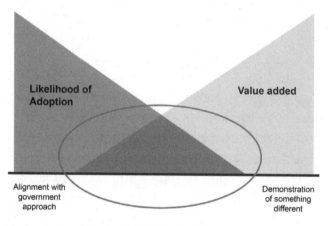

FIGURE 9.2 Increasing the Likelihood of Adoption.

and benefits of the program. This is the kind of incremental, in-the-weeds, trial-and-error, long-term process that Gawande lauds in his article. What about the left-hand triangle? The best way to temper the slope is to show governments or other system-level partners that it is possible to achieve *their own goals in a way that is simpler and more cost effective, that will be embraced by users, and that can be absorbed in a relatively easy way.* Oh, and by the way, the extent to which the changes can promote goodwill, good press, or other public acknowledgment for the government, all the better!

Only So Far, So Fast

The likelihood of governments or other partners adopting an ESE's program or program elements is also based on what Lev Vygotsky called the "zone of proximal development," or ZPD. Vygotsky, a Byelorussian psychologist who lived and worked early in the twentieth century, believed that people had range of knowledge that they could learn on their own based on their experiences and stage of development. The further away a new idea was from that ZPD, the more support a person needed to grasp it and incorporate it into his or her worldview.

This concept is central in Room to Read's approach to classroom instruction. When a teacher introduces a new letter or vocabulary word, she runs through a series of activities herself. She could introduce the sound using the letter at the beginning of a word—cat, car, can, crawl—or use the new word in a sentence: "The cat *crawled* under the car." Next, she could read a paragraph in the textbook with the new letters and words together with her class. Last, she could ask individual children to read the same or similar paragraph on their own. This approach is called "I do / we do / you do," and it is an excellent strategy for helping grow children's ZPD. It introduces new content gradually and in a way that children's minds can assimilate, especially when they are already familiar with the daily instructional approach.

Similarly, it is important to understand the zone of proximal development of the people whom you are trying to influence. Is support for girls' education a familiar concept, or does Room to Read need to help ease more traditional communities and government officials into the concept gradually? Are book authors in a lower-income country familiar with children's storybooks? Or might they benefit from seeing a selection of children's storybooks from another country to expose them to new ideas? A new technology can only be disruptive if the ultimate consumers understand it and perceive it to be valuable for themselves.

Plotting System-Level Adoption

Okay. Your ESE has developed strong programming, and you have hard data about its effectiveness. You have carefully organized your work to be primed for scaling (for example, you know that your approach can achieve impact at a system level, is easy to adopt, is enticing for users, and is cost effective) and are ready to go. What next? How do you plan for strategic influence and larger-level system adoption? What are your goals? How do you track your progress?

These are the questions that we have been asking ourselves at Room to Read over the past few years given that strategic government engagement is now a more explicit organizational goal. One of the biggest questions that we had to answer was how much we cared about maintaining the Room to Read brand. In other words, how much did we care that governments adopt "THE Room to Read approach" as part of their scaling efforts?

This is not a selfish question. ESEs work hard to develop their approaches. Shouldn't we be recognized for our work? In addition, as we have discussed previously, letting go of one's ownership allows others to change *your* work based on *their* own views and brand. Are you ready for that? Most importantly, if an organization becomes invisible because it is giving away its approach (its "intellectual property"), then how can it sustain itself financially? How can it ensure that it can continue to grow brand awareness and revenue to continue to do good work in the future?

Our current view is that we genuinely want our materials to be shared as widely as possible, and, given the hard work that we have put into the development of our programs, we strongly prefer to be paid for our work. At the very least, we feel that it is appropriate for governments and other partners to acknowledge Room to Read's contributions to new policies and practices. We also want to be able to tell our investors about successes so they know how their contributions continue to make a difference in the world. Our investors tend to be quite happy when a ministry of education adopts our work for extended use.

Most important to us is that governments and other system-level organizations ultimately adopt the elements of Room to Read programming that we believe lead to children's educational success, irrespective of whether they explicitly adopt the Room to Read approach. When we believe that governments understand the importance of a program element and have incorporated it into their own work, we can then relax, and we can focus on getting them to adopt a different program element or focus our time and attention on another country.

To be more proactive in promoting system-level adoption, where appropriate, we have created a "government adoption" tool for countries to use in their long-term and annual planning. The challenge in working with governments is that a policy is just a lot of words on paper unless governments act on it. We have seen this in several countries in which there is a conceptual commitment to improve reading levels, promote school libraries, and even support girls to stay in school longer. Often, however, governments take very little action to ensure these outcomes. Entrepreneurial social enterprises can be important "fire starters" with governments to catalyze and mobilize action.

So, at Room to Read we created a tool that helped us hold ourselves accountable for playing this important fire-starter role. The tool, reproduced in Figure 9.3, includes a section for our Literacy Program and a section for our Girls' Education Program. The rows in the tool reflect the core elements of Room to Read's programs that we believe are important for children's educational success. We have tested many individual elements empirically through various assessments and rating systems; others need further testing but have been checked with many country and school-level staff as key parts of our programming.

The assumption, after substantial internal discussion and analysis, is that if a school, district, province, or country were to have these program elements in place—irrespective of whether they were implemented by a ministry of education, Room to Read, or some other organization—young children would

Literacy	Understanding	Agreement	Preparation	Use	Success
Overall					
1 Family support for reading and writing					
2 School support for reading and writing					
Literacy skills development					
3 Effective student learning materials for reading and writing instruction					
4 Effective training and teacher support for reading and writing instruction					
5 Effective use of classroom strategies for reading and writing instruction					
6 Effective tools for student assessment					
Habit of reading					
7 Designated spaces for book collections (libraries or book corners)					
8 Child-friendly environments for reading					
9 Systems for checkout and management of books					
10 Effective activities to build interest and enjoyment in reading					
11 Effective use of books in the learning process (in addition to textbooks)					
Supplementary reading resources					
12 Sufficient quantity and diversity of developmentally appropriate reading material					

Level: ☐ Individual ☐ School ☐ Block (India) ☐ District ☐ Province/State ☐ Country

Girls' Education	Understanding	Agreement	Preparation	Use	Success
Girl-level interventions					
1 Effective life-skills training opportunities					
2 Effective peer tutoring					
Family- and school-level interventions					
3 Family support for girls' success					
4 School support for girls' success					
5 Effective tools for school-level assessment of girls' material support needs					
6 Effective tools for school-level assessment of girls' academic support needs					
7 Effective tools for risk management					
8 Effective activities for mentoring and referrals					
9 Girl-friendly classrooms and schools					

FIGURE 9.3 Government Adoption Tool.

achieve substantial success in their early grade reading and many more girls would complete high school with skills to succeed in the next phases of their lives.

The columns in the tool reflect the various stages of system-level adoption. The first column represents the first step in government adoption, "Understanding each element." Do government officials understand what we mean, for example, by "Systems for checkout and management of books"? Second, do they agree that the program element is important enough to incorporate into their overall programming? In other words, officials can understand what we are trying to do but still not agree with the concept or prioritize it enough to build it into their system.

If there is agreement, we move to the next stage, which is preparation. Has the government started to build the element into its policies or practices in a way that demonstrates its seriousness of intent? India's 2009 right-to-education law, for example, includes a provision that all schools should have school libraries. The Ministry of Education in Cambodia is developing an integrated life-skills curriculum with targets for children's success and related tracking measures.

Next is actual use. Is the government implementing the program element? In Nepal, for example, five districts are piloting the national reading curriculum that started with Room to Read's approach. The textbook and related teacher's guide have already been rolled out in more than 1,600 schools and are being used by 128,000 children. Grenada is building libraries in all its 57 government elementary schools, with five completed and the remainder scheduled for the next two years.

Last, are the program elements being implemented with success? In system-level implementation, are children developing the habit of reading and the necessary reading skills? Are girls completing high school in larger numbers and demonstrating more success in university and the workplace?

Each Room to Read country team completes this tool as part of its multiyear planning process based on the best information at hand. It is not a scientific process. Much of the work is subjective. However, completing the tool initially gives a good baseline for where a community or country might be in adopting essential program elements. It also helps Room to Read think about its strategic engagement activities. It helps us to see that we do not need to continue to work on an issue if the government is already on board and achieving success. We can shift our attention to other issues.

After country teams complete the tool, the last task is to identify a few of the elements to focus on strategically. The team then builds a set of activities to help move the system from one stage of development to another. If government officials are not yet aware of the importance of family support for reading and writing, the Room to Read country team could decide to meet with government officials, work with newspapers to tell stories of effective parental involvement in their children's education, or host a policy forum. If ministry of education officials have already *agreed* to the importance of parental education, we could work with them to *prepare* and *implement* a national reading campaign.

Networks of Influence

One important strategy for increasing an ESE's influence in a broader system is to identify key stakeholders and develop strategies to influence them. For Room to Read, the most important stakeholders in countries are governments and communities. Our greater set of stakeholders includes individual investors and partners, corporate and foundation supporters, volunteer chapter members and ambassadors, and partner organizations and institutions in the international development community. All are passionate about our joint mission and resources to build momentum for social change. These networks of influential investors and partners lend a bigger voice to the collective movement for change in education systems.

The Power of Convening Critical Friends and Advisors

One of the fun aspects of working in the social impact space is witnessing the collaboration between organizations and individuals. They both are committed to sharing knowledge and experiences to promote peer learning and developing "communities of practice" for key social issues.

To leverage this collaboration and improve Room to Read's work, we have regularly convened a diverse group of thought leaders to provide input on big issues we are grappling with as an organization. We call these meetings our "convenings of critical friends and advisors." We invite a wide variety of stakeholders, including education experts from other nonprofits, academic institutions, bilateral and multilateral development institutions, as well as private investors, corporate investors, and staff members. The idea is to bring as many different voices and perspectives into the room when discussing and debating strategic issues. We always hold these gatherings as part of our global strategic planning process.

Global Board of Directors

Another influential group of stakeholders for Room to Read is our global board of directors. The relationship between a board of directors and the management of a for-profit business is a multifaceted one, and it is not any different in the social sector. For nonprofits, boards of directors of course provide fiduciary and strategic oversight, as well as bring additional revenue and influential networks with them. We are fortunate at Room to Read to have always had a global board of directors that sees one of its primary goals is to build connections, awareness, and, most importantly, revenue. Like in other parts of our growth story, we went through a lot of trial and error before we found the right balance of how to engage and leverage our board for maximum impact.

In the early stage of an ESE, the board of directors is often most aligned and connected to the founding team. Many boards at this stage really act as personal boards of directors for the social entrepreneurs. Given the ups and downs of making it through the start-up years, having a supportive board capable of giving sound advice and cheering you on is enormously helpful. The challenge comes when the organization starts to grow rapidly. The board of directors needs to evolve along the same trajectory as the organization.

We've worked hard at Room to Read to ensure that our board grows with us and brings new skills and expertise as we need it. Today it is made up of committed individuals from a range of different industries, geographies, and experiences whom we trust to help guide our strategy and direction. Several of our board members come from the corporate sector. We also have a couple of key board seats for international education experts. Many board members are CEOs and executives who have struggled with similar issues when growing their own businesses. Here are some of the principles that we have learned over the years of how to best manage our partnership with these individuals.

Role Clarity Providing strategic, fiduciary oversight in an informed and constructive manner is the primary role of a board of directors. Executing on the agreed-upon plan and managing the operation is the role of the management team. Problems arise when the board oversteps its role and tries to take on management duties, or management does not fully inform or engage the board on important strategic decisions or compliance issues. We've found boards of directors of social enterprises to have three main needs. First, like all boards, they require regular and sufficient information to feel secure in performing their fiduciary oversight role. Second, they desire opportunities to be educated more deeply on the social impact issues the organization is working on and the challenges of the mission, and have the chance to participate in conversations that help come up with solutions. Third, they have "community" needs of wanting to connect and develop meaningful relationships with each other as a board and more broadly with others involved in the cause. The second and third needs are likely greater in the nonprofit space as members are volunteering their time because they care deeply about the social issue the organization is working on and want to feel connected.

Structure   One important way to ensure each person understands his or her role is by having a clear structure for the board and the various committees. We have found it works best at Room to Read when we have an independent board chair who is not a founder or the current CEO. This is a recommended best practice for nonprofits to ensure independent oversight role of the public charity. Nonprofits also benefit in decision making and strategic outreach by having outside perspectives from a diverse set of board members. Creating space for independent leaders at the board level to step up and act as chair helps bring together the most dynamic group of board members.

Additionally, we have an executive committee, audit committee, investment committee, human resources committee, and nominating and governance committee. We have never had a fundraising committee because our global board of directors is generally 12–15 members, and we strongly believe every one of the independent board members has a responsibility to assist management in revenue generation. We also don't have a programs committee. A couple of key members of our board have international education expertise. They, along with our critical friends and advisors, provide the technical programmatic input and connections we need.

Effective Management of Board Meetings The other way to ensure all board members play their roles effectively is to have clear, two-way communication. An important component of communication is ensuring meetings are managed well. We have developed a successful formula for board meetings. The most important part is a well-structured agenda with prereading materials sent out well in advance of the meeting, generally two weeks. The prereading is in the same format every time and has an overview of the key metrics and information for each area of the organization. By maintaining a consistent format heavy on quantitative data, the time required for board members to prepare for the meeting is minimized, yet we are still providing them with sufficient information so they are well informed when they arrive at the meeting.

Growth Mindset The ESE board's role is to challenge and motivate the management team constructively to embrace growth. However, board members should also inquire about any stresses or strains on the ESE as it attempts to scale. Throughout Room to Read's high-growth transition years, the pressure was to grow, grow, grow, but the board meetings were often not the places to talk about the very real pressure that growth was putting on the organization. Boards, at times, can have a "deliver or fail" mentality, which doesn't always set the best tone for a management team seeking guidance and advice. We work hard to ensure the management team and board have a collaborative relationship.

CEO Performance Management and Succession Planning The annual tasks of setting goals and managing the performance of the CEO are critical board functions that are often not done well in small organizations. Having a clear process in place, scheduling a performance review meeting in an agreed-upon timeframe, and setting expectations for how the board chair will approach these activities helps to make this less of a high-stakes conversation and instead more of a regular talk about the organization.

Erin remembers leading one investor trip in South Africa. A board member was in attendance as well as a dozen other investors and their families. At the kids' table one night at dinner, Erin's daughter and the board member's son, both around 10 years old, started a conversation about who was the boss of whom between their parents. Was Erin as the CEO the boss or was the board member ultimately the boss of the CEO? The kids came over to the adults' table and presented their debate since they couldn't resolve it themselves. Another investor on the trip who worked for a major Swiss bank explained it to them this way: Technically, the board of directors hires, fires, and holds the CEO accountable for performance, but anyone who has served on a board knows that in a well-run organization it is critical to support the CEO as he or she has a very tough job. The board should not get overly involved in operational details and instead focus on helping support the CEO to have a clear strategy and a solid plan for execution, and be sounding board for critical issues. Having this relationship be mutually supportive is ground zero for any high-performing organization.

Strategic Planning   We use our strategic planning process as the key opportunity for the board to review our direction and weigh in on our strategy. Strategic discussions, of course, happen in small ways at every meeting. However, big strategic pivots need to be managed, as these can have major consequences on a social organization's long-term impact. Developing a mutually agreeable strategic plan keeps the debate around the big issues, what is working, and what needs improvement, with negotiated timetables for actions and results. We have seen far too many ESEs spend valuable time trying to be all things to all people or changing tactics too frequently. We will discuss strategic planning in more detail in the final chapter, but this is certainly one of the most important issues on which nonprofit boards should spend their time.

When a strong and constructive relationship exists between the board and the management of the organization, it becomes a cornerstone in ensuring an organization achieves its highest level of impact, full growth potential, and largest sphere of strategic influence.

Influence in the International Space

Finally, there are some additional considerations for ESEs that seek to influence policy and practice at the global level as well as raise funds from a geographically diverse base. The challenge is to create a presence worldwide that allows Room to Read to engage in meaningful ways across multiple geographies. There is never enough time, people, or money to be everywhere we want to be, so we have had to focus our efforts on building a global network.

When it comes to influencing policy, ESEs such as Room to Read play a particularly important role because community-level experience in multiple countries provides critical information for international institutions seeking to scale effective strategies.

At Room to Read, we have started to build time for our global office staff to engage in strategic policy discussions and forums. We believe now, as the world community has ratified the Sustainable Development Goals to achieve by 2030, information from organizations like ours is more critical than ever. However, like our work in country offices, we must be rigorous and disciplined in what we choose to do. We run on a razor thin margin without much room for unplanned activities. So, during our annual planning process, we plan our strategic engagement activities carefully.

Room to Read has built credibility in international policy forums over the years, primarily because of our long-term commitment and follow-through in countries and communities. We have been able to make these commitments due to the fact that we are primarily privately funded. One key way we have cultivated this independent source of funding is by building a constellation of regional development and advisory boards in the various key markets we fundraise in from Europe to Asia-Pacific to Australia. These are "boards for busy people," in which the focus is on growing our brand and networks in each market. Our regional advisory board strategy accelerates the collective movement as Room to Read leverages influential people from corporate, media, and philanthropic networks. These people represent our local presence to unlock the leadership and investment required to support Room to Read in being a world-class, global organization.

Key Takeaways

- ESEs are organizations that seek to influence large-scale policies and practices. **Planning for strategic influence** should be part of an organization's overall planning process, but short-term aspirations **should be aligned with an organization's stage of development.**
- **Outlining your pathway to scale and end game** helps define many aspects of your operations, who your key stakeholders are, and **how you seek to influence the broader system.**
- Most important early on is to **develop proof of concept** of your core activities, with clear, easy-to-understand statistics, case studies, and testimonials about your good work. **Organizing activities for scalability** is also key.
- An organization's visibility and trustworthiness increases with each year of good work to the point that ESEs

can become more **influential in policy discussions** and successful in getting higher **system-level buy-in for scaling your activities.**

- **Partnering with governments to adopt and adapt** your approach is one essential pathway to scale and sustainability. Open models, replication, and commercial adoptions are other ways. Regardless of the path, plans should be **focused enough to track progress in system-level adoption** as well as **flexible enough to take advantage of unexpected opportunities** along the way.

- **Planning for strategic influence** should take into consideration the **system-level zone of proximal development.** It should include activities that shepherd key stakeholders toward understanding the value of your activities and helping guide them toward larger-scale change.

- **Developing strategies proactively to creatively engage key influencers** is important for building a collective movement and momentum around your approach and giving a wider voice to your cause.

- It is helpful to create a **constellation of influential groups** that are a part of your organization, from your global board of directors, to regional development boards, to critical friends and advisors and volunteer chapters to leverage **a wide range of stakeholders in your global movement.**

NOTE

1. Atul Gawande, "The Heroism of Incremental Care," *New Yorker*, January 23, 2017.

10

Government Funding: Damned If You Do, Damned If You Don't

The Triangular Partnership

It was supposed to be called the "Triangular Partnership." Room to Read was going to develop the teaching and learning materials, UNICEF was going to fund the effort, and the Ministry of Education in Zambia was going to ensure that teachers were trained and materials were being used in classrooms. This was an exciting opportunity. Room to Read had been creating a lot of buzz in Zambia for the rigorous strategies that we were using to help young children learn to read. Officials from all levels of the government had visited the pilot schools in Kafue district, near the capital of Lusaka, to see our work with children in grades 1 and 2. Children were learning to sound out words in ways that had never been seen before.

Although Room to Read's reading materials were supposed to supplement the government curriculum, some teachers had been ignoring the government textbook completely and were just using the Room to Read student books instead. Teachers, school principals, and government officials were gaining so much confidence in what they had been seeing that UNICEF was keen to scale the approach nationally. The Ministry of Education seemed enthusiastic to support it.

In September 2012, Cory and Room to Read's global director of literacy traveled to Zambia to work with the country team in the preparation of a proposal for UNICEF's consideration. Our proposal was to scale the program in another Chinyanja-speaking area of the country in 2013, expand into a small number of districts with other majority languages in 2014, and go nationwide in 2015.

Just as we were busy crunching numbers and thinking about the logistics of the rollout and the details of the proposal, we received an invitation to participate in a meeting with the education team of the United States Agency for International Development (USAID). USAID had just established three new early reading projects with a total funding level of more than $120 million just for Zambia and wanted to make sure that the organizations currently supporting literacy in the country were working in harmony. The meeting was cordial, but it was clear that USAID had its own priorities and approach and that any collaboration would have to be rooted in its approach and its terms.

Room to Read offered USAID our materials and methods. Even though Room to Read had developed the materials using our own financial resources and staff time, we were excited about the possibility of scaling our successful efforts to benefit children nationwide. Why reinvent materials for millions of dollars and over the course of years when a successful model with local political support from the Zambian government was ready to implement then and there?

Unfortunately, USAID did not accept our offer. The agency had negotiated a bilateral agreement with the government of Zambia, already bid out these three megaprojects, and had approved the new contractors' scopes of work. It was on the hook for spending the money that was allocated and meeting the stated project objectives. The USAID technical staff were not interested in adopting what was already available but was still amenable to ongoing discussions and information sharing.

Room to Read's country and global staff spent many hours discussing the possibility of collaboration. Did we want to join forces and be involved in these mass efforts? Our team was uncomfortable that many of the people who would be involved in the USAID efforts were the same people who created the current national approach to reading, one that had pushed Zambia to the lower end of regional assessment scores. In the end, we decided to maintain our autonomy, continue to show the value of our approach as alternative or at least complementary to what USAID would be proposing, and exert our influence by continuing to demonstrate how well our programs were helping children learn.

At that point, although Room to Read still had UNICEF's trust, the launch of the new USAID projects left questions about the views of the Ministry of Education. We still believed that our literacy work was stronger than any other at the time and that the ministry had the opportunity to use the Triangular Partnership to help many new schoolchildren who otherwise might not learn to read.

However, even with excellent relations and positive support, it was difficult for the Ministry of Education to turn away from the new USAID projects. The projects brought vast new money to pay for textbooks and learning materials, hardware, software, technical assistance, vehicles, and study tours. The deep support of USAID also brought credibility and cachet, a signal of trust that could generate additional financial support from other investors and political goodwill of the international community.

Soon after the USAID projects began in earnest, negotiations regarding the Triangular Partnership began to fall apart. The Ministry of Education began to focus its attention on collaboration with the USAID projects and, over time, UNICEF decreased its enthusiasm for the rollout of Room to Read's approach to literacy instruction. This was not a surprise. It made perfect sense that a government entity would align itself with the larger sources of power and funding.

This is not meant to be an accusation or cynical point of view. A government entity such as a ministry of education only has limited time and staffing resources. With the best of intentions, ministry officials must make decisions about how to deploy those resources to achieve the best results for its children. It is therefore quite reasonable that the Ministry of Education in Zambia would shift its time to the partner that could provide many times more resources and better positioning in regional and international policy discussions.

Similarly, the logic of USAID's decisions also makes sense. The agency has its own constituents. For example, it is only able to do as much work as funding allows, and funding is approved each year by the U.S. Congress. Agency officials must be able to demonstrate the specific value that they add to countries' development and goodwill. Room to Read could have participated in one or more bids for the ensuing USAID projects, in which case we could have brought our experience directly to bear on one or more of these large-scale activities. However, we didn't do so at the time. Therefore, why shouldn't USAID promote its own approach and its own implementing partners?

All the logic in the world, though, could not diminish our disappointment. We felt that our position as a trusted government partner in Zambia was being eroded—and by activities that would not support children's learning in the same way that we would have. We had painstakingly invested in, monitored, and improved with thought and care our approach long before the USAID projects arrived. We perceived ourselves to be the tortoise that was being outpaced by the wily yet somewhat clumsy hare, the honorable David aiming his tiny slingshot at the all-powerful Goliath. Our global and country staff felt a keen sense of bitterness and frustration at the time that what we thought was a highly successful approach was being overshadowed by bigger forces.

This experience in Zambia was a huge wake-up call for Room to Read. It made us appreciate more starkly that having excellent programming is simply not enough to win a seat at the table in national policy discussions. Newer, less-experienced players can quickly leapfrog long-standing, steady organizations such as Room to Read in their positioning and programming if they are awarded large-scale grants and contracts and given an automatic role in national educational planning. We needed to rethink our approach in a world with increasing competition and real challenges to our historical expertise. We needed to consider whether to join these government-funded projects.

Whether to accept government funding is a decision that many nonprofit organizations face at one time or another on their journeys to scale. Is government funding a reasonable way to achieve your mission and grow your impact? This chapter is meant to help you be more proactive and deliberate in how you think about your choices.

To Take Government Funding or Not to Take Government Funding—The Ongoing Question

Room to Read has always struggled to determine the appropriate role of U.S. government funding and other bilateral foreign assistance funds as part of our organization growth and development.

On the one hand, our reticence to take government funding has been something of a badge of honor. Part of our brand from our earliest days was to be lean, cheap, and cheerful, a scrappy upstart organization that was willing to get its hands dirty to get the best educational services to underserved communities. We often illustrated this image in photos of local partners riding bicycles on dirt roads with bookshelves strapped to the back and set in stark contrast to other photos with international development staff driving shiny, white, USAID-branded Toyota Land Cruisers with all-terrain tires and exhaust snorkels. Again, this was part of our pride, what made us feel special, and what resonated with so many of our early investors.

In many ways, we have continued to hold true to these values. For the most part, we still do not buy large vehicles, hire international staff with big benefits packages, or use maximum allowable U.S. government *per diem* rates when traveling. We continue to hire country nationals to lead country teams, prioritize effective and efficient implementation, and steer clear of the many meetings and debates that can overwhelm organizations and stymie progress.

Very early in our development, Room to Read took seriously the cautions against government funding. We were told by thoughtful advisors that taking government money can change the entire culture of an organization. Participating in government-funded contracts and grants can reduce autonomy, shift the balance of power in organizational decision making, and generate a self-perpetuating culture of red tape that could infuse the whole organization. Decisions begin to be made based on clients' expectations, or with an eye to anticipating clients' expectations and satisfying their paperwork requirements, which does not always produce the most effective solutions.

Accepting government funding can also create dependencies that alter long-term planning. It can even, in extreme situations, push you to act in a way that could compromise your organizational values and mission. It can force organizations to chase funds and contort their programmatic directions to respond to project needs instead of maintaining an efficient organizational focus.

Yet government funding is alluring. When a contract or grant is awarded, it is often at a funding level that is substantially higher than any other single source of funding and provides resources over an extended period. It can also allow you to pay for organizational overhead costs and even, in the case of contracts, offer a lucrative fee. This helps organizations invest much more heavily in their overall work. They can hire staff with competitive salaries and benefits and have the security of multiple years of funding. High levels of guaranteed, multiyear funding create a much different opportunity for longer-term planning. All of this is quite appealing for organizations that are passionate about an important social issue and see a potential opportunity to accelerate their impact.

Government funding also brings a very different culture of compliance than is otherwise necessary. For example, Room to Read has always been serious about its financial management. We have had rigorous financial oversight from our board of directors, including its world-class audit committee, strong financial oversight from our chief finance officers and finance teams, topnotch auditors, and effective financial processing and management systems. Room to Read is one of the very few organizations that have been awarded Charity Navigator's top four-star rating for 10 years, since 2007, which is every year that the rating system has been in place.

However, our organizational systems have not been set up with U.S. government compliance as our top priority. We have not kept time sheets across the organization. We have not opted to fly U.S. airline carriers exclusively on flights that depart from or return to the United States, nor have we organized our programmatic or financial reporting systems around U.S. government project reporting criteria.

We have therefore realized that participating in U.S. government projects would require a completely different approach that might not be consistent with the successful systems that we have had in place thus far. It would be a major organizational change, and one that we have been reticent to pursue.

The Challenge of Big Box Development

Part of Room to Read's reluctance to jump into government funding is a philosophical concern about "big box" development. This phenomenon is like when a large retailer such as Walmart or Home Depot moves into an area. These stores are appealing because they have a huge diversity of goods and lower prices, given their economies of scale, that beat what any other retailer can offer. Consumers are drawn to these stores because the stores meet so many needs in efficient and effective ways.

The problem is that big box stores crowd out local retailers who go out of business because they simply cannot compete. The consequence can be more limited options, less diversity of choice overall, and a consolidation of power such that a smaller number of people control retail offerings and labor market wages and conditions.

Similarly, in international development, the power of bilateral and multilateral agencies is equally as consequential. As was demonstrated in the Zambia example, a major infusion of bilateral support can crowd out local innovation. Organizations that may be doing excellent work but are not a part of the big projects can lose their influence as well as their staff to better-funded contracting organizations, some of which are for-profit businesses. The big projects often capture the attention of government officials and national planning, hire staff with higher salaries and more benefits than local organizations can provide, and bring a sense of momentum and prestige that is difficult to ignore. Like the big box stores, the influence of the bilateral projects can then limit the diversity of otherwise promising practices and wipe out a set of civil society organizations that were otherwise meeting local needs.

This consequence is not inherently bad if the large-scale bilateral projects help achieve at least as much success for children as was being achieved prior to their implementation. But this is not always the case.

As we were developing the vision for Room to Read Accelerator, one of the biggest questions was whether we wanted to undertake government-funded projects as part of our technical-assistance portfolio. Large projects can at times do more harm than good. For example, while large-scale projects bring with them vast amounts of financial resources, many low-income countries do not have the absorptive capacity to use those resources effectively. The consequence can be higher costs for materials and services, bloated labor markets with unsustainable salaries and benefits, and a sense of optimism and promise that often cannot be sustained beyond the three-to-five-year project windows.

In these situations, equipment and materials purchased for the projects cannot be refreshed, trainers and monitors can no longer provide ongoing support at project sites, and the promise of positive outcomes to be achieved in such a short period begins to dissipate. The result can be unmet expectations, cynicism, and reluctance for the next big project, all at the time that local organizations have been marginalized at the expense of the big projects.

Yet, at the same time, it is through large-scale projects that organizations can exert substantial influence and, under the best of circumstances, contribute in a way that really *can* have positive longer-term results. Prior to joining Room to Read, Cory had overseen national projects in countries as diverse as El Salvador, India, Yemen, and Zambia, and had seen how the power of working with ministries of education on targeted projects could improve educational opportunities for millions of children. In addition, as Room to Read began to think about expanding into government-funded activities, we realized that there was also a consequence for *not* participating. Opting out of large-scale projects can undermine current organizational efforts and undo previous progress and success.

For these reasons, we've had to think hard about participating in future U.S. government–funded projects. What trade-offs were we willing to make? What would be our strategy going forward?

Limited but Strategic Participation in Government-Funded Projects

The real discussion about bilateral funding came when we were preparing Room to Read's 2015–2019 strategic plan. Several factors spurred our interest. The first was that Room to Read continued to receive regular requests from governments and other nonprofit organizations to help them implement literacy and girls' education programming. It was always very difficult to decline such gracious requests, but we just did not have the operational expertise to implement such different projects. We were used to implementing full-country programs, with local staff and a long trajectory of work in collaboration with host-country governments and communities. We had not served as technical advisors. And even though we had slowed down substantially in our new country expansion, full-country programming was still our expertise and the operational approach with which we were most comfortable.

Second, as described earlier, given the huge influx of international funding for the literacy part of our work, we were starting to see substantial new competition from other organizations for host-country governments' time and support. Participating in government-funded and other technical assistance projects could be an important way to maintain our leadership in countries where our programming was strong and could make an important contribution to national educational reforms.

Of course, this was also a partly defensive play. After all, we otherwise risked losing staff or approval to continue working. This was particularly true in countries in which newer USAID projects were developing teaching and learning materials to be used across an entire country. If we were not a part of these projects and did not influence the new national planning for literacy, then we would either be forced to support an approach with which we might not feel comfortable or simply lose the opportunity to work at all.

Third, if we could manage government-funded projects appropriately, they could represent a good way to build our organizational capacity over time. These projects could provide multiyear funding at a high enough level to reduce pressure on our annual fundraising targets. At such a level, projects could finance organizational priorities that might not otherwise be possible.

Last, the fact that we had started to create more standardized worldwide curricula and instructional materials for our regular work meant that we now had well-defined materials that could be shared with others, such as through government-funded activities. In the past, when our operational approach was focused exclusively on implementing full-country programs, it was difficult to figure out how our work could accommodate project activities. Now, with strong program modules in place, it was easier to think about moving past full-country programming to activities organized by a short-term project approach.

For all these reasons, we built a new technical-assistance practice area, Accelerator, into our 2015–2019 strategic plan. The expectation was that we would experiment with large-scale technical assistance projects, including government-funded projects, at least as a short-term trial. We would try it for a few years to learn whether the benefits would be worth the costs and the shift in at least some of our focus to this new way of operating. We would then conduct a review midway through the strategic period to reflect on the extent to which we would build this approach more broadly into our future work.

A Slippery Slope

In some ways, the bridge to government-funded work had started to be built even before we made the full commitment in the 2015–2019 strategic plan. Our first forays into government funding felt innocent enough. In fact, our first grant from the U.S. government was like funding from other investors. It was easy to accept, as it did not bear consequences any different than anything else we had done in the past—a starter drug, to be sure.

Room to Read had received a generous government grant through the support of a Room to Read advocate at the State Department, who learned about Room to Read through the U.S.-India Business Council. In addition, the U.S. ambassador to Sri Lanka heard about Room to Read's programming part of the national recovery efforts after the deadly tsunami swept the country. Impressed with our work, he championed ongoing State Department support for Room to Read's reading and girls' education efforts not only in Sri Lanka but also in India and Nepal.

Administratively, we treated the grant like funding from any other large-scale investor. We used our regular tracking systems to monitor the implementation of project activities and our regular reporting systems to update the State Department on progress over time. Our State Department grant liaison also helped us substantially in the requisite paperwork and even advocated for more expansive project opportunities. The result, beginning in 2010, was a fantastic collaboration between Room to Read and the State Department that extended four years and served thousands of children across Bangladesh, India, the Maldives, Nepal, and Sri Lanka.

Room to Read's second U.S. government project also came about more by happenstance than strategic planning. Catholic Relief Services (CRS) reached out to Room to Read in 2010 to ask whether we wanted to partner with them on a competitive proposal for a food-assisted education project in the Lao People's Democratic Republic. This cooperative agreement was sponsored by the U.S. Department of Agriculture. Although food-assisted education was far from Room to Read's expertise, CRS was looking for a partner to provide the wraparound reading activities that would be required for the project. Room to Read was one of the few international educational organizations that was operating in Laos at the time, and we thought this could be a good way to augment our impact. We agreed to join CRS's bid, contributed the concept of "reading circles" to the proposal per CRS's guidance, and with CRS, were successful in winning the competition.

Over the next few years, Room to Read served as a sub-awardee to CRS in what was admittedly a difficult experience. We worked through many challenges during that period, from delays in overall project implementation to shortfalls in our own performance, to figuring out how to account for project activities within our organizational planning and accounting processes. The experience was an important one in that it helped us begin to understand the on-the-ground challenges of implementing services with very different considerations and reporting requirements than in the past. We realized that success in government-funded projects was not necessarily defined in terms of growing impact; it was just as much about responding adequately to U.S. government expectations.

Country and global team members were not completely naïve in going into the Laos project. We realized at the time that the project was going to be different from our normal implementation and tried to gear up as much as possible. Nevertheless, it was new for us to work on a U.S. government project and as a sub-awardee. This required responsiveness to

U.S. government rules and regulations and to the management style of the prime implementing organization. Similarly, CRS had to balance its own leadership with the expectations of the USDA partners, the government of Laos, and the circumstances of the project, which created more complexities than anticipated in the original award.

One example is the province of Savannakhet, where the project was located. This province has substantial ethnic and linguistic diversity. Neither Room to Read nor CRS were necessarily prepared for the implications of this on Room to Read's ability to support the reading development of young children. As much as Room to Read believes in the importance of supporting young children's reading in their first language, we were not prepared for such language diversity at the time. Room to Read's expertise was in the Lao language only, and we were still a few years from being able to support programming for children who speak other Laotian languages. This constraint severely limited our responsiveness during the site-selection process and subsequent project implementation.

As Room to Read began to learn more about U.S. government–funded projects, we started to monitor this new potential funding stream more closely. Part of the rationale for accepting the early projects was that we could do so without substantial organizational changes. If we kept our funding under $500,000 in any single year, then we would not be subject to a higher level of U.S. government scrutiny and compliance requirements (for example, time reporting and recognition of revenue). This was not based on any kind of desire to cheat, be duplicitous, or hide anything. We were confident and proud of the systems that we had put in place to be good stewards of our investors' money, including investments from the first U.S. government–funded projects. We simply wanted to delay decisions about the larger changes to our systems that would require adjustments to our approach to operations and decision making.

Unfortunately, as part of this early period, we incorrectly recorded revenue in the first quarter of 2014—on receipt of payment—that was a reimbursement for expenses accrued in the last quarter of 2013. After making the necessary correction, we found that we had exceeded the government-funding threshold in 2013 at the lower level of scrutiny, and we were required to conduct what was then called an "A-133 audit." This reference was to the U.S. Office of Management and Budget's Circular A-133, which specified the audit requirements for organizations that expend at a certain level in a specific fiscal year. Not surprisingly, the audit results identified systems that needed to be improved to comply with U.S. government requirements for organizations that receive funding at this higher level.

In typical Room to Read fashion, we were open and transparent about the audit outcomes and began to chip away at the immediate audit recommendations. However, the findings also forced us to face the issue head-on that we had been resisting for years: How did we want to incorporate government funding into our overall organizational strategy going forward?

The good news is that the audit results came out at the time that we were beginning to think about our next strategic plan. We could therefore make government funding part of the larger organizational decision about direction over the next five years and ensure that we were planning appropriately. But should we start to consider participating more actively in government-funded activities?

A Complex Innovation

We approached the question about government funding as well as the broader issue of Room to Read as a provider of technical assistance as what Govindarajan and Trimble[1] call a "complex innovation." This is the kind of project that goes far beyond ordinary day-to-day process improvements and what can easily be absorbed relatively easily by the existing organizational infrastructure. Complex innovations require dedicated teams, different processes, and strategies for coexisting with and supporting the existing "performance engine" as smoothly as possible. Perhaps the most important challenge with complex innovations is figuring out how to ensure that the innovation complements the overall organizational mission while not choking the existing systems that are the reasons for the organizational accomplishment in the first place. The success of such an endeavor requires a deep appreciation of this challenge, thoughtful planning, and goodwill between everyone involved in the process.

As part of the 2015–2019 strategic planning process, we realized that investing in U.S. government–funded projects would require changes across the board. It would require a new level of detail in our standard procedures for spending and accounting, staffing, program development, and operations. For example, it would require us to "Fly America." This is a U.S. government regulation to fly on U.S. carriers on outbound flights from and inbound flights to the United States, even in situations in which flights are more expensive than with non-U.S. carriers. It would also require staff to record hours in dreaded timesheets.

This is a tracking system that some private companies, such as law firms, use one way or another. It is a process that helps organizations keep track of people's time and allocate costs across projects. It is a common and reasonable request that is not difficult to implement but is perhaps an intimidating and off-putting cultural change for nonprofit organizations that have not had such systems in place in the past.

Having Our Cake and Eating It, Too

After many hours of debate, discussion, expert opinions, cautions, points, and counterpoints, Room to Read committed itself formally to government funding as part of our 2015–2019 strategic plan. We had already started to go down this road with a few small projects anyway and decided to take the bigger leap. We made what many people believed was a Faustian bargain to become proactive in seeking U.S. government funding and investing in the necessary planning and systems that go along with it. We believed that the possible benefits outweighed the costs. The question was how to do so in a way that would minimize the negative consequences and, importantly, not compromise our organizational values.

This issue was extremely important, as Room to Read's success to this point had been rooted substantially in people's passion, not only for our mission but also for our approach. Our staff and investors liked the fact that Room to Read was scrappy, cheap, and cheerful, and rejected Land Cruisers for bicycles. This orientation was important not only for staff around the world but also for the people who had invested in Room to Read's first 15 years of success.

The consequence was to create safeguards that would, ideally, allow us to benefit from government funding but also to retain as much of Room to Read's positive culture as possible. For example, we made the decision that we would not allow government funding to exceed 30% of all funding. (Even now, government funding accounts for less than 10% of annual operating expenses.)

In some ways, this threshold was somewhat arbitrary. It could have just as easily been 20%, 35%, or something else. The idea, though, was that we would cap the overall proportion of future work from this funding source at a meaningful level but also to make sure that we maintain our strong focus on other funding sources.

The most important question for any project was about opportunity costs. How does the decision to take on a government-funded project compare to the decision to take on a new privately funded project, or simply to continue to support direct implementation? What are the relative benefits to children? Are we helping enough children and at a deep enough level to be worth it? What are the relative costs in terms of staff time and the need for new organizational compliance infrastructure? Could we successfully incorporate the new systems and approaches into our work in a way that would be additive, or, as Govindarajan and Trimble have warned, could they possibly damage or break our existing performance engine?

Early Impressions

As of the writing of this manuscript, we are now more than two and a half years into the new strategic plan period. Our experiences to date with government-funded projects have already exceeded our initial expectations. These include four new U.S. government–supported projects. In all instances, we seem to be achieving or set up to achieve substantial strategic influence on large-scale state and national educational reform efforts.

In three of the four instances, we are a subcontractor on nationwide early-grade reading efforts. The first is as a subcontractor on a national early grade reading reform project in Nepal. In seconding three country office staff members to the project, Room to Read's role had been to lead the overall technical work on the project, and, in particular, to support the development of the early grade reading curriculum as well as the teaching and learning materials. The project also selected Room to Read's core grade 1 and 2 reading curricula as the basis for the larger-scale curricular rollout across the country. Second, Room to Read is serving as the lead in reading and writing materials development for a large project in Tanzania serving 6 of the 25 regions in the country; third, we are serving as the technical lead in reading and writing activities for a national early-grade reading project in Rwanda—the goal of which is to support more than 1.5 million primary schoolchildren throughout the country.

Our roles in all three of these projects came about through regular USAID contracts. In the case of Tanzania and Rwanda, Room to Read joined prime contractors on competitive proposals that ended up winning the bids. For Nepal, one of those contractors asked us to join its project after it had won the contract. All three projects have enabled Room to Read to play strategic roles in scaling effective literacy programming at regional and national policy levels.

The challenge in all these projects is that Room to Read's contribution to the technical work is substantial, but the price is also very high. In Nepal, for example, Room to Read seconded three of our most senior staff members to the project. These included the country director, program manager for instructional design and teacher support, and program manager for quality reading materials.

These critical positions are difficult to fill on a temporary basis for the project period at a time when Room to Read also has a comprehensive work plan and existing commitments. It takes a considerable amount of time to recruit new staff members and prepare them for their new responsibilities. This task becomes that much more difficult when the positions are only two to three years in length, as experienced professionals are looking for longer-term job security.

In addition, Room to Read contributed its grade 1 and 2 reading curricula to the project to be the starting point for the new national approach. It has already been rolled out in six districts, with many more planned this year. A few years ago, after the project leadership and government of Nepal realized that it would be too late to develop a new curriculum, the project asked national and international organizations working on literacy reform to present their approaches for consideration. Room to Read was honored that its curriculum was selected through this competition to be the basis for the national model.

We are very pleased to contribute our staff and organizational materials for larger-scale implementation. This outcome fits extremely well with our organizational goals and is consistent with our 2015–2019 strategic plan to "do more with less." This project has given Room to Read the opportunity to leverage its thought leadership and materials to benefit many more children in Nepal than would have otherwise been the case. At the same time, Room to Read's total financial compensation for this contribution is less than 1% of the total contract value. We receive funding for the staff salaries and a small amount of technical assistance but were not compensated in any way for our thought leadership in developing the teaching and learning materials in the first place. More on this later.

The opportunity cost for this work has been immense. And while Room to Read receives a fee for its services, these funds are nowhere near the costs for setting up the organizational systems to implement the work, the unaccounted time of organizational staff to support the efforts, and the drain on administration for our regular program implementation. However, even with the high costs, we still plan to consider similar kinds of projects in other countries, too, as they give us a real opportunity to help more children and increase our impact.

One possibility could be for Room to Read to become a prime implementer on future USAID projects. This would give us the opportunity to play a larger role in project design and implementation, as well as receive the kind of compensation that would really help to grow our organizational work overall.

The challenge is that the entry cost for becoming a successful prime implementer on USAID projects is astronomically high. It requires a completely different operational structure built on U.S. government regulations and planning for competitive proposals. Building this administrative infrastructure is possible and could even be justifiably charged to the government over time as required compliance costs.

Many of the prime organizations with which we work devote hundreds of thousands of dollars to compete for large USAID contracts. They maintain regular communications with USAID staff around the world and monitor program cycles to learn up to 12–18 months ahead of time when new project competitions will take place. They track the international travel of USAID staff and send their own staff to countries months ahead of any new project to gain an edge in the competitive process. They set up new country offices, often begin some work with their own money to demonstrate some working history in the country, develop new relationships with government officials, recruit for international staff, and secure exclusive partnerships with international and local organizations to advantage themselves for new projects.

By the time a new request for proposals hits the street, most competitive organizations have already spent months in strategic positioning, learning the nuances of USAID's interests, and even writing the more standard parts of proposals. In this kind of competitive environment, organizations such as Room to Read that do not have these systems in place or the experience in writing competitive U.S. government proposals are at a substantial disadvantage.

One exciting development is Room to Read's fourth USAID project, which *does* provide a substantial leadership opportunity for longer-term, large-scale change. This is a five-year cooperative agreement that Room to Read and USAID launched in India in 2015 to support reading for children in two large states: Chhattisgarh and Uttarakhand. The combined populations of these two states is approximately 35.6 million people, which would place them between Canada and Uganda as the 38th most populous country in the world. The opportunity for large-scale change in this project is therefore as large as any of our other activities to date.

The history of this partnership goes back a few years when Room to Read was considering the future direction of our work in India, one of our earliest countries of implementation. From our earliest days there, our country director had wanted us to spread our work around the country to gain visibility and credibility for our activities. The challenge was that in a country the size of India and with the limited financial resources available, our footprint was never big enough in any one state to create a critical mass or a proof of concept for scale. Over time, we realized that we would be more successful if we were to focus our efforts and therefore made the difficult decision to consolidate our work in fewer locations to make a bigger difference and use the results from more concentrated activities to advocate for future growth.

Although the logic of the decision was strong, the change had huge consequences for our work. This required changes in staffing—either relocating or laying off staff members—as well as stressing positive relationships with local and state governments that we had developed over many years. The state leaders of Chhattisgarh and Uttarakhand were particularly vocal about their disappointment. They had appreciated Room to Read's partnership, realized that there was much more work to do, and had hoped that Room to Read would work with their districts for many more years.

It was through difficult discussions with state leaders that we realized exiting an area could be just as challenging or even more so than starting up in a new area. This process required thoughtful planning, excellent diplomatic and transparent communication skills, and, just as importantly, some way to ensure that the good work we had done in a region could be sustained over time. As part of our exit strategy, we began to work closely with state educational officials to share our methods for library development and reading instruction so the states could continue to support their schools over time.

Room to Read staff and state officials were so enthusiastic about this collaboration that we decided to petition USAID to fund these sustainability efforts. USAID was happy to support this kind of a partnership. After more than a year of negotiations and planning, the result was a five-year project in which Room to Read would provide intensive support to 50 model schools in each state and then train state officials to continue Room to

Read–type support in approximately ten times more schools in the future.

This requirement for scale was a key point in the agreement. USAID chose to fund this activity directly instead of through a competitive request for proposals. The resultant "cooperative agreement," as distinct from a contract, represents a true partnership among USAID, the two states, and Room to Read. This is the kind of model of demonstration and scaling that has real potential for learning and would be an ideal approach to replicate with USAID and other bilateral and multilateral donors in the future.

Who Owns It?

One of the unexpected consequences of government contracting has been about intellectual property. These are the products and services that we have created using private funds that in part make Room to Read's contributions so valuable. As we started to think about government-funded projects, we were excited about the opportunity to share our storybooks and program activities with larger numbers of children. After all, that was the overarching purpose of joining these projects. We were even happy to contribute these resources to projects free of charge. We thought that was a pretty good deal given the sunk costs of research and development that had gone into these products.

It is for this reason that we have been somewhat surprised by the U.S. government's interpretation of this kind of contribution. The current view is that once in-kind products such as these children's storybooks are included in a project, the U.S. government has a right to use it in any way that it wants. It uses a licensing approach created by the nonprofit Creative Commons called "Creative Commons BY" as the basis for how it expects to use the materials.

Specifically, this means the contributing organization gives the government the irrevocable right to share (that is "copy and redistribute the material in any medium or format") or adapt (that is, "remix, transform, and build upon the material for any purpose, even commercially") the materials in any way that it sees fit. This can include use outside the project or country and in any languages. What this means is that when Room to Read would like to donate a storybook or a teaching resource to a project, the U.S. government has the right to let anyone use it, modify it, and charge for it as long as Room to Read receives attribution for the original work.

If the donated content in the project is modified in a substantive way (though what constitutes a substantive modification is not very clear and, at least at this point, decided unilaterally by the government), the contributor must give the actual ownership to the U.S. government. The government can then keep the copyright or assign it to another organization. For example, Room to Read recently donated a set of storybooks to a project. The contents of the books were modified slightly and then incorporated into a larger reader for students to enjoy across the country. Again, the positive outcome is that Room to Read's work is reaching more children. However, the U.S. government then assigned the ownership of the readers to the host country government. The upshot is that, according to the letter of the law, Room to Read would now have to ask permission to use the modified materials!

In our not-so-humble view and in contrast to our ordinarily progressive view of the world, this appropriation of preexisting material is a huge government overreach. In practical terms, the U.S. government has co-opted our organization's intellectual property. We do believe that the intent behind the overreach is a good one: more children accessing opportunities to read in a world that has too few books and examples of good teaching and learning materials for children at the earliest stages of their reading skills development. However, there are many ways the government can achieve this goal without seizing an organization's intellectual property.

We have recommended several strategies in our government-funded projects for ensuring the maximum distribution of materials while maintaining the integrity of Room to Read's intellectual property. For example, we recommended making the materials available freely in the original languages and formats in which they were published. We also recommended opportunities for other organizations to make derivatives of our publications if they checked with us first to ensure at least some kind of quality control. However, the U.S. government has not yet accepted these recommendations for most projects. We have had to agree to the government's approach or simply not contribute existing material to these projects. It has been "all or none."

These are not easy decisions. We have not yet come up with a satisfying approach and still make decisions about in-kind intellectual contributions on a case-by-case basis. We hope to identify better ideas about how to address these issues in the future in a way that is a win for everyone involved.

Key Takeaways

- **Timing is everything!** When to make a decision to accept bilateral and multilateral funding is important and can affect many aspects of your organizational development.
- Even though government funds can be large and game changing, **there are huge costs** in terms of change to organizational culture, implementation of new systems, introduction of new compliance and auditing requirements, and work on a reimbursement basis. Costs can be overwhelming and, in the case of building compliance systems, can be difficult to sustain financially without

feeling compelled to grow this part of your work even more rapidly over time.

- If you do decide to accept government funding, be particularly mindful to **minimize the negative consequences of "big box development."** Do everything you can to continue to promote innovation in local organizations instead of crowding them out.

- Make sure that participating in government-funded projects **never puts your organization in a position to compromise its values** or forces you to do something that is contrary to your mission.

- **Be careful when you contribute existing materials** to government projects that you understand what rights you will have to own and use the derivative products.

- In addition, if you decide to accept government funding, **be clear about why you are doing so**, and let that reason drive how much you accept. For us, the motivation was to help more children, remain competitive, and continue to provide thought leadership in our core program areas.

NOTE

1. Vijay Govindarajan and Chris Trimble, *Beyond the Idea: How to Execute Innovation in Any Organization* (New York: St. Martin's, 2013).

11

Strategic Planning: Wrapping It All Up

I t was one of our favorite weeks of the year: country management conference time. The brain trust of Room to Read's global leadership was meeting in Siem Reap, Cambodia, to align ourselves and set the direction for the organization for the coming year. It was June 2014, and the key agenda item was to debate the organization's next five-year global strategic plan for 2015–2019. Erin was also kicking off her annual five weeks of work visits in Room to Read countries and personal leave this week with her mother and eight-year-old daughter in tow.

As a way of balancing motherhood and work, ever since her daughter was three years old Erin had taken the three generations of women on the road to Asia and Africa so she could spend quality time with both her families—her own, and the Room to Read family. As they exited the Siem Reap airport after the long cross-Pacific flight, Erin's daughter made a beeline past the air-conditioned taxis and begged to take the preferred local form of transport, the three-wheeled tuk-tuk, to the hotel. As frequent travelers, they packed light, so Erin agreed to the adventure of the three of them piling into the tuk-tuk. The driver requested the name of their hotel, which Erin couldn't immediately remember. As she searched in her purse for their travel itinerary, the driver said, "Ma'am, only when I know where the end is, can I take you the most direct and best way."

In this town full of ancient Buddhist temples, Erin laughed to herself that even the tuk-tuk drivers sounded like sage philosophers. She also realized this was a great aphorism for the upcoming week of strategy conversations. As a global leadership team, we needed to review our pathway to scale and end game and then set clear goals to ensure we were traveling there in the most efficient and effective way.

As part of the strategic planning process, the week would be full of discussions refining the best ways to grow our programmatic work in Asia and Africa, concentrating on streamlining our model for consistent and high-quality delivery, as well as brainstorming about additional replication approaches to grow our impact faster. Each country would share its greatest pain points, and we would jointly commit to the key global initiatives that had the greatest cross-country implications for the next five years.

This conference was just one critical milestone in our 2015–2019 planning process that would take about nine months to complete. We would have staff roundtables in each country and global office department. We would engage our board of directors and critical friends and advisors, seek feedback from our base of supporters both through online surveys and interviews with key investors, and work with consultants to research the landscape of possibilities open to us for continuing to evolve and grow to challenge our thinking with outside perspective. We undertake this exercise only once every five years, as it is a large investment of time and resources to develop an ambitious, constructive, and thoughtful strategic plan.

Strategic Planning: Bringing It All Together

We take strategic planning seriously at Room to Read. It is one of the main ways we have established clarity in our thinking and goals, built organizational grit and discipline to continue to accomplish major milestones, and focused on ourselves as a learning and evolving organization throughout our different organizational phases. For us, strategic plans don't just sit on shelves as nice summary documents of our ideals. Instead, we use them regularly to guide our priorities and activities to help us fulfill our mission with maximum efficiency and impact. Room to Read's global strategic plans articulate specific goals and describe the action steps and resources needed to accomplish them.

We have had three strategic plans in our history at Room to Read. In many ways, they mirror the stages of organizational development we have discussed throughout this book: start-up, transition, and maturity. We developed our first plan in our fifth year of operation when we realized we needed to communicate a greater vision for the organization than just making it to the end of each year still intact. It was titled, "Room to Read Five Year Strategic Plan 2006–2010: Building a Trusted Global Organization That Brings Millions of Children the Lifelong Gift of Education." While it was admittedly not the most detailed plan, it did outline and solidify the vision, mission, organizational operating principles, core values, theory of change for our core programs, monitoring and evaluation overview, country expansion plans, work plans by department, and budget and impact projections. It was instrumental in rallying and aligning the fast-growing staff, board of directors, ever-expanding base of supporters, and volunteer chapters' members at the time.

The next two strategic plans built off this solid foundation. Our "Global Strategic Plan 2010–2014: A Roadmap for Learning: Literacy and Girls' Education" outlined how we would deepen our programs to be more focused on educational learning outcomes, not just educational infrastructure outputs. We committed to incorporating early-grade literacy instruction, as well as mentoring and life-skills curricula, into our core programs. This plan encapsulated the largest programmatic pivot we have made at Room to Read.

Our third strategic plan, "Global Strategic Plan 2015–2019: Scaling Our Impact," described how we would grow our impact at an even faster rate by investing in our core business to drive for efficiencies and greater effectiveness. It also launched our new Accelerator delivery model, intended to assist us in scaling our impact faster by building capacity in others to implement Room to Read–like educational programs. This plan focused more on our operations and delivery to build a sustainable organization than on our programmatic model that we felt was stable and achieving strong results.

So why have a strategic plan for your organization? Here are a few compelling reasons we have found from our experience:

- Being value- and mission-driven organizations, entrepreneurial social enterprises are served well when they can clearly articulate their visions for social impact. Developing a strategic plan is a great forcing mechanism to do just that.
- ESEs are most successful when they have passionate stakeholders involved, from staff to advisors to volunteers. A strategic plan is a useful tool in aligning these groups and leveraging their efforts for maximum productivity. Plans are key in helping you build a strong organizational culture based on clear and ambitious goals with accountability for performance.
- Boards of directors in nonprofits can gain confidence and understanding of where the organization is headed when they are engaged through the lens of a strategic plan. The plan assists them in remaining involved at the strategic level and resisting the potential desire to micromanage day-to-day operations.
- Investors, especially investors who make large, multiyear commitments, appreciate the ability to understand the future direction of the organization. Strategic plans can be great engagement tools with investors so you can outline

your shared vision, shared purpose, and shared discipline to execute with their valuable support.

Tips for Managing the Strategic Planning Process

As we have discussed throughout this book, when building and growing an organization, it is important to be disciplined in what you do. Getting to where you want to go requires an intense focus. For our strategic plans to be most useful, we have developed a certain rigor in the process that is outlined in the following overarching principles and approaches.

Participation is a key tool in gaining buy-in ("Tell me and I forget. Teach me and I remember. Involve me and I learn." —Benjamin Franklin)   This is the underpinning of good, participatory classroom management, but it also applies to strategic planning and, frankly, everything we do. We have found wide participation in developing the strategic plan is key to getting the most out of the plan as it gets implemented. First, it is beneficial to hear a wide range of feedback from staff and other key stakeholders to challenge and expand your thinking. As we already mentioned, we do this with country and global office staff through a series of roundtable discussions. Staff have deep knowledge about what is working, how it is working, and what might be able to work better. Their experience is often more relevant and practical than general research or theoretical constructs. This engagement is also important for eventual buy-in for the final plan. We have found that people appreciate their feedback being heard and considered, even if not ultimately the direction that is selected.

We also invite a wide array of our supporters to provide feedback. The invitation helps get everyone into the tent and remain committed long term to our mission. Strategic planning conversations are great ways to engage in an authentic way about our work and the challenges posed in it. They build a shared responsibility in jointly owning the future direction of the organization and encouraging people to invest their time, networks, and financial resources in achieving the plan.

Define who the final decision makers are up front ("Input by the many, decisions by the few." —Anonymous) A decision-making body should be defined for clarity and transparency. The management team, consisting of all the heads of departments, along with our board of directors, are the final decision makers at Room to Read. It doesn't really matter as much who the body includes (though a very large group can make decision making more challenging), just that it is defined up front, so that when you inevitably encounter some thorny, controversial issues, everyone is aware who will make the ultimate decision. We select a subcommittee of our board of directors for each strategic plan that helps work closely with management throughout the process to ensure no surprises toward the end when management is seeking final approval from the board. Strategic planning is a great opportunity to engage board members deeply in the vision for how the organization plans to continue to evolve, and to enable you to chart a course together.

Leadership matters ("Great leaders don't set out to be a leader...they set out to make a difference. It is never about the role—always about the goal." —Anonymous) The CEO must be fully committed to driving the strategic planning process and executing on the final plan. This commitment is one of the deciding factors in whether this is a make-work exercise or a game-changing, transformational one for the organization. And there must be an equally strong commitment on behalf of the board chair and members to engage in the process. Before undertaking a strategic planning process, the CEO must ensure there is sufficient time and adequate resources for all key executives to participate fully. It is important that this is a collaborative process owned by management so that organizational silos and turf wars are avoided and leadership comes together to jointly lay out the road map for the future.

Get help ("Ask for help, not because you are weak, but because you want to remain strong." —Les Brown)
There is a lot of additional work required in the year a strategic plan is developed. One way to support management is to bring in reinforcements for key staff who will be heavily involved, where necessary. We always engage external consultants for our strategic plans. They are particularly useful in facilitating tough, high-stakes conversations and ensure all perspectives are heard and considered. The CEO, or any one person for that matter, shouldn't dominate conversations to the point that it squelches honest reflection and rigorous debate. We use consultants to share outside research about alternative approaches and ideas. As unbiased facilitators, they are also the best people to conduct interviews with partners, competitors, and key investors.

Cast your net wide and challenge the status quo ("Nothing wilts faster than laurels that have been rested upon." —Percy Bysshe Shelley)   It is important to be open to a wide range of new ideas and approaches at the beginning of a strategic planning process. This is the best time for the organization to do some blue-sky thinking. Additionally, you must assess the organization's strengths and limitations to being responsive to your environment. We do this generally in the form of a SWOT analysis (strengths, weaknesses, opportunities, and threats). We seek to understand the current landscape and define how we might need to evolve to maintain our comparative advantage and continue to grow our impact. Once we go through this broad brainstorming process, we narrow it down by selecting what we believe Room to Read is best suited to do. In our last strategic plan, for example, we considered nine different options for scaling our impact before we selected launching our technical assistance arm of the business, Room to Read Accelerator.

Convening our critical friends and advisors group is one way we seek objective and unbiased feedback on how we are doing. We ask them to be brutally honest about where our weaknesses are and where the opportunities exist for even greater impact. This feedback is not always easy to receive, but constructive feedback has the potential for being the most transformational. In our second strategic plan, which centered on deepening the impact of our programs, our advisors questioned the organization's commitment to girls' education since they felt we had a more developed literacy approach. This challenge garnered our focus to invest even more attention and resources in the Girls' Education Program to ensure we became a thought leader in issues around gender equality in education.

**Use data to inform decisions ("Trust, but verify."
—Ronald Reagan)** It is important to use data to balance the advice and perceptions of your staff and other key stakeholders. We use our management- and country-level dashboards along with our monitoring and evaluation reports to root the conversations in a comprehensive picture of how the organization is doing. A balance of qualitative and quantitative analysis is essential.

**Always have a BHAG—Big Hairy Audacious Goal—to rally everyone around ("He who is not courageous enough to take risks will accomplish nothing in life."
—Muhammad Ali)** Strategic plans work best if they have a BHAG that motivates and inspires your staff and supporters.

In our current plan, our big organizational goal that drives the whole plan is, "By 2020, Room to Read will have invested in the futures of at least 15 million children by developing literacy skills and the habit of reading among primary school children and by supporting girls to complete secondary school with strong life skills." When we show up in any Room to Read country of operation, the staff there know we are driving toward impacting 15 million children, and they feel accountable for their important role in achieving the goal. Annual planning, resource allocation, and country reviews are rooted in this goal. A BHAG is important for motivating external audiences as well. We regularly reference this number when we solicit funds and report back to our investors or communicate with our chapter network. It helps us create a sense of urgency that everyone needs to work hard and ensure we achieve this goal together.

Make sure you define your "no, not yets" ("The essence of strategy is choosing what not to do." —Michael Porter)   When you get right down to it, strategic planning is about trade-offs. Eventually, after considering many possibilities, you must decisively choose what you are going to do and, even more importantly, what you are not going to do. This is often the hardest principle for Room to Read to follow, as we have an ambitious nature. However, we have also realized the strain on the organization of pushing too hard within an inevitably resource-constrained environment. This can result in negative backlash as well. Naming what we will not attempt to accomplish yet (for example, working in preservice teacher training instead of in-service training or providing university support for girls) helps set parameters for us.

Hope for the best and plan for the worst in strategic planning ("Do what you can, with what you have, where you are." —Theodore Roosevelt)   Trying to get the balance right of setting ambitious yet achievable plans is the aim of strategic planning. Some goals can be identified as stretch goals, but it is helpful to plan for most of your goals to be achievable, with reasonable effort, during your strategic plan period. Otherwise you risk demotivating instead of motivating your staff and stakeholders. No one wants to be on the losing team, forever clawing its way out of a self-imposed hole of a well-intentioned but overwhelming set of goals. We try to be ambitious yet keenly aware of what is realistic given our human resources, expected budget growth, and comparative strengths so that we can set targets that we are cautiously optimistic we can achieve.

Be specific about how you intend to operationalize the plan ("A goal without a plan is just a wish." —Antoine de Saint-Exupéry)   Clear priorities and implementation plans are essential. Developing and writing the strategic plan requires a disciplined effort. However, operationalizing the plan is where the real work begins. For our last strategic plan, we outlined 12 cross-departmental initiatives the organization would undertake in the next five years and wrote detailed charters for each. Each had a management team champion, project manager, and core team that identified the activities, timeline, and budget required to execute the initiative. The management team then regularly tracked progress on implementation plans and centered each year's annual plan on progressing the overarching strategic plan. This eye on execution and driving for performance is the difference between just having a plan and genuinely realizing the plan.

Communication and utilization ("A problem well defined is a problem half solved." —John Dewey)   The final deliverables of our strategic planning process are a detailed internal version of the plan, a summary external version, and a strategic plan presentation. Communicating the final strategic plan to all participants is key for building momentum to achieve the goals set in the plan. We ask every new employee joining Room to Read to read the plan. Erin as CEO has provided an overview of the plan and a status update on how we are progressing on the five-year plan during onboarding sessions, when she visits country offices, at the chapter leadership conference, at the country management conference, in board of director meetings, and in meetings with major investors. Effective, repetitive communication about how we are progressing in our global strategic plan is an anchoring tool for every major aspect of our organization.

All this is not to say that plans are completely static. We are no better at predicting the future than anyone else, and situations evolve over the period of five years that always require adjustments. Nevertheless, clearly outlining when you have overachieved, just met, or underperformed in a plan is important for transparency and accountability. A lot is learned from plans that do not go as well as expected. Throughout the strategic plan period, it is important to recognize the small wins in progress and reinforce the efforts going into delivering on the plan. At the end of a plan period, doing a rigorous postmortem review helps set up the organizational assessment for the next strategic plan.

This disciplined and transparent approach to managing has helped Room to Read tackle a wide range of challenges through our different stages of organizational growth; make the right investments for building a sustainable, high-performing organization; and continue to improve our work in delivering educational outcomes for children. With a clear road map, we know we have a much higher chance of successfully reaching our goals. A common vision and execution strategy goes a long way in bringing together the multifaceted aspects of a dynamic social enterprise.

Conclusion: Wrapping It All Up

We are ending, thus, with the beginning. Well-defined strategic plans are a great starting point to support the growth of your organization. They can drive the people, priorities, and performance of your organization for greatest impact. They define your goals and intended impact as well as process through your theory of change, identification of key stakeholders and influence with them, and provide guidance for your organizational activities. We have found that using strategic plans as well-conceived road maps has helped us drive hard and fast toward scale.

This rigorous and strategic approach to managing Room to Read has allowed us to grow our impact from a few thousand children in 2001 in one country to more than 15 million children to date across 14 countries. We are working in our 20,000th school community this year, and more than 50,000 girls have benefited from our Girls' Education Program. We have built a sustainable institution that is weathering the ups and downs of the nonprofit sector. Improving the educational outcomes of eager and deserving students around the world is our true north star that guides us at Room to Read.

What matters most to all of us who have been a part of the Room to Read journey—the global movement of staff, volunteers, investors, and partners—is that this scale has allowed us to help rewrite the futures of children, each with his or her own unique and special story. Their stories are what motivate us during the long days and miles of travel. Stories of students like Bonolo, six years old, who is in Ms. Makwela's first grade classroom. Ms. Makwela teaches at Mohwelere Primary School in South Africa in which nearly one-fourth of the students have been orphaned by AIDS, and the surrounding community is wracked by unemployment, high illiteracy, and poverty. After Ms. Makwela learned the teaching techniques in Room to

Read's Literacy Program, she transformed her classroom from an intimidating place of unfocused repetition into an inviting, print-rich, child-friendly environment. She encourages sharing and has learned new methods of delivering impactful lessons in the Sepedi language that has accelerated the rate of students' reading. Bonolo says his proudest moment was when he once read at the assembly in front of the whole school. When he finished, everyone clapped.

Stories of girls like that of Miriam, who was the first participant in our Girls' Education Program in Zambia and later was a social mobilizer working as part of our staff delivering the program itself. Miriam's father died when she was just a baby, leaving her mother to raise six children on her own. The family struggled to survive selling tomatoes by the side of the road. Miriam had challenges staying in school, but she believed education was the ticket out of the trap of poverty. "I admired how determined, passionate, courageous, and composed the social mobilizers were. I still wake up in disbelief when I think about how far I have come," Miriam said. She took the same approach when she was a social mobilizer, sharing her personal experiences and life story as an example for the next generation of young girls, that hard work and determination to stay in school pays off.

Education has been instrumental in the lives of so many of our staff members across the globe as well. It is one of the reasons why we all work so passionately, especially for our country staff who often witness firsthand in their home countries the transformative power of education to change the destiny of their lives, their friends and families, and the communities in which they work.

So, what do we think are the fundamental issues that entrepreneurial social organizations can learn from our experience at Room to Read? Core to who we are is the organizational grit we describe in various ways throughout this book to be proactive and disciplined in how we approach almost every decision at each phase of our growth. It is the dynamic relationship between organizational approaches and phases of organizational development that we summarized in Table 2.3 in Chapter 2. We analyze and debate the options, we make the decision of what to do, we go do it, we measure the result, we reflect and improve upon it, and we work hard to scale what is working. And then we keep doing that repeatedly. If our history were a children's storybook, we might be *The Little Engine That Could*, which teaches children the values of optimism and hard work.

Our belief is that with a thoughtful, disciplined approach, any entrepreneurial social enterprise can achieve an equally impactful growth trajectory. The nature of ESEs is to disrupt the *status quo*, innovate, and scale new approaches. Just as important as innovation, ESEs must also develop the ability to manage through the organizational stages of development required to support scaling their impact. Only in building a strong organization can their impact be maximized. ESE leaders must embrace the delicate balance of being disciplined and yet at the same time nimble enough to continually navigate through numerous key business decisions that we summarize below.

Programs and Operations   At Room to Read, our theory of change has guided us to focus on the most important and strategic activities to achieve scale. It defines our core program and outlines how we are pursuing scale and system-level change in education. We have tracked and measured our results in terms of reach and impact. We have never tried to be all things to all people and have kept a narrow and consistent programmatic agenda. This has required us to say no to many opportunities that would have otherwise resulted in program creep. Remaining focused allowed us to keep our eye on the prize of having governments adapt and adopt our approaches as our end game. We have also placed as great a value throughout our organizational history on the "how" of our work, our operations, as the "what" of our work in terms of our programmatic models. Effective and efficient implementation and building the capacity of the governments and communities in which we work to sustain our programs supports us in our pursuit of excellence in execution, which increases our impact.

Communications and Fundraising   From the start, we realized we were in the collective movement–building business. Carefully managing our brand, investor, and volunteer experience has been key in growing the global movement that keeps supporters engaged and empowered to join us as social change champions. At Room to Read, we have always embraced the power of storytelling as a key component in our ability to build the momentum of this collective movement, which is instrumental in generating the revenue required to support our growth and impact. We prioritize fundraising and communications, find ways to create a sense of urgency for our mission, and see our investors as true partners in our movement. We don't want to lose another generation of children to illiteracy or gender inequality. The cost of ignorance is too high for society when children don't grow up educated and empowered to create solutions for tomorrow.

As one of the early entrepreneurial social enterprises, Room to Read has helped demonstrate that philanthropy and social entrepreneurship are two sides of the same coin. Social enterprises have unique approaches to critical social issues facing the world that need to scale. Philanthropists want to support change that will improve the lives of the neediest. This is not a zero-sum game. We must work together to achieve the best results for the greatest number of people.

Leadership and Culture   A strong organizational culture has been one of Room to Read's best assets in navigating well through the organizational stages of development. An organization's culture is defined and built right from the top by its leaders. Being a mission-driven organization with enduring core values is a nonprofit's number one recruitment and retention tool for top talent. We know that people stay at Room to Read when they feel they are thriving in a positive, supportive work environment that provides opportunities for growth and development.

Creating such environments requires entrepreneurial social enterprise leaders to have well-developed leadership skills. Leaders must connect with and inspire a wide array of stakeholders, including staff, community members, governments, corporate partners, and investors. Great communication skills are essential. Resilience is key. There will be many times you will think you have failed, but you must keep trying new things, persevering, and moving forward.

For most social challenges in the world, there is rarely a silver bullet. Instead, it is a matter of consistent hard work that over time produces results. Leaders must be prepared to double down and keep working on solutions and driving for scale against the odds. Only in hindsight, over nearly two decades, have we grown to appreciate what Room to Read has accomplished. In the face of adversity, we choose action every time and keep moving forward. Every organization will go through crisis and tough times. You are not defined by the crisis that strikes your organization. Instead, you are defined by how you respond to it.

One of the most important parts of our organizational culture over the years has been a sense of optimism and fun. We have regularly used the power of pause to have some fun, especially when we have been in our fast-growing phases. Team off-sites and meet-ups have allowed us to get to know the people with whom we work so hard. These strategic pauses have also allowed us a moment to think and reflect as a team. The other ingredient critical in building our organizational culture is optimism. Having an uplifting and optimistic narrative for Room to Read's future has been a powerful intoxicant, especially in those start-up and transition years when you must overcome so many hurdles.

Social entrepreneurs are best when we lead with values and visions. We make choices each day to inspire people to be better, make better choices for our planet and humanity, and show up fully and participate in creating a better world. All those involved in the social impact movement choose not to let doubt, failure, or fear rule the day. Instead, we choose action, hope, and compassion. We are not waiting for someone else to solve today's problems. We know that each of us can be part of the solution. If not you, who else? We may act and fail, but we believe that is better than never trying in the first place. We are doers, not talkers. We start simple and build up. We are first movers and early adopters. And we hope the knowledge, experience, and wisdom we build collectively will help improve our global society for all. It will take all of us—social entrepreneurs, civil society, philanthropists, corporations, media, and governments—working together to make the biggest difference. The world needs us. There is an opportunity now to make the world a better place that is an incredible responsibility we all have.

Cory and Erin are profoundly proud to be a part of the social impact movement. Most entrepreneurial social enterprises start with a team that has a deep personal conviction that something is wrong. Then an idea germinates and takes hold about how to solve the problem, and that in turn grows into an organization, and more people join the movement. Room to Read's story is like many others in this regard. We must hold ourselves accountable for maximizing the potential of our organizations to reach the greatest scale and impact possible.

What is our advice in conclusion, then, for those social entrepreneurs and social change champions who want to learn from Room to Read's history and experience? In many ways, it can be summed up as follows:

- Be driven by passion, and ensure you always sustain that mission-driven core in yourself, the greater team, and in the fabric of the organization's enduring values.
- Take risks. While success is the ultimate goal, one must sometimes fail. So, fail fast, fail often, and fail forward,

as the ethos of Silicon Valley entrepreneurs prescribes. Large, disruptive change to unjust and inequitable systems is unlikely to come easy or without trial and error. If you don't fail sometimes, you are not taking enough risks or being innovative enough. Learn from each bump along the road.

- Think short term, and work on the things you can solve now, but have a vision and road map for the long run of how you are building a sustainable institution for scale. Define your end game for seeking broader system-level change at the beginning.

- Persevere one decision at a time, one pivot at a time, one crisis at a time. Build resilience into your team and the ability to adapt continually to the landscape and externalities you are not able to control.

It is not an easy path that entrepreneurial social enterprises choose, but know that you are not traveling the path on your own. Many entrepreneurs across industries feel similar challenges. There is a well-known story that entrepreneur Bradley Smith shared about the psychological toll and internal struggles of entrepreneurship. He said, "It's like a man riding a lion. People think, 'This guy's brave.' And he's thinking, 'How the hell did I get on a lion, and how do I keep from getting eaten?'" Despite the challenges, we have still found working in the social impact space to be the most rewarding aspect of our professional lives because at the end of the day we know we are making a difference working to ensure all children have quality educational opportunities in their local communities so they reach their full potential in life.

The growth and expansion of the global social entrepreneurial movement has had a profound positive impact on the world. In the face of adversity, it has brought new thinking and drawn out people's desire to see a more just and equitable world for all. You see it changing the thinking in board rooms, in classrooms, in community centers, and in chambers of government. The movement is still young and growing, and the impact is just beginning.

For us, the best way to end is with the words of the students who have inspired us to keep going through the ups and downs and twists and turns in working toward positive change in the world. Students like Charmaine, a sixth-grade student Erin had the pleasure of meeting at a library supported by Room to Read at a rural primary school in Mpumalanga Province in South Africa. Charmaine was an unusually articulate and dynamic girl. She wrote us a poem on our visit to thank us for working in her school, because the library had become her favorite place and unleashed her creativity. All of us social entrepreneurs and the social change champions who support great causes around the world are choosing love, compassion, and optimism. Charmaine's poem beautifully represents the power of all of us coming together, unleashing the possibility of change.

Love Poem

Love is my religion

I could die for it

Love begins at home where it is not how much we do or how much we have that matters

But how much love we give each other that matters …

The degree of loving is measured with the degree of giving

The giving of love is an education in itself

Love is the foundation from which your decisions about your life should be made

In every living thing, there is the desire for love

If you could love enough, you could be the most powerful person in the world

If you want to be loved, be loveable

At the touch of love, everyone becomes a poet

So, let's meet each other with a smile

For smiles are the beginning of love

Index

Page references followed by *fig* indicate an illustrated figure; followed by *t* indicate a table.